Samuel Langdon

The Appeal to the Serpent

Or, life in an ancient Buddhist city. A story of Ceylon in the fourth century A.D.

Samuel Langdon

The Appeal to the Serpent
Or, life in an ancient Buddhist city. A story of Ceylon in the fourth century A.D.

ISBN/EAN: 9783337237370

Printed in Europe, USA, Canada, Australia, Japan

Cover: Foto ©ninafisch / pixelio.de

More available books at **www.hansebooks.com**

ON MIHINTALA.

(From a drawing by E. A. King, Esq.)

[See page 15.

THE
APPEAL TO THE SERPENT

OR

Life in an Ancient Buddhist City

A STORY OF CEYLON IN THE FOURTH CENTURY A.D.

BY THE

REV. SAMUEL LANGDON

MEMBER OF THE ROYAL ASIATIC SOCIETY (CEYLON)
AUTHOR OF 'MY MISSION GARDEN' 'PUNCHI NONA, A STORY OF
VILLAGE LIFE IN CEYLON' ETC.

THE RELIGIOUS TRACT SOCIETY
56 PATERNOSTER ROW, 65 ST PAUL'S CHURCHYARD
AND 164 PICCADILLY

CONTENTS

CHAPTER	PAGE
I. ON MIHINTALA	11
II. THE WESTERN FOREIGNERS	34
III. IN THE PREACHING HALL	49
IV. AT THE ASTROLOGER'S	63
V. THE JEWESS	74
VI. OUT OF THE CITY	90
VII. THE NEW RELIGION	103
VIII. THE BURNT HAND	114
IX. THE PANSALA	129
X. PASTORAL	141
XI. THE NEW FRIEND AND THE OLD	156
XII. WITH THE 'RECONCILERS'	172
XIII. OMENS AND REFLECTIONS	184
XIV. WITH THE GOSSIPS AT THE GOLDSMITH'S	197
XV. LEAH'S CONFESSION OF FAITH	210
XVI. CONVERSATION AND CORRESPONDENCE	225
XVII. IN WHICH ABHAYO THERO GOES TO MIHINTALA FOR THE LAST TIME	239

CHAPTER	PAGE
XVIII. FRIENDLY CONTROVERSIALISTS	251
XIX. TROUBLE AT 'SABANA'	262
XX. AT THE 'BRAZEN PALACE'	279
XXI. THE APPEAL TO THE SERPENT	295
XXII. THE MONSOON COMES	301
XXIII. AFTER THE MONSOON	312

STONE IMAGE OF BUDDHA IN THE FOREST.
(*From a photograph by Scowen & Co., Colombo.*)

THE APPEAL TO THE SERPENT

CHAPTER I.

ON MIHINTALA.

Men, driven by fear, go to many a refuge,
To mountains and forests, to groves and sacred trees.
BUDDHAGOSHA.

To Mihintala, men had gone as to a refuge during many centuries, even before the time in which our story opens. The natural features of the hill, and its solitary majesty, had invested it in the earliest days with a sacred character. To the builders of Anuradhapura it was a favoured habitation of the gods, and it is possible that the nearness of the holy mountain influenced their decision as to the locality in which the royal city should be built, as much as the constellation under which it was founded, and from which its name was partly derived.[1]

The old Pali chronicles are full of the praises of the

---

[1] Founded about 450 B.C. by Prince Anuradho, and called after the constellation of that name.

sacred hill. Before it had been honoured as the spot selected for the introduction of Buddhism, it was called 'The Superb Missa.' And if that epithet was meant to describe the view to be obtained from its summit, or from the peak which forms the most sacred feature of the hill, called by the old historian Mahanamo 'The Delightful Ambatthalo,' the adjective was well deserved, as anybody will say who has had the opportunity of looking from its giddy heights on the vast plain which surrounds it, and enjoying one of the finest views to be obtained even in Ceylon. Probably, nobody makes the ascent now without trying to realise in some way the magnificent vision which lay spread beneath when the great city came up close to the 'holy mountain' itself, if it did not include it; when a road, lined with shrines and statues, called by Tennent the *Via Sacra*, connected this vast natural dagoba with the scarcely less imposing artificial hills erected by the kings of the 'great dynasty.'

On the adornment of the hill the pious kings had lavished much wealth, skill, and labour. No sacrifice was too great and no offering too valuable to be devoted to the enrichment of the hill on which Buddhism was first preached to the Sinhalese. And the entire hill, with its two thousand steps cut out from the hard granite rock, its aqueducts of solid stone, its great galleries, wiharas,[1] the massive sculptures of Buddhas, kings, and sacred symbols, formed one great monument to Mahindo, the Indian Apostle of Buddhism, who, more than three hundred years before the Christian era, brought the doctrines of Gautama, the Buddha, to Ceylon.

[1] Temples or image-houses.

It is impossible for one to stand there now, looking down on the forest-covered plain, without being deeply impressed, as he thinks not only of the wilderness beauty of the scene, but of the historical associations which cluster around the mountain, and of the story of the ancient city which once covered with a busy life so vast a portion of the plain below. There I stood some time ago, trying to realise, with the help of old chroniclers and modern writers, some idea of the life on the plain in the days of Anuradhapura's glory. And as I stood thinking of the 'might-have-beens,' of magnificent pageants, of gorgeous processions of kings and priests, of the great tank-makers and dagoba-builders, of contending armies, of bloody struggles between Sinhalese and Damilos, of the millions of men and women who had marched in a vast procession of life across the plain through the centuries, shouting the three 'Saranas' or 'Refuges,' their only hope, and of the 'holy mountain' standing immovable in the midst of it all; and as I thought also of the faint glimpse which an ancient Greek traveller[1] gives us of a Christian church existing in Ceylon in those early centuries, a dream of the past, which may possibly have some meaning for the present, outlined itself dimly before my mind, and this was what I saw:

It was the afternoon of a fine day, early in the month of Jattho, which corresponds in the Buddhist calendar to our month of May. A great festival was to be held on Mihintala, and everything betokened that it was to be celebrated with the utmost magnificence. A grand torchlight procession was to be made that

---

[1] Cosmas Indicopleustes, about 510 A.D.

night to the shrine of Mahindo, in which the king himself, Sri Meghawarna, would take part, in honour of the recent arrival in Anuradhapura of the sacred tooth-relic, which, it was stated, had been rescued more than eight hundred years before from the funeral pyre of the Buddha, and which had now been sent to Ceylon with much secrecy from Kalinga, that it might be saved from falling into the possession of the Brahmins, the victorious opponents of Buddhism in India.

This was to be only one of a series of functions to be held in celebration of the great event which had filled the royal city with rejoicing. Mihintala was covered with garlands, which made it look as if the entire mountain had blossomed into flower. A hundred arches of beautiful design, ornamented with fruits and flowers, and festooned with moss and the young palm-leaf, had been erected on the stairs of the ascent, and over the street which nearly surrounded the foot of the hill. The dagoba domes, the galleries, and the statues on the summit and on the hillside, had been similarly adorned with banners and with flowers.

Small groups of visitors wander about the hill to look at the preparations, in a variety of costumes which indicate various ranks and nationalities. There is one small group standing near the gallery known as the 'Bed of Mahindo,' where the father of Ceylon Buddhism breathed his last, which attracts our attention. From the way in which this group is regarded—we might almost say worshipped—by other visitors to the hill, as well as by their attire and general bearing, we gather that it is composed of persons of distinction. One of them, who appears to be altogether a stranger to the place, is an elderly man of average height, with clearly cut features, clean shaven, a dark countenance with bright eyes, and a most intelligent expression. A loose muslin robe covers the tunic and closely fitting shirt in which he is clad. This is Dharma Sen, a visitor of high rank from India. He is accompanied by Detu, the royal artist, the king's younger brother, who is dressed in the heavy fantastic costume of the Sinhalese nobles.

Within the last few days these two have been renewing an acquaintance formed some years ago, when Detu visited the celebrated 'Deer-park' monastery at Sarnath, near Benares, for the purpose of studying the carving and sculpture for which that monastery had become famous throughout the Buddhist dominions of India and Ceylon.

One of the little group is a Buddhist priest. He would be the first of the three to attract attention, but we have taken him last because we wish to describe him more particularly, as he forms one of the principal personages in this story of the old city. We may as well say at once that he is its hero. His figure is tall and commanding. It is a figure which is strikingly set off by the yellow robe which indicates the Buddhist mendicant, thrown lightly and gracefully over the left shoulder, leaving the right arm free. His head and face are not so completely shaven as is the general rule with his brethren, but the hair is closely cut. He is much taller and of lighter complexion than is usual amongst the Sinhalese. His eyes are large and often bright and restless-looking; and often again they settle into a far-reaching gaze like that of a stone Buddha in meditation.

Comparatively young as he is, about thirty, Abhayo holds a high position in the adjoining monastery, and is known far and wide as the leading Thero[1] of Mihintala, though much the junior, and therefore inferior in official rank, to several members of the community. But he stands high in royal favour because of his great gifts; and his reputation with the people as a preacher is unequalled. But his colleagues shake their shaven heads when his eloquence is referred to, and everybody knows that significant shake of the head, which means a 'but,' and indicates that there is a flaw somewhere. In this case it means that the character discussed is singular and—'bring your ear down!'—'unorthodox.' His colleagues, while acknowledging his talents, regard him as a man of mysterious habits, with a conceit acquired in travel, which makes him dissatisfied with the life of the monastery. They had begun to say also amongst themselves that his travel had given him a want of reverence for sacred things.

He had travelled as the companion of Detu, the artist prince, in the journey to India already referred to. They were fast friends, the prince and the priest, though as unlike as possible in temperament. Detu's life was apparently devoted to the purposes of his art, and was characterised by great calmness. To the ordinary observer he appeared phlegmatic; not so to

---

[1] This is in Pali the equivalent of Presbyter or Elder. It is applied to members of the priesthood of a certain standing. Honorifics and Sinhalese terms, where they are not really necessary, are dispensed with, as far as possible, in the story.

his intimate friends, or to his pupils, to whom he voluntarily gave lessons in carving in wood and stone, and who regarded their teacher with enthusiastic admiration. The prince would appear to a casual observer better fitted for the passionless repose of the priestly office than his friend, the impassioned preacher, the restless monk.

The three stood for a time, looking in silence on the view which presented itself to their gaze, while the prince's retinue, composed of Sinhalese men of high rank, kept at a respectful distance. It was getting near the time of sunset, and a cool, gentle breeze shook the garlands of flowers which covered Mihintala. A magnificent sweep of country lay before the three friends, comprising the greater part of the dominion immediately under the rule of King Meghawarna. It was a vast plain, stretching away with faint undulations to the sea on the east and west, and on into the north country as far as the eye could see. To the south the view was broken by solitary hills which appeared to be crowned with rocky fortresses, and then stretched on beyond to the mountain ranges which marked the hill-country of Malaya.

'Is it not a splendid vision?' said Detu, waving his hand towards the great city in the west, interspersed with groves and rice-fields, and turning to his Indian friend.

'It is a splendid vision, as you say. You may well be proud of such a land as this. Do the people share your pride in the natural beauty of the land?'

'I fear not. But some of my pupils are becoming appreciative. To most of our people, however, if we talked in this glowing way of the scenery, we should be regarded as if describing a dream.'

'And a dream it is,' said the priest, 'and, like a dream, it may at any moment fade. Let the embankments with which our kings have formed those beautiful lakes, which shine like inland seas, be broken down, and what would remain of the picture then? What would become of those vast tracts of living green, in the thousands of rice-fields that we see, on which the peace and comfort of the village homes which cluster around the sacred domes depend, as well as the existence of the city itself? Every day, as I look out on this great city with its gilded palaces and its immense dagobas, and down into its busy streets, and then let my eye wander over that sea of green, dotted with the white domes, and watch the curling smoke rise above the forest, I ask myself, 'How long?' and in my dream it dissolves like the cloud yonder, which the sun is breaking into such glorious fragments, and the city lies in ruin, and the vast plain is a desolate solitude.'

As he spoke, his eyes brightened into a look that was fiery; when he finished, they settled down again into the old far-off gaze of the meditating Buddha.

'We may congratulate ourselves,' said Detu, 'that the dream is not very likely to be realised. But that kind of talk is just like our friend. Nothing seems to satisfy him. Now, I rejoice in the beauty on the surface of things. This wonderful view of the city and surrounding country thrills me with delight whenever I behold it, and I do not feel like thanking my friend for pointing out the possibilities of decay and destruction underneath. While I am rejoicing in the beauty of the countenance, he is saddened with the thought of the struggles and sorrows of the soul. The thought of the troubles of the rice-cultivators in the villages yonder—who, after all, are mostly the serfs of the Pansala[1]—mars all the enjoyment of the scenery for him. I suppose it is all right for a priest to have such views, though very few of his brethren would agree with him. But I am forgetting that you are not acquainted with the objects of interest to be seen from here. Let me point them out!'

'Both Nature and art appear to me alike magnificent from this point of view,' replied Dharma Sen. 'One could stand here for ever looking on such a scene as this. I think I can understand, however, the feeling of our friend the Thero. Often have I looked in that way from the towers on the topes of Sarnath, and reflected on the transitoriness of all things except the eternal rest. And I have lived to see something like our friend's dream begin to come over the glories of that hallowed spot, and the "order" established by the Vanquisher breaking up under the fierce assaults of the Brahmans of Benares. But enough of this; tell me, prince, what is that stupendous pile yonder which seems to vie in massiveness with Mihintala itself?'

'That is the Abhayagiri (the mountain without fear). The temple near, as well as the dagoba itself, forms a monument of a king's gratitude. It was built more than four hundred years ago by Walagam Bahu, to commemorate the assistance rendered him by the

---

[1] Residence of Buddhist monks.

great priest Tisso in the expulsion of the Malabar invaders. The immense dome which is nearer, flashing like gold, surmounted by what looks like a spark of fire, is Ruwanweli, the last work of the great king Dutugemunu. There, on the platform beneath, the king was brought out to die, that he might depart gazing on that great work of his life. It was not complete then, but was made to look complete with a covering of cloth. The plates of burnished metal have been laid on in more recent times. The thing which sparkles like fire at the top is a piece of crystal, placed there for protection from the fierce lightnings which sometimes stream over the city in the changes of the monsoons. Naturally, to me, the most interesting of the dagobas [1] is the massive one away more to the north there, the Jetawanarama, built by my father, Maha Sen. The smaller dagoba, nearly in the centre of the city, is the oldest, the most beautiful, and most venerated of all, surrounded as it is with the most hallowed associations. That is the Thuparama, built more than six hundred years ago by Devenipiya Tisso, to whose conversion to the faith of the Buddhas the hill on which we stand may be regarded as a monument. It was built to enshrine the sacred relic, the divine collar-bone of the holy Tathagato.[2] It is fitting that the unspeakably precious treasure which the princess has brought us should find its resting-place near.'[3]

[1] The word 'dagoba' is derived from *Dhātu Gabbhan* = a relic receptacle. For detailed descriptions of the principal dagobas see Tennent's *Ceylon* and Burrows's *Buried Cities of Ceylon*. The Abhayagiri dagoba was originally 405 feet high—fifty feet higher than St. Paul's, London.

[2] One of the titles of Buddha.

[3] It is said that the sacred tooth-relic, of which the Buddhists in

'Do the people know of the difficulty with which the treasure was brought?' inquired Dharma Sen.

'Why, all the city is filled with admiration at the ingenuity which led the princess to conceal the holy relic in the luxuriant tresses of her hair. Our poets are already singing hymns in her praise, as well they might to one who has come like a bright goddess from the heaven of Indra, with such blessing to Lanka.[1] Henceforth our country will be envied of all the kingdoms of the earth, for the possession of this treasure, and the memory of the princess honoured with the most illustrious names that Anuradhapura has ever known. But what passes my comprehension is this, that the Brahmans, who were so anxious to secure the palladium, should have allowed it to pass so easily out of their reach. But, of course, they would never have expected that it would be carried off in that manner. It must have been a great sacrifice on the part of the king. It was like taking away the eye of the Kalinga kingdom.'

'The metaphor is scarcely inappropriate, my lord prince; it was the eye-tooth!' This was said in Sinhalese, with a little chuckle, by a stout personage who had now entered the gallery, and who knew enough of Pali, the language in which the friends had been talking, to understand what the prince was saying as he approached.

'This is Kapuranda, our great astrologer and phy-

Ceylon are so proud, was brought to Anuradhapura early in the fourth century in the manner indicated in the story. It is not likely, however, that the present relic in Kandy is the one originally brought.

[1] The ancient name for Ceylon.

sician,' said the prince, introducing the new-comer to his Indian friend. 'You have not seen in all India, I'll warrant, a greater man of science than he. You would scarcely think him to be a man who spends his nights in searching out the mysteries of the stars, and his days in practising the healing art. His familiarity' (this in an aside) ' is the result of high royal favour, which, however, he has lately lost in great measure through the influence of the Thero, who has no high opinion of his honesty.' Then addressing the astrologer, 'But let me give thee a word of caution, my big man of science, to speak a little more respectfully of the divine gift which to-day makes our country the envy of all the heavens of the gods, especially in the presence of the Thero.'

The astrologer, who was breathing like a porpoise, from the difficulty of the ascent, laughed, shaking his fat sides, in compliment to the prince's allusions to his great rotundity of person. And then, with a little leering look towards the priest, putting the palms of his hands together as if in adoration, replied: 'My lord, the priest will forgive me, I know, since it is rumoured that he himself does not always speak with reverence of the holy places and sacred relics. My lord knows that I am punctual in all the fasts and observances, and that the feast-days never see me absent from the reading of the Bana,[1] though I am not a priest.'

The priest appeared to ignore the astrologer's existence. He had been absorbed in meditation, and had apparently heard nothing of what was passing. Sud-

[1] The Buddhist Scriptures.

denly he broke out with the exclamation: 'Great Buddha! Can it be possible that these vast monuments of laborious uselessness can appropriately do honour to such a life as thine?' Then, turning to Dharma Sen, and pointing to the Abhayagiri Dagoba, which, in the light of the setting sun, threw a great dark shadow over the city, he said: 'Look at that, the glory of kings, a dark shadow of death for the people! The shadow is significant. That building contains bricks enough to build a city. The wealth and labour expended on it, employed in the supply of water, would have made a nation happy with a more lasting source of joy than even the possession of the sacred tooth itself. I do not forget,' he added, 'the works of beneficence wrought by the late king, thy royal father, prince. Generations to come will bless his memory for that glorious gift,' pointing with his long naked right arm to the shining expanse of the Mineri Lake in the east, 'when these immense dagobas are overgrown with forest and trampled under foot of beasts.'

'He, he, he!' chuckled the little fat astrologer, with a look which said, 'I told you so.'

'You would think my friend was sitting in the rostrum of the preaching-hall,' said the prince; while the Indian noble appeared to be impressed, and looked as if he thought it marvellous that a priest should talk in that strange fashion.

The prince went on describing the most prominent objects in the city which lay spread out like a map at their feet—the royal palace with its magnificent halls and its pleasure-gardens, the palace of the queen, the royal harem and the beautiful bathing tanks. Palace after palace and temple after temple were indicated, and their historical associations recounted. The glittering roof of the lofty Brazen Palace, built by Dutugemunu to contain cells for the accommodation of a thousand priests, shone like a sheet of gold. The sacred Bo-tree, almost in the middle of the city, from which all the more important streets appeared to radiate like the spokes of a wheel from the axle-tree, was of course pointed out as the central glory of the capital, though the tree itself was scarcely discernible, but the structures which constituted, or belonged to, the Maha Wihara,[1] on which the wealth of successive kings had been lavished, left no doubt as to the position of the sacred tree.

The description grew vivid, and the speaker's face glowed with an unwonted enthusiasm as he talked of monuments which were commemorative of great national victories. The Elala Dagoba, not far from the Holy Tree, he said, was a monument which had been erected to honour the memory of a brave foe and a magnanimous king. It was on that spot that Elala, the Damilo chief, was slain in war by Dutugemunu, and there the victorious king raised that lofty pile in honour of his courageous enemy.

'You appear to be full of Dutugemunu here,' said the visitor. 'He must have been a remarkable man and a good friend of the faith.'

'None more so in all our history. He built monasteries for the priests, of which the Brazen Palace was

[1] The great temple attached to the sacred Bo-tree. The Bo- or Boddhi-tree, still living in Anuradhapura—the 'oldest historic tree in the world'—grew from a branch of the Peepul (*Ficus religiosa*), under which Gautama attained Buddhaship, brought from India to Ceylon by the sister of Mahindo, and planted by King Pia Tisso 307 B.C.

THE ISURU MUNI ROCK TEMPLE.
(From a photograph by Scowen & Co., Colombo.)

the largest and finest. And at the "shout of refection" thousands of the yellow-robed brethren appeared in response to the royal invitation to the daily meal. The rice-fields which you see stretching away into the dim distance, like seas of vivid green, are the gifts with which the priesthood has been endowed by pious kings, and chiefly by the king of whom we have been talking, whose glory it was to call himself "the slave of the order." The city itself may be said to have been a gift to the priesthood.'

'All for the priest and nothing for the people!' interjected the Thero.

'At any rate, the Pansalas have no cause of complaint,' was the rejoinder. 'But let me get on with the description, for the light will soon be gone. It was Dutugemunu who made the pleasure-gardens on this side of the city, and set them apart for the service of the priests.'

The gardens were bright with yellow robes moving hither and thither over the green sward, and amongst trees covered with an abundant variety of foliage and flower. Some of them were ablaze with a crimson splendour, but the white of the champaka was the most prevalent colour. And these varied contrasts made the gardens a striking and beautiful scene to look down upon in the light of the setting sun.

'Away towards the south, and not far from the Tissa-wewa, the immense tank which lies there glittering yonder, beyond the tomb of Elala, you will observe the towers of the Isuru Muni Wihara, so called from the Esara Munis' (illustrious ascetics), 'who were fed on that spot by the pious king Tisso.

'Now look away to the west again, in the direction

of the king's palace. That is the secular quarter of the city, and there, between that big dagoba and the palace, you perceive the gleam of the small lake where you bathed this morning, and near which is the building in which I have the honour of entertaining you. The small street away to the north of the lake marks the place where the community of Western foreigners resides.'

'I have heard of them,' returned Dharma Sen, 'the white merchants who are not of our faith. It is a wonder that the late king tolerated them after his return to the religion of his fathers. But I presume they are not like the Wytulians, and are not a source of danger to the kingdom. I should like to know more of them.'

'If report speaks truly, the Thero could tell you much more about them than I can. Hitherto they have not appeared dangerous, and have confined their religious practices very much to themselves. Perhaps the Thero will tell you of them afterwards.'

'You spoke just now of the ancient temple of Isuru Muni. Is it not somewhere near that famous spot that the holy sisters live?' asked Dharma Sen.

'Yes. Not far from the temple towers you may observe a large rock rising out of a small garden, where it is just possible that you may see figures moving, which but for their white robes would be invisible. They are the female recluses to whose use the garden and the rock-chambers, with certain buildings that can scarcely be seen now, were devoted by the most religious monarch whose name I have mentioned so frequently already.'

'That is to say, Dutugemunu!' said the Indian visitor, with a smile. 'Then that is where the princess is lodged. It will please Anula well to have such opportunities of study and research as such a place must afford.'

'Anula; what Anula?' asked the prince, with sudden interest. 'Not the beautiful daughter of our old friend the guardian of the chief temple at Sarnath?'

'The same. She was one of our party, and joined the suite of the princess on the way, at the request of the princess herself. On her father's death, she made a vow that she would visit the holiest places in the south. Admiration has been given her freely in every place, not only because of the beauty of her person, but because of the excellent qualities of her mind, and her devotion to the faith of the great Sakya.[1] At Dantapura, where we stayed for a time, she astonished the royal court and the most learned of the city by the ease with which she wrote and conversed in Pali, in matters pertaining to the faith. It was chiefly through her influence that the princess came, and the secret mode of conveying the city's chief treasure was due in great measure to Anula's ready wit.'

'This is news, friend. I had no knowledge that you were so accompanied. We have been so full of the princess that we have overlooked most of her companions. This will be of interest to the Thero, who knew her at Sarnath, as the beautiful girl who could read the inscriptions on the pillars with which Asoka

[1] The tribal name of Gautama, the Buddha.

adorned your ancient city. But, after all, of what interest can such news be for one who has renounced the world for the ascetic life?'

A low chuckling laugh from behind, at which the prince frowned, indicated that the astrologer was still in the neighbourhood.

The priest looked as if he had heard not, but there was a faint tremor in his voice as he said, 'Our friend has not yet seen the statue of the great king Tisso, nor has he seen the stones on which are engraven the regulations for "the order." The day will soon have left the sky, and we should lose no time in seeing that excellent work of thine, my prince.'

They turned towards the wihara, where, on a great pedestal of granite, stood the statue of Mahindo's royal convert, the first of the Anuradhapura kings to walk in the 'eight-fold way.'

The visitor made a slight motion with his hands as if of reverence. The astrologer, who still attached himself to the company, bowed himself before it as abjectly as the corpulence of his person would permit, while an expression of disgust flashed into the face of the priest, as he looked at the little squat figure of the astrologer in obeisance.

The artist did not expect enthusiastic admiration from his Indian friend, whose eyes had been accustomed to the exquisite work in stone with which the temples and palaces in the kingdom of Benares were decorated, and he was not disappointed at receiving no rapturous compliments.

'It is a piece of excellent work,' said Dharma Sen; 'but why did you not make it more massive, like your colossal Buddhas?'

'There was a thought of that when the late king, Maha Sen, gave the order, and the king would have wished it so. But it was agreed in council with the priests that such massive shapes should be reserved for the Blessed One alone, because the greatness of that wisdom can only be represented in such greatness of mass, and but feebly then. It was done in our workshops, under my direction, but you know how greatly I am indebted for whatever skill I possess to what I saw in India.'

'Your workmen must also be skilful to carve so well as this.'

'Our workmen, with few exceptions, are from India. My countrymen, alas! have but little skill in the arts. We are indebted for much to India. But listen! what is that?'

It was the shout of praise—'*Sádhu! Sádhu!*' rising from hundreds of voices on the sacred hill. Coming out of the image-house, the little party found that the sun had set, and that the pilgrims on the mountain, their numbers greatly increased, were all gazing intently on the eastern sky, up into which banners of red light were apparently streaming, to form the splendid phenomenon known as 'Buddha's rays.'

It was witnessed by the crowd with the greatest enthusiasm, while many bowed before it in the attitude of worship. And when it was found that at that auspicious moment a procession of nuns, accompanying two ladies of the Princess of Kalinga's retinue, on a visit to the shrine of Mahindo, was ascending the stairs of Mihintala, the enthusiasm knew no bounds, and the reverence and praises were diverted from the sudden glory of the sky to the procession.

The popular attention was fixed not so much on the nuns with shaven heads and white robes as on the two stately figures at the head of the procession, also clothed in white, but with robes of richer material and unshaven heads, who carried on trays bedecked with flowers offerings for the shrine. They were both handsome, and formed a striking contrast in personal appearance to the shaven-headed nuns. One of them was Anula. The prince recognised her at once. The priest looked away at the sky, but with an inward struggle which he managed well to conceal, and then turned again into the image-house. Her appearance was such as would rivet the attention of utter strangers, to say nothing of those who were acquainted with her qualities of mind. Her head was well shaped and well carried. The face, statuesque in its lines, with the dark beauty of her race and country, but without insipidity. There were dark eyes that could flash into fire at a word, with a passion which was kept subdued in continual exercises of devotion.

On reaching the wihara, and having laid their offerings on the stone altar, the ladies prostrated themselves on the ground, pronouncing the three Saranas,[1] 'I take refuge in the Buddha. I take refuge in the doctrine. I take refuge in the order.' This done, Anula, notwithstanding her great self-control, could scarcely refrain from an exclamation of surprise, as she recognised in the attendant priest, standing by the altar, the tall form of Abhayo, immovable and emotionless as a statue.

A few brief moments, and the visitors had gone.

[1] The Buddhist confession of faith, commonly called the *Tun Sarana*, or 'Three Refuges.'

The priest walked around the hill to the rock-cells, saying to himself, 'It was a necessary penance.' And as he walked the night fell, and a thousand lamps seemed to burst into sudden flame all over the hill. It was the illumination in honour of the sacred relic.

CHAPTER II.

THE WESTERN FOREIGNERS.

How shall we sing the Lord's song in a strange land?
PSALM cxxxvii. 4.

REFERENCE has already been made to the mingling of nationalities on Mihintala. Not only were various Buddhist nations represented in Anuradhapura, but the trade in ivory and precious stones brought to the city large numbers of the merchants of the West, whose distinguishing costumes might often be seen in the principal streets. The majority of them had come from Alexandria; and those who, by frequent visits or long residence, had acquired the language, often discoursed in the houses of the Sinhalese nobles, with a well-concealed indifference to the gems for which they were bargaining, of the glories of that queenly city, of its temples, churches, palaces, and schools, and of the Museum which made the Brazen Palace of Anuradhapura sink into insignificance.

The Sinhalese listener would receive these stories of the greatness and splendour of the Western city, of the Pharos, and of the mighty monuments on the banks of the Nile, with a 'grain of salt.' It was a traveller's tale, and it had long been an unchangeable article of faith with him that nothing in the world could exceed in magnificence and majesty the vast buildings and stupendous piles with which Dutugemunu had adorned the mighty city in which he dwelt. He was not so impressed by the vividness of the description as to neglect his interest in the bargain. And we may be sure that the Alexandrian gem merchant had not altogether lost sight of the thing in hand, while apparently absorbed in his memories of the wonderful city which he called 'Home.'

Some of these traders were Jews, who would turn their faces away, and utter anathemas under their breath when they passed the statues of Buddha; or they would speak with indignation of 'the groves of Baal' when they met the pilgrim processions bound for the 'illustrious Bo.'

Others were Greek Christians, some of whom were more than tolerant of the idolatry and superstition by which they were surrounded. Some of them were more than half pagan themselves, and would often make their language 'strong,' by mingling the names of the Grecian gods with the holiest names of the Christian faith. A few were cosmopolitan in their religious tastes, believing that all religious systems had a common basis, and they might be seen worshipping with the Syrians on the Christian Sabbath, and laying garlands before the shrine in the Ruwanweli image-house a few days after. This 'universal charity' might have been born of cowardice;—it might have been thought useful in the 'interests of trade,' or it might have been owing to the absence of any real and deep-seated religious feeling, and often it was undoubtedly due to the most superficial acquaintance with the religions which were affected.

But certain it is that their eclecticism gained for those who professed it great popularity amongst the Sinhalese, who made much of the foreign converts, as they called them, from Alexandria, the centre of Western thought and learning; and would speak of their standing in Alexandrian society, and their learning, in the most exaggerated terms, in order to enhance the value of the conversion. Looked at from a purely worldly or business point of view, the eclectic life was a success. It gave the man who followed it the entrance to society which would otherwise be barred to him, and it also furnished him with splendid opportunities for the purchase of gems.

Let us follow a young Greek of this class down the street which leads to the sacred Bo, and on towards the palace from the Isuru Muni temple, the oldest in the city.

It is the morning of the day on which our story opens, and the city is busy with all the excitement of the occasion. Alypius is in a hurry, an unusual thing for him, for he glories in being able to maintain an equable calm, and in never being excited. His figure is of the average height. He wears a toga fastened by a brooch evidently of great value, which, with the jewels which flash on his fingers, may be taken as indications of some wealth. The toga is thrown back over the shoulders—exhibiting the neat and closely fitting tunic underneath—that he may walk the faster. His face shows that he is in deep thought. The face is undoubtedly Greek, with the straight features which characterise the Grecian statues. The eyes, however, are too close together, and just now the eyebrows are lowered. The face and head indicate power, and might be called handsome but for a certain sinister look about the eyes, and the fact that he never looks you straight in the face. There was a lack of sincerity in the expression even when, as now, he was absorbed in an unusually exciting vein of thought. It was the look of a man who could not be sincere, even with himself.

Groups of yellow-robed monks pass him unnoticed. Small processions conveying distinguished pilgrims under canopies of white cloth, with all sorts of floral decorations, are met without the beaming smile of 'universal charity' with which Alypius usually greets such spectacles. He turns down by a preaching hall—where yellow robes pass in and out among the great stone pillars of exquisite workmanship—to be out of the crowd, when, just as he reaches the Elala Dagoba, he finds the crowd bigger than ever. Men are clearing the way with the cracking of long whips, and shouting the titles of Kirti Sri Meghawarna, the king, who has been visiting the Thuparama, to worship the sacred tooth, and is now on his way to the Isuru Muni temple.

There is no help for it, he must stop till the procession has passed, and very long the time seems to the impatient Greek. Suddenly the whips stop their cracking, the bands of music cease, the tomtoms are hushed, and the shrill pipes are silent. A universal quiet pervades the crowd as the king's elephant kneels, and the king, in obedience to the traditional veneration which the Sinhalese maintain for the memory of the chivalric chief of the Damilos, walks past the mound which covers the ashes of Dutugemunu's great foe. The king, like most great bodies, moves slowly. His corpulence, which is a great virtue in the eyes of his subjects, will not admit of haste. The ministers of the king and the chiefs who follow are nearly as corpulent, or, if they are not, they try to make up for it in appearance with folds of many yards of muslin about their waists, which compels them to adopt that undignified method of locomotion called 'waddling.'

The dark face of Sri Meghawarna is almost as Greek in its outlines as that of Alypius himself. The young Greek has often been struck with the similarity of type in the contour of face which many of the people of this Eastern land bear to that of the Greek colonists of Alexandria, and has caught himself wondering sometimes whether they may not be, after all, branches of the same stock. The crown which rests on the king's head is not unlike a mitre in shape, broad at the top and adorned with splendid jewels and a nodding plume.

Alypius bows low to the ground and puts on the 'universal charity' smile as the king and his ministers pass, and then he rushes by the tail of the procession with an imprecation in Greek, stumbling against a priest, who says laughingly:

'What, my eclectic friend? You are generally more careful in picking your way.'

Alypius was about to do reverence, when he saw that he was standing before the towering form of the Mihintala Thero, whose eyes always appeared to look right through him, and in whose presence he never felt at ease.

'I was hurrying to the house of Joseph the Syrian, when I was met and delayed by the royal procession. What brings the king and you abroad so early? I suppose it is this precious tooth.'

'That sneer, Alypius, sits very ill on lips which have pronounced the " three refuges " at the Dalada shrine.'

The Greek blushed to the roots of his hair, but immediately retorted: 'It is not more anomalous than the Thero's own frequent visits to the family of the Syrian disciple of the Nazarene. What would the fathers and brethren of the sacred college say to that, my lord? But my anxiety now is to visit that same family, which, as the Thero knows, is abundant reason for anxiety and haste.' And saying this he rushed off, while the priest walked to the Brazen Palace, into the great hall of which he passed.

Alypius was not long in reaching the 'foreign quarter' of the city where the Christian community dwelt, and where the merchants of the West chiefly resided. There was a little church in the centre of this community, small and insignificant compared with the splendid temples and mighty piles of the great heathen city, but it was a most sacred and precious thing to many of these exiles. That plain building of stone and mud was very dear to the heart of Joseph the Syrian. It was suggestive to him of many happy memories and hallowed associations. He had come, a political exile from Antioch, with his young wife first to a small colony of his own people in South India, and then, attracted by the wonderful stories which had been told him about Lanka and its jewels, he threw in his lot with a firm of gem merchants, and settled in the royal city. He had not been there long before he succeeded, with the help of his friends, in building a house for the worship of God. And after a time a presbyter, Thomas, of the Syrian Church, whom he had known in old days, came to act as minister to the little community.

The presbyter was a man of great reserve. He was known to but few beyond the small congregation to which he ministered, and they knew him as the 'one-armed Christian priest.' It was said that by some accident he had lost his right arm. He never referred to it himself, and the deftness with which he used his left hand in turning pages of manuscript seemed to make the absence of the right scarcely felt. He always appeared in a long, thin black robe, which covered his person, with the exception of his long, active left arm. Though not a very old man, his appearance, with his long beard and long hair, was scarcely less venerable than that of his friend Joseph, who was some few years older. There were lines in his face that indicated sad memories and much suffering in his past life; but with that past few, if any, were acquainted except his friend Joseph. And perhaps it was that knowledge which made the merchant regard the minister with a tender reverence, given to a life sanctified by trials which were greater than any he himself had been called on to endure.

All these arrangements for worship were, to the surprise of Joseph, made without opposition from the Buddhist authorities. Buddhist princes, in Ceylon at any rate, have not often been intolerant in regard to other religions, except when associated in their minds with political danger. Even through the revolution which followed the recantation of the Wytulian heresy by Maha Sen, when the king's zeal was turned against the heretics, the little Christian community had remained untouched. Perhaps it was too insignificant for the zeal of the penitent king.

To Joseph the church was a bright bit of home in the strange heathen land. The plain walls and pierced windows, without ornament, in order that they might emphasise the contrast between the purity and spirituality of the Christian faith and the idolatry in the midst of which it was set, as a light in a dark place, the solemn liturgy set in Scripture phraseology, and the simple ritual, all lessened the exile bitterness in Joseph's heart, and made him feel that he was still in his Father's House. And over the rostrum where the preacher was wont to sit with the roll of the Gospel manuscript in his hand, Joseph had given expression to this thought of home in the Hebrew characters cut in stone, which formed the word ' Bethel.'

This feeling of attachment to the Bethel had been strengthened by another tie. Joseph's wife, Rachel, the companion of his exile, had died many years ago, leaving him a baby-girl to fill the place occupied by her in his heart and home. The mother was buried in the little church, just under the sacramental table, and there Joseph held up the infant daughter to receive baptism, and he called her name Irene, for he said, 'God hath sent the dove to me in my grief, to tell me that the world is not destroyed.'

He built his house as near to the church as he possibly could. There was nothing pretentious about it. It was a square building of stone, and in that respect differed from the mud houses of most of his Sinhalese neighbours. It also differed from them in having a flat roof, while the Sinhalese houses were thatched. Joseph used to say in the dry season that he wondered the people did not see the advantage of the flat roof and its canopy of plaited leaves; but in the burst of the monsoon he would acknowledge that the advantage was a doubtful one. Like the houses of the better class amongst the Sinhalese, the buildings connected with it were arranged in quadrangular form, every room looking into a square which Joseph's Greek and Italian friends called the *atrium*. This part of the house was Irene's delight, and Joseph had gratified her desires to the full in its adornment. In it she trained with the utmost care plants of the kinds which flourished in the land of her fathers, which the gem merchants, out of their affection for Joseph and his daughter, had brought her.

And Joseph would sit in the verandah looking at the flowers and dreaming of his old home, or he and his friend Thomas would sit in the hall watching the lithe and graceful figure of Irene, as she, with the help of her little Sinhalese maid Kumari, trained the flowers and tended the birds. Irene was accustomed to say that she would not exchange that little spot for all the palace of the chief queen, with its cool corridors and its richly sculptured bathing tanks. And Joseph said that looking there was like being in church, that it took him altogether away from the heathen city, and made him re-live his childhood and youth.

And truly there was not a more beautiful sight in Anuradhapura, even on that day of magnificent spectacles, than was presented on this morning within the quadrangle of the house of Joseph the Syrian. Irene, moving about amidst rare dwarf palms, was assisting the tendrils of a beautiful passion-flower to grasp the next highest bar of a trellised arch, unconsciously showing the full beauty and grace of her figure. Tall and queenly she looked as she stood there in her simple, white, loose morning costume, her long black hair folded and bound up, Grecian fashion, with a fillet of jasmine, which Kumari had brought her. Kumari stood by her, looking with profound admiration on the grace and beauty of her mistress. This state of mind was almost chronic with the little Sinhalese maiden. She herself made an effective contrast. The bright, dark-eyed, dark-skinned beauty of the girl in her more tightly fitting Sinhalese dress made an admirable though not intentional set-off to the beauty of the fair young Syrian.

Joseph was sitting on his favourite couch in the verandah, and father and daughter talked, as the latter attended to the plants nearest to the old man's seat.

'Do you think, my father, that the Thero is at all impressed with the truths of our Holy Religion? His eyes were filled with tears the other day while Thomas was reading and you were interpreting the story of the death and resurrection of Lazarus from the manuscript of the Holy Gospel by John the Elder.'

'Yes, daughter, I noticed that, and immediately after it he had that look in his eyes characteristic in some of his moods which I have never seen in other men except one, whom I heard when I was a mere youth in Antioch. He often looked in his excitement while talking as if his soul had been carried away and his eyes were trying to follow it, and so sometimes does our friend the Thero. Of the story of Bethany, he said, speaking in that absent way: "Great Buddha, there is nothing in thy life like that. If thou hadst the sympathy, thou hadst not the power—not the power." He repeated the last words over and over again. It was evidently that which had struck him most in the story.

'On my asking him why he apostrophised Buddha

when he knew him to be in Nirvana, he replied that it was a habit which most of them had in their times of self-forgetfulness. "Does it not seem at such times," he went on to say, "as if an instinct compelled us to cry out to a God somewhere in the universe? But the masses of the people never realise the meaning of Nirvana. Buddha is for them but one of their many gods. It is difficult, extremely difficult;" and then he paused and turned the talk, and asked me if I had ever heard the story of " Buddha and the mustard seed."'

'What was it, father mine? I had left the hall before that; tell it me, I pray thee, while I train these tendrils of the passion-flower. How like poor human souls they look as they feel about in space for something to rest upon!'

'He said that, shortly after Gautama had obtained the knowledge of deliverance by his long fast under the tree of wisdom, a young girl, by name Kisagotami, who had been married to a wealthy man, came to him one day in great distress. She had one child, but when the beautiful boy could run alone he died. The young girl, in her love for it, carried the dead child clasped to her bosom. She had been directed by a mendicant who said: "The Buddha can give you medicine; go to him." She went to Gautama, and doing homage to him, said: "Lord and Master, do you know any medicine that will be good for my child?" "Yes, I know of some," said the Teacher. Now it was the custom for patients or their friends to provide the herbs which the doctors required, so she asked what herbs he would want. "I want some mustard seed," he said; and when the poor girl eagerly promised to bring some of so common a drug, he added, " You must get it from some house where no son or husband, or parent or slave, has died." " Very good," she said, and went to ask for it, still carrying her dead child with her. The people said, "Here is mustard seed, take it;" but when she asked: "In my friend's house has any son died, or a husband, or a parent, or slave?" they answered: " Lady! what is this you say ? The living are few, the dead are many!" She returned to the Buddha, saying: " My Lord, I have not found the mustard seed; the people tell me that the living are few and the dead are many." He exhorted her to take comfort from the fact that she was not alone in her suffering, which she did, and became a disciple.'

'I can understand how he would contrast the two stories. He must see that none but a living Saviour can deliver the world.'

'My daughter, to us it is a marvel that any can resist the influence of that Gospel which the holy Apostle Paul said was "the power of God unto salvation to him that believeth"; but nothing can be harder than for a man to cast off the creed of the generations of his people, of his birth, even though it be the cold, dark atheism of Gautama. How long have we declared Jesus in this idolatrous city, and with what results? Do not Thomas and I, as we look out from the roof on their heathen processions as they go to the Idol tree, cry with all our hearts: " How long ? O Lord! how long?" By the way, Prudentius, the Italian merchant, was telling us yesterday that acts of worship are being paid now in Christian churches in Rome to relics which are said to have been miraculously discovered.'

'Surely that cannot be in a Christian church, my father! But were you not saying the other day that the natural man is always an idolater?'

'It is true, my child; and even with the best—and God knows that I am not among them—our sacred places are apt to become idolatrous shrines.' And Joseph sighed as he thought of the slab under the communion-table in the little church, how he had looked towards it in his devotions, as if it had been the door of heaven.

'But about the Thero, my father; he is good and sincere, I know, and will follow the light when he sees it. He is different from other wearers of the robe, if one may judge from the stories Kumari sometimes tells me of them.'

'Yes, child, head and shoulders above them spiritually as well as physically. He is a great orator, they say, in his native tongue, and is appointed by royal command to give the address to-morrow night at the dedication of the new hall in honour of this new object of idolatry, the sacred tooth.'

'How I should like to be there! Would it be possible, my father?'

'Peace be to this house!' This was said by the young Greek gem merchant, who had stood in the entrance for a few moments in astonishment at the beauty of the scene.

'And likewise to thee, Alypius,' replied Joseph, rising to welcome the visitor, while Irene, with a slight inclination of the head, drawing on a veil, went on quietly with her work.

'My daughter and I were just talking of our friend the Mihintala Thero' (Alypius's brow darkened), 'and of the dedication of the new preaching hall at the king's palace, in honour of the relic. Thou wert saying, child, thou wouldest like to be there; but knowest thou not that any such act of thine would be construed into a participation in the sin of idolatry, with which this fair land is cursed?'

This was said as much for the benefit of Alypius as Irene. His 'universal charity' and 'philosophical affinities' in religion were not at all agreeable to the Syrian, and often made their intimate business relationships repugnant to him.

'But this is not to be an occasion for the worship of false gods or relics. If report speaks truly, the priest has but scant reverence for such things himself. Kumari says that her mother will take me to the part of the hall which the women occupy.'

'We will see, child; but I like it not. In the meantime Alypius and I have business of importance to discuss.'

The men withdrew to a room which was Joseph's place of business, from whence came sounds as of earnest persuasion on the part of the young Alexandrian, and opposition on Joseph's part. The young man had made himself almost indispensable to the old Syrian merchant, who had trusted the plausible Greek and had admitted him into the firm of dealers of which he, up to that time, had been chief. There were many things in the younger man's character beside his eclecticism which displeased Joseph, but he had on two or three occasions rendered important services in business, and, in common gratitude, Joseph felt loth to think evil of him.

If Alypius was sincere anywhere it was in this house.

About the sincerity of his own ardent affection for the fair daughter of his partner there could be no doubt. But his love was not returned. His presence chilled Irene, and his quick perceptions soon discovered that fact. But he could wait, he said to himself.

CHAPTER III.

IN THE PREACHING HALL.

Earnest among the thoughtless, awake among the sleepers, the wise man advances like a racer, leaving behind the hack.
BUDDHAGOSHA.

THERE was a vast crowd gathered that evening at the new hall. The relic had been exhibited to many thousands of people, and a royal procession had taken the shrine which was to cover it through the principal streets of the city and down the sacred way to Mihintala on the previous night. The first Bana-reading in the new hall lately built by the king, and dedicated to the tooth, was to be one of the chief events in the celebration of the week. The hall itself was of considerable dimensions, but it had been made larger by means of huge verandahs and pandals on wooden pillars, decorated with a variety of leaves and fruit, and covered with plaited leaves, so that a multitude of people could be accommodated, who could look between the elegantly carved pillars of the hall and see all that passed, if they were not able to hear all that was said.

'The Mihintala Thero has a voice like a bell,' Irene heard a Sinhalese man say to his neighbour, as she passed the outskirts of the crowd with Kumari's mother, to a place outside the pillars of the hall, but near enough to see and hear well, allotted to distinguished ladies.

'There is no doubt that we shall be able to hear him,' responded the other; 'but the question is whether we ought, as good Buddhists, to listen to what a man has to say who, if rumour may be credited, has so little reverence for our holy relics and sacred places.'

'Let us not judge harshly, my friend. The king and the artist prince favour him, though, it is said, rather for his skill in speech than for his opinions. He has travelled much, and he doubtless has seen much in other religions and peoples that he likes. Our Thero may be affected somewhat by what he has seen in foreign lands. On the other hand, look at that Greek there, pushing his way in at the right. He has travelled more than the Thero, and knows all the religions of the world, and yet they say that he has come to the conclusion that ours is the best, and I know he has pronounced the "refuges," and taken "Sil."[1]

'People say that he wants to start a new religion, to be made up of the best in all religions; but look, there come the priests!'

A long procession of yellow-robed, shaven-headed monks entered at the end of the hall, and ranged themselves on an elevated platform erected for them, so

---

[1] The ten silas are ten precepts for regulating the conduct of Buddhist priests. The first five are binding on all good Buddhists. These may be observed either for a definite or indefinite time, gaining proportionate merit for the person who observes them, who begins the observance by having the precepts repeated to him by a priest. This is called 'taking Sil.'

that none should be above them, with their faces turned slightly away from that part of the hall set apart for females. (On such occasions the rule of the order, that no mendicant may look at the face of a woman, was strictly observed, though in the streets and in ordinary life it was not so closely adhered to.) Foremost came the old high priest of Thuparama, but conspicuously above them all might be seen the Mihintala Thero.

The Indian visitors, a prince of Kalinga, with Dharma Sen and others, sat on the left of the platform, and with them was Detu, who acted as interpreter, when anything of special importance was said, for the visitors, who, although they could converse in Pali, of course as yet knew but little of Sinhalese.

At the back of the hall, on a framework covered with baked clay, were pictures taken from scenes in the life of Gautama, painted under the prince's superintendence. On the sides of the platform there were also rude pictures illustrating the Játakas or Birth-stories.

Alypius had managed to get very near the platform, and was engaged in conversation with a priest who appeared to be an old acquaintance. There was a cynical sneer on his face, which the priest did not see as he looked on the pictures, which, it must be confessed, were but uncouth and rude specimens of art, while he said in a smooth, laudatory tone: 'It is a wonderful production. Very realistic indeed, and must have an effect in educating the people with regard to the life of the Blessed One. They are beginning to put pictures, I hear, in our—I mean—in Christian churches now.'

Detu was not satisfied with the work; he said to his Indian friends, half in apology: 'We are not painters. We do try to execute something worth looking at in sculpture, but even in that we are far behind you. It may come to us in time. You will see that some of the scenes are the carvings in your temples reproduced from memory. But here comes my royal brother the king.'

The bands of music were giving vent to their most deafening sounds as Sri Meghawarna entered the hall, followed by his ministers and attendant chiefs, with Sinhalese men of high rank, who carried lamps which emitted sweet perfumes, holding them down low near the monarch's feet as he walked. It was an imposing spectacle. Alypius remarked to his friend the priest that the whole scene reminded him of the representations of Egyptian ceremonies which he had seen in carvings and paintings in some of the old temples and palaces on the banks of the Nile. In fact, there was the most striking resemblances between that ancient faith and that of the last of the Buddhas.

'Is that a bit of your new universal religion?' asked the priest.

But all further conversation was stopped. The king had seated himself on the gorgeous throne-seat, while all the multitude bowed their heads low in reverence, and those who could do so on the outside prostrated themselves on the ground. The priests alone stood upright, in token of the supremacy of the 'order,' to which even kings must bow. Gautama had taught them that they were not to do reverence to any mortal; the caste of Buddhist mendicants was to be worshipped, even by Brahmans.

Soon after the king was seated a young priest went into the rostrum, and, sitting there with a book of ola leaves spread before him, read the Buddhist Scriptures from one of the three Pitakas, which contain the doctrines of Gautama.

This ended, the Mihintala Thero came forward. After a breathless pause, which lasted for a few seconds, during which he appeared to be in profound meditation, he chanted a few stanzas of Pali verse. It sounded like a dirge, a wail of bitter sadness, as if it contained the sorrows and disappointments of a life. The voice was thin and penetrating to begin with. It was delivered, apparently, with little effort at first, and there was the far-away look in the speaker's eyes, as if the king and the multitude were not present, and the soul were struggling to attain distant heights, which soon grew into a mighty passion of earnestness.

Irene could not understand the Pali; indeed, but few, comparatively, of those present could. She knew Sinhalese well, for Joseph and she had studied it together, that they might be of service, as he had said, to the cause of their Lord and Master; but she felt the struggle and sorrow in the quotations, just as if she knew every word. Sympathetic natures can often read without words.

Anula, the Indian lady, had heard the words repeated a hundred times, but felt that she had never known them before. Was it possible that there could be all that suggestion of doubt and disappointment in them? Did the Blessed One speak the words with all that depth of sorrow? She had been accustomed to priests who spoke like machines, who always spoke the sacred words mechanically. This was a new experience. It was a man who felt and thought, and not a statue. And so she pondered as the Thero left the Pali to speak in the language of the people, a language which she as yet could not understand, but which she determined soon to acquire.

The stanzas repeated by the Thero were the following:—

>   Long have I wandered! long!
>   Bound by the chain of life,
>   Through many births:
>   Seeking thus long in vain,
>   Whence comes this life in man, his consciousness,
>   his pain?
>   And hard to bear his birth,
>   When pain and death but lead to birth again.
>   Found! It is found!
>   O Cause of Individuality!
>   No longer shalt thou make a house for me:
>   Broken are all thy beams,
>   Thy ridge-pole shattered:
>   Into *Nirvana* now my mind has past:
>   The end of cravings has been reached at last!

'Thus spake the All-wise, the Blessed One,' he went on, 'on attaining the knowledge of all things under the Tree of Wisdom. So he describes his search, the object of his seeking and struggling, and the victory gained at last. It is a picture of the hope and the hopelessness of even what is best in human life. Life is full of desire, and we are taught that desire is the curse of existence. The Holy One teaches us to look forward with hope to the rest of Nirvana, where desire and life are together extinguished. But in order to this there must be a repression in our own heart and life of every wishful thought and feeling. This is the

one great conquest in humanity. The only conquerors
are the Arhats,[1] who have overcome desire and conquered self. As the hosts of Mára tempted the Lord
of all the worlds, so are we tried by our desires and
passions.' (He pointed to the pictures of the struggle
with Mára, the prince of evil, whose seductive daughters
were represented on the painted clay, as beseeching
Gautama, and trying to allure him with their beauty,
away from his quest, and from the throne of his firm
resolve under the sacred Bo.) 'That is the struggle of
life. To resist Mára is to live, nay, to die—for why
should we live?—and rest for ever. Followers of the
Blessed One, can any life be noble—is it not rather
low and ignominious?—which is not characterised
by a stern resistance of temptation and of lust? Is
not gratified desire the beginning of disgrace and perdition?

'But how few are the conquerors! How few are
the delivered! And what is there in all births and in
all worlds more difficult than the resistance of desire?
My brothers, my partners in the evils of existence, be
firm and courageous. Bend not before the assaults
of Mára, yield not to his seductions, and then deliverance and rest must be ours. But I know the cry that
rises at once to your lips, the cry which rises so often
from my own, the cry of the sinning and suffering ones
all over the world: " We are so weak, and the foe is so
strong. Is there none to pity, none to help?" Be
brave, my brothers, there is pity and help somewhere
in the universe, though the Blessed One has passed
away.' (Some of the priests exchanged glances.) 'We

---

[1] Saints who have conquered human passions—ascetics.

know not how it will come, but help must come to those who follow the "eight-fold path."[1]

'We dare not put ourselves by the side of the Tathagato. Look at the history represented there. No one of us can look at it and say, "It is ours; I may become that." You say it may be reached by the accumulation of merit. But what is the merit of all our births when placed by that of all the lives of the last of the Buddhas? Oh, my brothers, the Buddhas are far away from us! There is not one of us but feels that a great gulf is fixed between them and us, over which they cannot pass to us, nor we to them. I am as one standing on the edge looking into that gulf to-night with straining eyes. Millions of living beings in the world are doing the same, crying, "How may we cross to the blessed shore?" Keep the precepts! Gain merit. The Karma[2] of a thousand births, and all in holy living, will at last be our deliverance. Meanwhile we wander on these shores in doubt and despair through repeated transmigrations, as these Jatakas say the Bodhisatwa[3] did. We have the precepts, and we have been taught the way. But the way is so difficult, and we are so weary of it all, so often vanquished by Mára. And to look at the Buddha, to look at that calm face in repose, or the uplifted finger of the Great Teacher of

---

[1] The first of the 'Four Paths' which summarise the teaching of the Buddha, consisting of the following eight virtues: (1) Right convictions, (2) right emotions, (3) right words, (4) right deeds, (5) right means of living, (6) right endeavours, (7) right memories, (8) right meditations.

[2] Karma or Kamma is the sum of a man's deeds, which, according to their Kusal (merit) or Akusal (demerit), determined his condition in the next birth.

[3] The title of him who is to become the Buddha.

mankind, is only to remind us of our own weakness and despair.

'My brothers, we want help. We want help from outside ourselves. The world in its misery is holding out its hands imploringly into space for help from without. That is what all this statue and relic worship means. It was never sanctioned by the Blessed One. That is what all the worship of demons around us means. That is what this new mixture of Brahmanism and Buddhism means. It is the world imploring deliverance and crying for help from outside its own poor weak self. And is there none to pity, none to help? The imploring world will not believe it. Men look at the wonders of the heavens and the earth, they look at the sun-god, at the star-houses, at the days and the seasons, and all that is wrought by the great forces of Nature, and they say, "Will you tell us that there is nothing behind all that? Nothing that can help and save?"

'Brothers, the Buddhas that have gone have shown us the path. We are thankful for that; but they give us no help but example. We are thankful for that. But example is not enough. It will not deliver me unless I have the power to follow. Look again at these pictures, and think of the history. Are we of the same race as the Buddhas? There is that gulf between us. Who will save?

'This is our hope. Think of it. There is a coming One. He will bring the help that we need. Let us, while we look at the past—let us, while we look with reverence, but not worship, at the statues, pictures, and relics which remind us of the last of the mighty conquerors of Mára—let us also look forward to the promised One who shall come amongst ourselves from the Tusita heaven, and finish the deliverance revealed by him whose disciples we are.

'Is it not possible that he has already come? That somewhere in the vast world the Maitri[1] Buddha hath already appeared to men with manifestations of that mighty power which alone can save, and that infinite merit which alone can compensate for all our demerits? These, my brothers, are some of the strugglings of my own mind. Why do I tell you of this? Why give you my doubts? Because I know that often in some shape or other they are your doubts also. Because I would not have you despair. I ask you to look for the coming One. There is our hope. Let us arise and seek Him, the greatest of all, the Maitri Buddha, our deliverer, our friend!'

The attention of the crowd was riveted on the speaker, not altogether by what he said. Many of the audience could hardly follow him in the strife of doubt and belief to which he had given utterance. There were some who felt that these were burning words flung out from a soul on fire with the thought of the mysteries and destinies of life, and who hailed the gleam of hope with which the address had been concluded. There was a responsive flame in their own soul which went out to that expressed in the words of the impassioned priest.

[1] *Maitri* is the name of the Bodhisatwa who is to be the next Buddha. It is said that he will come to the world from the Tusita heaven. Gautama, the Buddha of the present Kalpa (era or dispensation), was preceded by many Buddhas with Kalpas stretching over incalculable periods of time.

But all were deeply impressed with the man. His figure, as he stood on the front of the platform, was in the highest degree impressive and commanding. 'It revives the orations in the Academy,' said Alypius to his friend. 'I could almost believe that I was listening to an eloquent Greek in the Alexandrian schools, where they love, and grow enthusiastic over, themes like that. And again it was not altogether unlike a Christian enthusiast, and there was as much Christianity in the address as Buddhism. You will have to watch your eloquent brother closely, or you will see him throwing off his robes some fine day. That was not a bad suggestion, however, about the Maitri Buddha. Is it true that another Buddha is expected? I never heard of that before.'

'Quite true,' replied the priest; 'but our Mihintala brother is surely wrong about the time. The dispensation of Gautama is not yet finished. I must look that up.'

'Well, at any rate, that part of the address was worth something. The hint may be useful in—in——'

'You were going to say in the "new universal religion;" but you will not get the preacher to agree with you there. When I spoke to him about your scheme the other day, he said he had no faith in any scheme of the kind which did not proceed from a pure heart and clean hands. What did he mean, do you think? I cannot understand where he picked up his strange ideas. I am pretty sure he didn't get them in the Pansala.'

'But I think I could throw a light on it that would make the brethren of the Pansala stare, and more than stare. You may be sure of this: that priests do not get ideas of that kind by adhering strictly to the rules of the "order." But I would not say a word to discredit his orthodoxy for one moment, especially in the presence of his brethren. I must not stay. Long life to you! There is some one that I know.' And the young Greek edged his way to the place where Irene with Kumari's mother was trying to emerge from the crowd of women.

The acclamations which had rent the air at the conclusion of the discourse had died away, but the magnetic spell of the speaker's presence and voice still lingered with the dispersing multitude. The king had retired at the close of the address. Detu lingered with the illustrious visitors, and went over again what the Thero had said for their benefit. He was profoundly moved by it himself, and therefore repeated it with much impressiveness. But of them all there was not one so deeply impressed as Anula. She united the translation with the voice to which she seemed still to be listening. A great resolve had taken hold of her. Her own doubts and struggles had been set before her in the speaker's words, and henceforth she too would look for the coming Buddha.

The Greek Alypius accosted Irene, and said in Greek: 'It is not fit that the daughter of Joseph the Syrian should mingle with the multitude in the city with only the Sinhalese nurse to protect her. Let me, I pray thee, offer my escort, to ensure a safe return to thy father's house.'

'I have no fear, Alypius. Kumari's father will join us soon, and the distance is not great.'

'But is it not possible that the passions of the mob

may be enkindled by the indiscreet though eloquent address to which we have just listened, that they may be angry because of its unorthodoxy, and may they not with some show of truth connect it with the house of Joseph the Syrian? I can have nothing but admiration for the Thero's profound talents—a little wild and incoherent, but very much in earnest. We, at any rate, ought not to complain of his unorthodoxy. I was thinking only of the influence of the address on the populace.'

'The populace will not think of it in that way, unless some kind friend suggests it. Oh, if I could but have dared to get up and tell them of One who is mighty to save! How cowardly we are! But the Thero would not be ashamed of the Lord Jesus if he knew Him. Thou seest we can have no need of thy escort, Alypius.'

And with that the Greek left, muttering maledictions on his luck, as he called it, but immediately comforting himself with the saying, 'The time will come when it shall be different.' He paused, hesitating as to the direction he should take, then, having come to a decision, walked briskly down an unfrequented street, saying under his breath: 'Ah yes, I will go to my friend the astrologer.'

Irene went home, thinking of the Thero's burning words and the struggles of his soul, and thinking also that perhaps none in the vast assembly understood the eloquent priest as well as she did.

There was another lady who went away with her party having her mind occupied with similar thoughts. It was Anula; she could understand him, she said to herself, although she knew scarcely a word except what was uttered in the introductory stanzas. And then she turned to her Sinhalese friends, to make inquiries concerning the fair girl whose beauty was discernible even through her veil, and who had listened to the Thero's discourse with such rapt attention.

CHAPTER IV.

AT THE ASTROLOGER'S.

A thing of dark imaginings.—BYRON.

THE Greek hurried with quick steps down the River Street, one of the minor streets leading to one of the numerous ferries by which the Malwatteoya—the river on which the city was situated—was crossed. Half way between the Ruwanweli temple and the river, he stopped before a high wall surrounding a large court, within which was a temple which in its construction was very unlike the ordinary wiharas of Anuradhapura. The architecture would indicate at a glance its connection with Hinduism, to say nothing of the images within of Hindu deities, which held their own with representations of Gautama. The religious observances at the temple formed a strange mixture of Buddhism and Hinduism, and attracted large numbers of the Damilos,[1] who formed the chief proportion of the artisan class in the city, as well as those who were still attached to the Wytulian doctrine, the heresy

---

[1] Ceylon was invaded early in Sinhalese history by the Damilos (Tamils) from Southern India.

encouraged by King Maha Sen in the early part of
his reign. There were but few temples in Anuradhapura that were more popular than the Khandarája,
into the spacious court of which Alypius now entered.
The heretical monastery connected with it had been
suppressed on the return of Maha Sen to the faith of
his forefathers, and the tall structure in which the
priests had made their home had been given by him to
the court astrologer as a reward for some successful
divination.

A new residence had been built for the priests since
Maha Sen's death, but the old monastery, built in imi-
tation of the Brazen Palace, broad at the base and
gradually diminishing towards the top of the five-storied
building, was in the possession of the chief astrologer
of the court, the son of Maha Sen's favourite. It had
been much altered since the time of its erection, to suit
the purposes of the astrologer. The highest story but
one, which had been the residence of the chief priest,
was now the hall of 'mystery,' and was regarded with
the profoundest awe by the populace, who would bind
their charms on more tightly and mutter the 'refuges,'
as they beheld strange lights flashing through the little
wooden windows at night, or listened to the peculiar
noises, sometimes like thunder, that issued from the
astrologer's tower, which nobody doubted were the
voices of the demons in conversation with the wizard.
Above this was a room only half covered by roof, where
the astrologer was supposed to read the signs in the
heavens. There were but few places more popular
during the daytime than this, which was really the
centre of the religious life of the lower classes, and a
not infrequent resort of priests and nobles, and there

was not a place in the city more generally avoided by night.

It was evidently not the first nocturnal visit that had been paid to the astrologer by Alypius. The servant who lay sleeping at the principal entrance, and who was wakened with much difficulty, recognised in the visitor, as soon as he could open his eyes, an old acquaintance of his master.

The Greek, not wishing to attract attention by shouting or clapping his hands, the usual method of announcing oneself, had rolled the sleeper over, as if he had been a log, with his feet. But, like a log, the porter remained at his post, with an occasional snort as the only evidence of life. Then the visitor laid hold of him by the long black hair which was hanging loosely over his shoulder. This at last had the desired effect. 'Kiri Banda,' said Alypius. 'Give me thanks! I have pulled thee back from Nirvana by the hair of the head. That woman's hair of thine is worth something after all. Thou wert going off to the eternal sleep too soon, my friend. Thy Karma is not yet worked out. Where is thy master?'

Kiri Banda stood rubbing his eyes, muttering plagues on the visitor with his 'Karmas' and 'Nirvanas,' and then said deferentially, 'My lord will find him in the upper chamber pursuing his divine calling. I heard him talking with the Dewas a short time since. My lord knows the way,' directing the Greek to a little stone staircase, where a small brass lamp with a floating wick was burning. Up went Alypius, and as he went a loud snoring became more and more distinct. 'Aha!' said he to himself, 'this is the talk with the gods heard by my good friend below. By my faith (which faith?), the conversation is very one-sided, and is sufficiently sonorous for all the gods in the Pantheon to hear.'

The astrologer's sleep was not so profound as that of his servant. Before the Greek had reached the hall of mystery the sound had ceased; a little chuckling laugh greeted him at the door and gave him a welcome. The fat figure of the little astrologer assumed an enormous rotundity as seen in the dim ghastly light shed from a small lamp which was fed by some chemically prepared oil, which lamp was, of course, a part of the magical apparatus with which the man of science surrounded himself. The walls of the room were adorned with rough paintings of the 'Star-houses,' and ola leaves on which various horoscopes were marked. Everything was arranged to make an impression. Human skulls and the skulls of animals, including the skull of a mighty elephant, formed a horrible pyramid on one side of the room, and a collection of masks more horrible still, used in demon ceremonies, was piled up on the other side. Serpents (their fangs extracted) of the most loathsome appearance crawled about the skulls, and a huge, detestable-looking Kabaragoya (like a small crocodile), ugly enough in the daylight, uglier still in the dim magic light of the astrologer's hall, lay motionless near the masks, ready to be cut in pieces for the most precious charms and incantations.

The eye of the Greek took in all this at a glance. Few people would dare enter such a place, but Alypius was one of the initiated, and was but little impressed, except with the thought of the effect all the room would probably have on the ignorant. He was most impressed with the small glittering eyes of the master of this temple of horrors, who stood in the centre of the hall motioning him to be seated on a roughly-made couch over which a leopard skin had been thrown.

'I had the utmost difficulty to waken that slave of thine. He had gone to Nirvana, and I had at last to drag him out by the hair of the head. He told me that his master was conversing with the gods. I heard the conversation as I came; pray let me not interrupt so sacred a communion.'

'He, he!' laughed the astrologer, 'we were not expecting to be honoured with a visit from the learned Greek to-night. I have an engagement at midnight, but before that we expected everybody to be at the great function in the new preaching hall. My honoured guest has just come from there, and would have preferred to have gone in another direction than this with fairer company, but the company was not so pleased with the idea of such companionship as I am, eh?'

'Now come, my friend, let there be no attempting to impose on me with your magic. That line does not accord well with such a corpulent figure as thine. It does very well for the crowd, but we are behind the scenes now. Let us talk like reasonable men. I have no doubt that you got to know from Kiri Banda that his brother and brother's wife were going to accompany the daughter of Joseph the Syrian to the ceremony, and you guessed the rest, and it was not a bad guess after all. I saw that thou wert not present to do worship to thy dear friend the Mihintala Thero, and therefore I sought thee here.'

'He, he! thou knowest how dearly I love him! My

affection almost equals thine own. What sort of an impression did he make? That is the man for your new religion, my friend.'

'Ah, if we could but persuade him,' replied Alypius, in sanctimonious tones, 'of its value and its beauty, and if we could but persuade him of our passionate affection for him personally, and all that concerns his welfare, our cause would be gained. But of this, judging from his manner, he seems to have no perception as yet.'

'He, he!'

'He has great influence, though. His preaching to-night took amazingly with the people, who cannot understand his heresies. And it would be difficult even for the priests to entrap him. He managed it cleverly to-night by introducing the Maitri Buddha.'

'He, he! And is he the Maitri Buddha? He will forestall thee yet, Alypius, with that new all-embracing religion of thine. If he can persuade the people that the Buddhist chronology is wrong, and that he is the Buddha to come, it will not be difficult to get himself recognised as the successor of the holy Gautama.'

'By Jove!—I mean by the sacred person of Tathagato—it is a good idea, and we, who are so very fond of him, might persuade him to take up that rôle of the leader of the new Graeco-Brahman-Buddhistic faith, the religion of the future.'

'He, he! but that might be only securing him greater influence than ever. It is just as likely as not that the people would accept him in that capacity; not, of course, but that we should rejoice all the more on that account.'

'Is it true that his resplendent majesty the king lavishes favours on him?'

'True enough that he is in high favour just now, and that I am out of favour somewhat. And my position is due to the Thero's interference with my business; he has had the hardihood to suggest doubts to my royal master as to the honesty of some of my experiments. I brought the king a message from the Maha Sen, who is now in the heaven of the gods, directing him to proceed in battle against the kingdom of Ruhuna.'

'And didst go thyself for the message, my volatile friend? It would have been worth the king's great sapphire to have seen thee flying through the air. But was that all the message?'

'No; it told him that the most splendid possession in the universe would soon be conveyed to Lanka, and that its arrival should be the sign of the authenticity of the message. It was a long message; it went on to say that Sri Meghawarna was to signalise the event by destroying all the heretics now under the canopy of his dominions, that but for his own (Maha Sen's) heresy he would have acquired merit enough to have carried him to Nirvana, but that black past prevented his progress. The message concluded with an exhortation to the king to profit by his father's errors.'

'An elaborate message, truly, and a most worthy messenger, my Sinhalese Mercury. We will have thy statue made—nay, we will embalm thee and put thee beside the glorious Greek divinity who was the messenger of the gods. One word more: did the Thuparama priest know of thy aërial flight?'

'He, he! Since I have gone so far, I may as well

tell all, especially as I know full well that it will not be to your interest any more than mine to disclose it. The chief priest of Thuparama is jealous of the Mihintala Thero, and he is, besides, angry with him for his heretical views.'

'Ah, ah! I see! The old Thero is for war and extermination, and extending the "canopy of dominion," which will mean new endowments for the favourite temple, and at the same time he would strike a blow at the heretic priest. It was well put that, and worthy of the gods. I shall address his reverence when I next see him with the titles belonging to his new godship Maha Sen. But why select such a messenger? I mean no offence, my worthy friend; it may be the popular worship of fatness, but our Western ideas of such functionaries are not of that kind. Why didn't the priest do it himself? He understands the mysteries of Arhatship.'

'That would not have succeeded. He believes in them, but does not understand. And it is no irreverence to say that the king is not overburdened with genius; but he would have suspected the Thero of some sinister design, and so it was thought it had better be done by a poor artless astrologer, who could have no purpose but the king's weal. I fell into a trance, in which state I lay for some hours, during which time I journeyed in my aethereal body—you may laugh, but it was you and Leah the Jewess who taught me how to do it, and the beauty and grace of that body of mine, my jewel of gem-merchants, might not be unfit to place beside your Mercuries and Apollos. I declare I am getting quite vain of it.'

'Well, that is a result of the new religion that I did

not anticipate; but there is an advantage in that. It promises beautiful compensations. All men and women are vain, and the majority of them are ugly. Well, my æthereal Apollo, never mind the journey and the gods who were all dazzled with thy wondrous beauty. Come down to this world again—how was the message received?'

'Why, when I became conscious, I found that the ola on which the message was written had been transferred from the hand of my æthereal body to that of the corporeal, which, after I had prostrated myself before his majesty, was handed to him by the chief Adigar. It made a deep impression. The king put me questions concerning my journey and the Dewa Loka.[1] He is against war, as you know. The spirit of the old conquerors is not in him. I can sympathise with him. I am not a fighting man myself, that is, in this body, but I make up for it—such are the blessed compensations of our religion—by being a warrior of undaunted courage in the other.'

'Thou takest most readily, my ugly-beautiful cowardly-courageous friend, to the new-old Buddhism. I presume it is this duality which makes thee so discursive. Come to the point, friend. War with Ruhuna[2] would suit me well. Gems would be more plentiful in Anuradhapura. But the other part of the message would not suit me—at least, it would not suit

---

[1] One of the Buddhist heavens—the heaven of the gods.

[2] Ceylon was divided in ancient times geographically into three parts: Pihiti Rata (corresponding to the modern Western, North-Western, North-Central, and Northern Provinces); Ruhuna (corresponding to the Southern and Eastern, with a large part of Lower Uva); while the Maya Rata, embracing the greater part of Malaya or the hill-country, lay between.

some of my friends. And I am not sorry that the scheme—I mean—the message of the gods—was not well received. But how did it come about?'

'A council was called to consider the message. In it were the Theros of Thuparama and Mihintala. The latter took the leaf and examined it closely. I could see a look in those eyes of his which boded no good for me. In short, somebody betrayed me, and that somebody shall suffer, if I can ever discover him. It is a pity these æthereal bodies cannot help us in extremities of this kind, he, he!'

'I know the rest—so the leaf was marked, and Abhayo Thero knew all about it, and declared that it was a disgrace to the faith of the holy Gautama, and a wrong to the memory of the king Maha Sen, and thou wert near losing the use of thy corporeal body altogether. Would that be a misfortune?'

'Well, I don't want to part with it yet, but I should probably have been compelled to, if Thuparama had not come to my rescue. He said that it was good and orthodox Buddhism, and he gave instances of such messages in the utterance of the Blessed One as well as in the narratives of holy Bhikshus, his disciples, who possessed the power of travelling through the air. He showed that it was extremely likely that in the process of transference from the æthereal to the corporeal body, the wicked demons, who were always warring against the gods, changed the leaf, in order that the good cause might suffer. Sri Meghawarna is easily persuaded. At any rate, I brought off my corporeal body safely. Though I must say the king regards me with suspicion at present; but my turn will come. A court astrologer may enter the king's favour by many avenues. The priest denied having marked the leaf himself, and that made it all the easier to believe that it was the work of the demons. But listen! The great procession has commenced its march; let us go up to the tower to look at it!'

CHAPTER V.

THE JEWESS.

> Black spirits and white,
> Red spirits and grey:
> Mingle, mingle, mingle;
> You that mingle may.
>   SHAKSPERE, *Macbeth.*

It was the night of the full moon, and, looked at from the astrologer's tower, the view of the city was weird and impressive. The stupendous piles of brick which formed the temples looked more immense still in the magic light which flooded the vast plain. Their great white and gilded domes rising above the palms looked as if they belonged to some magnificent city of dreams. The statues on the gallery of the Ruwanweli came out in bold relief. The king's palace and the bathing tanks were illuminated with thousands of small lamps, which looked like stars from the point of view occupied by the Greek and the astrologer. The lines of the streets were made clearly visible by the illuminations, especially in the streets through which the Perahera[1] was expected to pass.

The procession had just started from the Thuparama

---

[1] Procession. At the annual *perahera* in Kandy, the shrine of TOOTH is carried at the head of the procession.

THE PERAHERA.
(*From a photograph by Scowen & Co., Colombo.*)

temple when the two men looked out from the tower. They could see the dark, massive figures of the elephants, headed by the monster just presented by the king to the service of the Dalada shrine, as the torches were carried in the direction of the sacred Bo. They could also see the mighty creatures, a hundred or more, kneel in obeisance, as they drew near the foot of the tree, while the air was rent with cries of '*Sâdhu*!'

The occasional glimpse of grotesque figures on stilts, and the waving of torches, with the dancing and drumming of the demon-priests, all tended to make a weird and unearthly spectacle.

They watched the distant procession as it passed through the principal streets. At last the astrologer said: 'Let us go below again. It will be hours yet before the procession passes down this street on the way to the great ceremony of "cutting the water." Besides, if I mistake not those sounds below, my visitor has arrived. Did I tell you that I expected Leah, the Jewess? Does she not claim with you some active part in the foundation of this new religion of ours?'

Kiri Banda had evidently fallen asleep again, and required a great deal of rousing before he could be got on his feet. This time the visitor had come by another entrance, a smaller door opening from another street, and communicating directly with the house of the astrologer. The dogs had howled their loudest at the appearance of Leah's veiled figure, but the sight of a stout stick which she carried to walk with made them do their howling at a respectful distance. They were wide awake, thanks to the moonlight and the processional music in the distance.

This visitor was also evidently known to Kiri Banda.

He did not give her a hearty welcome, but that might be because he disliked being disturbed in his sleep.

'O faithful servant, to resist the temptations of the street on such a night as this. Wherefore art not with the giddy multitude? I knew the Sinhalese could sleep, but I never before found one strong enough to resist the attraction of a procession. But I am glad thou art here to let me in. Show me thy master!' All this was said in broken Sinhalese, but was well understood by the porter. Kiri Banda pointed surlily to the staircase, and muttered under his breath: 'I should have liked well enough to have been at the procession with my brother and his family, though there is a lot of foolishness in it; but when there are people like your ladyship and that Greek about, I think it may be worth while to stay here, and I may not be quite so sleepy as you imagine.'

Before the servant had repeated this long sentence to himself, the visitor had reached the Hall of Mystery, where she was received with most profuse expressions of welcome from the astrologer.

'A long life to you, pearl of wise women! he-he-he! a thousand welcomes to this poor temple of science!'

Leah threw aside her veil and revealed her face more fully. It was undoubtedly a Jewish face. It was the face of a woman on good terms with herself. She was not, and probably never had been beautiful, though it was possible that in her younger days she might have been attractive. Her head was set well on a good figure. Her eyes were not unlike the astrologer's, small, black and bright, and also restless. The expression on her face was agreeable, and her voice was melodious. She rarely failed to give a favourable first impression. Her age might be reasonably judged to be about fifty, though her travels and a long residence in tropical countries perhaps made her look older than she really was.

Her life had been one of adventure. She was reputed to be a widow, and as such allowed herself to be addressed, but nobody in Anuradhapura knew anything of her deceased husband, who was rumoured to have died in Alexandria, or, indeed, of her former life, except that the gem merchants, in whose company she had come to the capital of Ceylon, had intimated that her antecedents were of a somewhat doubtful character. Something was said about her having tried to revive the worship of Isis and connect it with Christianity, in Alexandria, and of her having professed to unravel the mystery of the Sphinx. For a time, so the rumour said, she had a large following in the great city of the West, her popularity being chiefly due to conjuring or, as the ignorant believed, miracle-working.

An attempt, however, to impose on a Christian bishop brought down on her head the thunders of the Church. The Church officials had no love for her as a Jewess by descent, and were highly indignant at her attempted revival of heathenism. Her complicity in a political intrigue, it was said, an intrigue which proved a failure, brought her life into imminent danger. She escaped from the city, her admirers said in a miraculous manner, and her enemies that she had been assisted by persons in authority who had been deluded by her teaching. All this may have been mere conjecture. The merchants said that she certainly did not bear the name of the Alexandrian unfolder of the mysteries of Isis. They did not know her religion, although she was so clearly of Jewish descent. She was mysterious, and they did not trouble themselves about religious mysteries. But she was a clever talker, and seemed to like talking with men and affecting masculine manners. They had gathered that she had come to Ceylon in search of some wonderful jewel, mentioned in the history of her people, but with that they had not troubled themselves. She was altogether a very agreeable woman, they said, and an excellent judge of gems, and that was enough for them.

She had been in Anuradhapura for a year or more, and during that time had ingratiated herself with some of the most important persons in the city, both in the priesthood and among the laity. Of the former, one of her most devoted adherents was the high priest of Thuparama, and among the latter it was said that Detu, the artist prince, might be reckoned among her disciples, although he had made no open avowal of it, and shrank as yet from any public identification of himself with the new doctrines proclaimed by the Jewess and her coadjutor, the Greek Alypius. It was no secret, however, that Leah had managed to secure the favour of the queen and other ladies of the royal household.

It was true that she had managed this chiefly by her public declaration of faith in Buddhism, and this was the excuse of the old priest of the Thuparama temple, when asked whether he thought it right that so prominent a member of the monastic order should be led by a woman. He said it was not the first time that women had rendered assistance to the great society founded by the Buddha. He welcomed Leah all the more, because she was a foreigner, and had been trained in a religion so arrogant and hostile. It was an indication of the universality which was destined for the religion of the Buddhas.

Leah had made her confession and accepted the 'refuges' in the presence of the old man and a large number of the yellow-robed monks. She had also given an address, which was interpreted to the congregation by Alypius, expressive of her dissatisfaction with the religion of her childhood and youth. She extolled Gautama as the grandest example of humanity that had ever existed in the world; and in the course of her address managed to attribute to the founder of Buddhism sayings which he had never uttered, and to show a very confused knowledge of the faith she had embraced. With the utmost dexterity, however, she was able to persuade her hearers that she had long been a good Buddhist, though under another name; and before she had finished she had more than half persuaded them that they themselves were only half-hearted disciples of Buddha, that they had lost the knowledge and power which characterised the faith and the order in earlier times, and that she was born to bring them into the right path.

Alypius in a short address eulogised the lady as a benefactress of her race. He spoke of her self-denial as worthy of a disciple of Gautama, and said that she was in constant communion with the holiest and most zealous beings in other worlds. This was the first public announcement of the new religion. The meeting at the astrologer's took place not long after that event.

Leah expressed her delight at meeting the Greek in the Hall of Mystery. The language would now present no difficulty. She would have found it slow

F

work and uncertain, conversing with the man of science
in his native tongue. The Jewess was quite at home
in the Hall of Mystery. It was not the first time she
had been there, and the astrologer evidently regarded
her as an adept in his own science. He had been consulted by her originally with regard to a tradition
which said that a celebrated sapphire in the possession
of the king had been taken from the head of a cobra.
Alypius paid her, apparently, the utmost deference.
That is, apparently to the astrologer. If he could have
understood the little 'asides' in Greek which passed
between the two, he might have thought otherwise.

'I told you, my scientific friend, that I wanted a
talk with you to-night about the best means of spreading our views, and I am glad of the presence of this
learned Greek. It could not have turned out better.
We are a goodly triumvirate. Why should we not be
the standing inner council of the new organisation?
It need not be divulged, but we know each other pretty
well, and we know what it all means, and we shall probably be of great use, nay of absolute necessity to each
other. Let us call ourselves the directors at once.
That will be so much accomplished. My dear astrologer, you can render us most valuable service, though
it will be premature to announce you to the public as
director. What do you say now?'

'He-he-he!' chuckled the astrologer.

'But first,' continued the lady, 'let me ask whether
there is any probability of our being overheard. I
selected this time because I thought we should be
secure from interruption. What about the servant
below?'

'As to Kiri Banda, I can vouch for it that he is

sleeping soundly and dreaming of the delightful curry he means to make for himself to-morrow. Listen, and you can hear him now—conversing with the gods, eh, astrologer?' replied the Greek.

In the pause which followed, clear indications of Kiri Banda's somnolence came up the staircase.

'H'm, it sounds near, but the Sinhalese snore well, I know. I was going to say that we have already made a favourable impression on the populace. And we have committed ourselves so far that we cannot go back even if we wished; but my main object in coming to-night was to secure the astrologer's assistance in a scheme which shall gain unbounded favour not only with the masses, but with the nobility, and even with the priesthood itself. I had intended coming at once to thee, Alypius, after seeing the astrologer, but it is better, after all, that thou shouldest be here. Did the astrologer invite thee?'

'Nay, I had been to the great function at the opening of the new hall, and had had enough of tall-talk to last me for a lifetime, and so came on here for a chat with our friend.'

'I was there. We have not done with our tall-talker. Did it occur to thee that he might be made useful to the cause?'

'That is what we have just been saying. If we could only get him to believe that he is the Buddha of the new dispensation, it would be a great gain. The people would not believe in it, perhaps, and the priests would see that there was something wrong in the chronology. At any rate, it would be a stern opponent got out of the way. But I have been doubting, since the astrologer and I talked of it, whether we could induce him to put himself in such a position. He is not a fool by any means.'

'There, you mistake, my friend; all men are fools enough to think well of themselves. And if you are to undermine the damaging influence of the Thero, it must be through his self-conceit. Introduce me to him, and see whether I cannot manipulate him.'

'Remember the bishop.'

'Ah, thou knowest that story; I trust nobody else in this city knows it. This is a different case altogether. Anuradhapura is not Alexandria, not quite, yet! It is all very fine, and very useful to us, to talk of the wisdom of the East, and bow before the name of the all-wise Gautama, but the work of fooling seems to me easier here than in any city or town I have yet visited, and I have seen a good many.'

'It is true, the people who could take in those addresses of thine can swallow a great deal. They have been prepared for the process, however, by their priests. But we shall find some, if I mistake not, who will not take to it so kindly.'

'That will depend on how we work them. Our friend here, the astrologer, is not to be classed among the big-throated majority, at any rate.' And Leah turned to their host with a compliment on his keen perceptions.

'He! he!' responded the man of science.

'That is because his whole life has been spent in practising on that majority,' said Alypius, 'and in widening that swallow of theirs. The breath of his being depends on it. But what is this new scheme? Unfold, and I will translate.'

'Briefly, it is this. We are already known to be

in correspondence with the great spirits of the higher worlds. We move amongst them in our æthereal bodies. Now what I propose is that we establish a shrine in the city where one of these "old masters" may be regularly consulted by those who enrol themselves as disciples of this new-old faith. It may be new in this form, but it is old enough for all that—old as the hills, old as our astrological friend's science.'

'Old as the art of fooling,' interpolated the Greek. 'I thought you said you would be brief. Sometimes I think that want of brevity in talk is thy only womanly characteristic.'

'I could be brief enough if it were not for thy rude interruptions, Alypius. Now my design is this: that a shrine be formed in a remote part of the city. This neighbourhood would do very well, but the astrologer would perhaps be suspected of having a hand in it, and the associations might not be suitable, and I propose that the "great spirits" should be consulted at the shrine by good Buddhists, and by the disciples of the new faith generally. I have said "great spirits," but it will be better if we have one mysterious, invisible head and teacher, whose earthly home will be the place we may decide on.'

'That is not at all a bad idea. There is nothing like a bit of mystery for attracting the people. The more mysterious the better. That invisible teacher will take, no doubt of it. But there must be some visible manifestation of his presence; and how will he communicate with the outside world? Like the "great spirits" we have already been in communion with, I presume. By the sacred Bo-tree, I am beginning to believe in him already! By what name is he to be known among men? Will it be something Judaic from the fertile brain of this daughter of Abraham? Will it be selected from Greek mythology? from the Brahman scriptures, or from Buddhist metaphysics?'

'The name is a matter of importance. I have thought of that. At first I thought of something supremely ridiculous; but that would only frustrate our purpose. Then I thought of modifying the name of one of the most credulous of our new disciples.'

'I know; you mean the Adigar Lihinichargaya.[1] Yes, but that is too long, and could not be very well adapted. Let us have something short and to the point.'

'Well, this is what I propose, as suggestive of his high office: Samarga Karanna, the reconciler. You see, we want to take in followers of all religions. It will be hard for anybody to find anything in Samarga to differ from. He is the most liberal-minded creature in the world. His arms are wide enough to embrace all. But his fists will tell heavily on those who are unreasonable enough to oppose him.'

'I see; you will leave small room for difference, but woe will descend on those who differ. Your acquaintance with the Gnostics is bringing forth fruit here. "The Reconciler" is an old friend in new surroundings. Buddhism has always struck me as being comprehensive enough, but Samarga will be more liberal still. Unless I am greatly mistaken, however, we shall find considerable difficulty in making Christianity and Buddhism embrace each other before the shrine of our great invisible teacher. Joseph the Syrian and Thomas the Presbyter are not unacquainted with the Gnostics.

[1] Minister of State.

We must take care not to follow that school too closely. You have burnt your fingers sufficiently in that direction already.'

'Ah, I know your anxiety to secure that household. They are not disposed to be friendly to me, and I have never seen Thomas. I think you said "Thomas." I knew— But few names are more common. Could you not get the members of that community to meet you some day soon, to discuss our religion of reconciliation? Our business is to persuade each party into a little compromise. When that is done, all difficulties will be overcome.'

'It is all very well to talk; saying is always easier than doing. It will be advisable, though, to try the work of reconciliation in the house of the Syrian. But we shall have to walk warily there. It will be a great advantage if we can succeed in winning them.'

'I am not so sure of that,' returned the Jewess; 'we could do very well without them; but I know that would not harmonise with thy wishes. Thy influence with them now is great, I know, in business, if in no other way. Thy position as hierophant to the new teacher, the invisible reconciler, would possibly give thee still greater influence. By the way, Abhayo Thero is a friend of Joseph, is he not? It ought not to be difficult to secure him. But I remember he is not a favourite of yours, and I know he and the astrologer here are not on the most affectionate terms. Well, we will flatter him to the top of his bent. There are but few men in the world that can stand that. The "Reconciler" shall send a message expressly for him. You were going to make him the coming Buddha, were you not?

'I am afraid that will hardly do,' replied the Greek, 'besides, I have another idea with reference to that. No; we must get him mixed up with something which will secure the disfavour of the king. That will be the surest way of dealing with him; but what about the astrologer here? What part will he play in this manufacture of a religion? I know, of course, that astrology and demon-worship will find a place in it; that has been arranged for—and here too we are not original—but what part will our friend take with reference to the "Reconciler"?'

'My dear friend, he will be in charge of the shrine, and will lend us important aid by means of his profession and his acquaintance with the secrets of the city. We shall make him superintendent of the apparatus of the shrine. He will not appear in the matter, but we shall depend largely on him.'

'But where do we establish ourselves?'

'I have thought of that. On the other side of the city, not far from the place of the tombs, there is a house which will just suit our purpose, and which will lend itself readily to the formation of a secret chamber. I have thought of a name for the shrine also. Let us call it SARANA! That will appeal to both Buddhists and Christians.'

It will be understood that the greater part of the dialogue was made clear to the astrologer by interpretation. The details of the scheme were here entered into, and it was resolved to set up the invisible teacher in his new home as soon as possible.

As the conversation concluded, the pipes and cymbals, and the loud thrumming of the tomtoms, announced the near approach of the perahera on its way to the 'cutting of the waters.' Kiri Banda could be heard snoring most profoundly.

'I believe if the procession went over his body he would sleep,' said the Jewess.

'Doubtless,' replied the Greek. 'Let us hurry away by another street before the procession arrives!'

CHAPTER VI.

OUT OF THE CITY.

> When, when shall I the country see,
> Its woodlands green—oh, when be free,
> With books of great old men, and sleep,
> And hours of dreamy ease, to creep
> Into oblivion sweet of life,
> Its agitations and its strife? — HORACE.

FOR some time it had been talked of in the house of Joseph the Syrian that arrangements should be made as the hot season advanced to spend a few days with some of Kumari's relatives in the village of Jambugama, about ten miles out of the city, towards the hill-country.

Joseph had rarely left Anuradhapura since he had settled there. His absences from home had been limited to a few brief journeys to Mahatota (great ferry), the seaport on the north-western coast which formed the outlet of trade for the capital and the interior of the country. Though he and his friend Thomas would never tire of anathematising (in a kindly way, generally) the idolatrous city, and the worshippers of Baal, as they called its inhabitants, yet there was one bright spot from which he never cared to be long away. But just now he was jaded and weary of business cares, and Irene had noticed that after the visits of Alypius a look of anxiety might be caught on his face, hitherto so placid; a look which he would compel himself to banish when conscious of his daughter's gaze. And now and then he would sigh heavily, as he followed Irene's movements through the rooms or in the little garden in the quadrangle.

Kumari was a village maiden, the daughter of a village headman, whose duty it was to wait on the chief of his district, who had been compelled to be in attendance at the royal court for two or three months of the year. The chief's duties in the capital were concluded, and the time had come for Kumari's father, Sikkhi Banda, to return with his wife to their village. They had come to see their daughter, and pay their respects to Joseph before leaving, and Kumari felt, as she said, like being cut in two by her love for her young mistress and her desire to go home with her parents. It was then that Sikkhi Banda had asked Joseph if he would honour him by bringing the lady who was 'as the bright star of good fortune,' to dwell for a time with them at Jambugama.

He was in the course of a long sentence about his own insignificance and that of his family, and the uncomfortableness of the house, when Irene broke in with, 'It is the very thing, my father; I believe this is Kumari's suggestion.' And she shook her finger at the laughing, tell-tale eyes, which shone brightly out of the dusky face of her little helper. 'We shall find it comfortable enough, and we can sit under the great mango trees which Kumari tells me spread a canopy over the house, and there we will sing our hymns and talk together.'

'And the mangoes will soon be ripe, and the jambus

too,' said Kumari, clapping her hands, and looking as if that argument ought to be powerful enough to remove mountains of objection. 'And you shall walk by the rice-fields that are like gold now, and you shall hear the women singing as they work in the fields, and you shall see Grunty, our one-horned buffalo! She is not very clean, and looks gruff, but she means well, and she always comes when I call her; and then there is the dear delightful bird I told you of, that imitates everything, and is as wise as a "Supanno." Sometimes I think it is one of those wonderful creatures; and then too, you shall see my little sisters!' All this was rattled off with the utmost rapidity; and the reference to the little sisters, who had been left at home, was made in a tone and with a gesture which made Joseph smile.

'We will see, little maid,' he said. Then turning to her father, 'I feel that the quiet of thy village, my friend, would do me good. We thank thee for thy kindness, and may possibly avail ourselves of it. May the God Whom thou dost not know, but Who knoweth and loveth thee, have thee in His keeping!'

This was an admission which Irene did not fail to take advantage of, and it was soon arranged that the headman and his wife should be followed in the course of a few days by Joseph and his daughter with Kumari.

The interval was a time of elaborate preparation, for it was necessary to take many things with them which would not have been needful in visiting their own people. Alypius had called on one or two occasions, and Joseph's face had worn, as before, the look of one wakening from a troubled dream when he had gone. And Abhayo Thero had come one evening during the preparations, and expressed his regret at their departure even for so short a time; but he talked with Joseph as if he could enter into his love for the country, and his longing for a quiet place where he might rest.

'The air of the city,' he said, 'is full of the great strife between man and man; here there is peace.' And with the faintest smile at his simple pun he looked for a moment at Irene, who had passed out, veiled, into the verandah for something which was to be brought in and put with other things intended for their village residence.

There was a cloud for a moment on Joseph's brow as he replied: 'Ah, my friend, little dost thou know of what lieth within the circle of such a life as ours. Whatever peace we have comes to us with our faith in the words which Thomas reads to us from the holy Gospels. Sometimes of late I have felt as if even that were not sufficient to comfort my soul, and when that is the case I am afraid change of scene will do but little for me. But come during our absence as often as thou canst, friend! and Thomas, who lives almost the life of a hermit in this secluded part of the city, he will welcome thee and talk with thee about the great themes on which we all three love to discourse.'

It was then that Abhayo told Joseph that he could distinctly see a storm gathering for himself. The suspicion of heresy, for which people had cared but little before, was being vigorously circulated with reference to himself. People in high places, he said, were beginning to avoid him, as one whose presence was dangerous to society. 'And from their point of view they are right,' he went on to say. 'What can a public teacher be but dangerous, who has nothing but doubts to put before perishing souls? They put their faith in the "Three Refuges," and I tell them that even the Blessed One had many doubts, that he cannot help, cannot deliver; that the Dharma is neither strong nor pure enough to be our guide, and that the Sangha[1] is unworthy. My brethren resent it, of course, as treachery to the order. Oh, why have I been led so far, and yet to know so little?' It was, no doubt, the thought of parting with one whom he had come to regard as an old friend which led him to open his heart in that way. And though the Syrian and his daughter intended to be absent only for a comparatively brief sojourn, he had a prevision, he said, that something important and unhappy was about to occur to him. He shook his head at Joseph's suggestion that he too should seek for a quiet retreat till the storm had passed. He would go on with the struggle, he said, and help others as far as he was able. And when he was leaving the house, he paused at the threshold and said simply and pathetically to the father and daughter who had followed him: 'May the Spirit of the Saviour whom you serve be with ye both and give ye peace!'

'And with thee, friend!' said Joseph and Irene, both as if in the same breath, as the tall, commanding figure walked away from the door, throwing the loose folds of the yellow robe over his left shoulder.

With the earliest dawn, a day or two later, the little party began their journey. There were two bullock carts of the clumsiest description, one carrying the little Syrian household, and the other various chattels which were thought to be necessary during their sojourn. In the one with the chattels lay Kiri Banda, who had got

[1] The monastic order of Buddhists.

leave from the astrologer, his master, to accompany the party on a visit for two or three days to his friends in the village. There, he no sooner laid himself down on his hard bed than he fell into a heavy, sonorous sleep, which neither the jolting of the cart nor the cries of the driver could wake him from.

It took them a long time to get through the city, the streets of which for a considerable distance in the early morning wore a deserted appearance, save for a Sāmanera[1] here and there, lazily sweeping the broken petals and the decaying flowers of yesterday's offerings into the causeway, from the shrines which stood at the corners of the streets.

Entering into Moon Street, they took a course towards the southern gate of the city, which was yet at a great distance. The awakening for the day was beginning. Soldiers with short swords in their belts, and holding long spears, walked to and fro in front of the palaces of the great nobles, which adorned the part of the city through which the first portion of their journey lay, some of the buildings being two or three stories high. Of course the sentinels appeared as if they had not slept a wink all the night.

People came out of their rooms to look up and down the great street, washing their teeth as they came. Some of the gentry came out to have a breath of the morning air, wrapping themselves from head to foot in white cloth, from fear of the cold.

Gradually little groups began to gather in the street. Yellow robes began to appear, and small processions of

---

[1] Often translated 'deacon.' The junior members of a monastery, who have not received the 'Upasampada' or higher ordination, are called 'Sāmaneras.'

women, dressed in white, carrying trays covered with flowers and spathes of palm blossom, to be laid before a distant shrine to which they were proceeding to take the vows of 'Sil' for a period.

The goldsmiths in the verandahs began to make their little charcoal-fires, and were blowing at them with their rough bamboo blowpipes. In the eating-houses, which were all open to the street, sometimes one, sometimes two, and sometimes even three women were pounding, each with a large wooden pestle, on the rice in a wooden mortar, with rhythmic thuds, while they related their dreams of the previous night, or gossiped about the neighbouring families. They were preparing the rice-flour for the little morning meal, while another woman got the black clay oven in the corner ready for cooking the same, for travellers would soon be calling for their early refreshment.

The barbers were beginning their daily vocation also. People were beginning to journey abroad, and after ascertaining that the day was auspicious and that the omens were favourable, came slowly in to the barber's little stall on the edge of the causeway, silently to await the barber's grasp on the nose with the left hand, while the shaving proceeded with the right.

Frequently, a large garden of mangoes and plantains would appear at the side of the great street, as the bullock carts moved slowly and ponderously along, or topes of bread-fruit trees surrounding a little dagoba. Into some of the gardens women went, and graceful, bright-looking girls carrying on their heads and at their sides chatties of burnished brass, to be filled with water from the well in the garden. And very pretty and picturesque they looked in the light of the early morning, with their bright faces, white and coloured garments and brass pots, as they moved among the broad leaves of the plantain trees.

In some of the smaller streets which led off from Moon Street, the work of the day had begun in real earnest, the hammers of the workers in tin and brass were ringing sharply on their little anvils, and the shopkeepers were taking their seats tailor-fashion in the midst of their wares.

All these varied sights, together with the clear morning air, were sources of exquisite pleasure to the young Syrian girl, and Joseph's brow for a time wore the smoothness of one who has forgotten anxiety.

In the southern part of the city, the buildings appeared to be all temples or monasteries. As they neared the south gate the houses became fewer, and the gardens more numerous, and even rice-fields occasionally bordered on the street.

At the gate itself a busy life became manifest. Pilgrims passed out on their way to Malaya and Ruhuna, returning from a pilgrimage to the sacred tree, rejoicing that they had been favoured to take part in the demonstrations connected with the reception of the holy tooth-relic, for they had acquired such merit as would make themselves regarded in their villages as pre-eminently righteous. Sinhalese men passed laden with pingoes, which reminded Joseph, as they had often done before, of the Egyptian yoke carved in stone on some of the structures which he had seen in Egypt.

Soldiers lounged about, resting on their spears, while some of them tried the strength of each other's bows sitting on the ground, pulling the bow between their toes and hands. Elephants passed and repassed, and occa-

G

sionally, though rarely, a chariot, containing a grandee, was drawn along by a horse, the bridle being drawn through the horse's nostrils, as in the case of the bullocks that were being taken out of the carts, to be succeeded by another relay from the sheds outside the city wall. And among the crowds of people who passed in, Kumari pointed out some rough and fierce-looking men from the hill-country, of the class, so the little maid said, who would sometimes make a raid on their village rice-fields. They were like the demons who lived with them in the mountains, she said.

Some Malabars, of truculent aspect, stared at Irene and her venerable father, and laughed. They then looked into the second cart, where Kiri Banda was rubbing his eyes and arranging his hair; the cart having stopped to be examined by the officer of the gate. After some chatting in the Malabar tongue, in which Kiri Banda was not quite at home, they turned away on the approach of the examiner.

We must not linger, however. The city is soon left behind, although the large traffic and the numerous passengers on the road still show our travellers that they are not yet far from the city walls.

It is the road to Dambulla, and Kiri Banda says that it goes on—though much of it is not fit for carts to pass over—through Laggala, the country of Kuweni, the demon-queen of Wijayo, to the holy mountain of the sacred footprint itself.[1]

We can scarcely stay to speak of the deer which ran across the road, and the jackals which ran before them, and the monkeys that played in the trees by the roadside; all of which gave much delight to the

[1] Adam's Peak.

Sinhalese girl and her young mistress. Now and then Irene would clap her hands in the excitement of watching the monkeys, and Kiri Banda, who had raised his head to look out of the cart, would lie down again, grumbling that it was all 'a woman's foolishness.'

And when the time came for the mid-day meal in the cart, both the mistress and maid were in their glory. Irene declared that it beat the grandest dining-hall in the city. And Kiri Banda, who was a proverbial philosopher in his way, overhearing this remark, made to Kumari while he was straining off the water from a chatty of rice, muttered in an undertone, 'Crow's flesh near at hand is better than peacock's flesh at a distance.' At which they all laughed, Joseph included; and Irene laughed again, to see her father laugh.

I shall not have given a correct impression of the Syrian's daughter, if the reader has imagined her to have been always a sad, solemn, and stately young lady. To-day she appeared to enjoy everything with a liveliness which was unbounded. And when they had to leave the carts for the footpath which led to Jambugama, she protested that she would not use the litter which had been sent to the road by the headman, with several villagers (recognised with delight by Kumari), to carry her over the rough ways which connected the village with the road. She would run along between the paddy-fields with Kumari, she said, and would enjoy it much better than being carried, especially as the day was cloudy and the sun was in the west.

Kiri Banda, who walked, or rather waddled, by Joseph's litter, said, looking at the girls as they ran on in front: 'To those who can walk, even the jungle is a royal road.'

Then Joseph tried to get him to converse about his master the astrologer, and his mode of life, intending to show him the folly of such superstitions as were fostered by his master's science; but the man immediately relapsed into a condition resembling sleep-walking, with only an occasional grunt to indicate that he was awake. Although, when reference was made to the Mihintala Thero, and the trouble he might bring on himself by the suspicions which were being roused against him with the populace, he became wide-awake and grunted out—'Will the barking of dogs reach the sky?'

Joseph had put leading questions, to ascertain how far the suspicion which had been referred to by the Thero on parting had gained ground, and he was delighted to find a partisan in the astrologer's factotum. It was not much that Kiri Banda said, but the little he did say left the impression on Joseph's mind that there were powerful enemies at work against the priest.

On the way to the village they passed little groups of people watching buffaloes, and here and there where the crop had been early, a threshing-floor, where the oxen were being driven in a circle, treading out the corn. And the oxen would be stopped while the inquisitive owners would request Kiri Banda to inform them as to who the strangers were, where they were going, and what their business was. And Kiri Banda would inform them with the utmost gravity that it was the venerable Emperor of the West country, travelling *incognito* with his daughter, the princess, to visit the far-famed villages of Lanka; adding, in an aside, that they would get favour from those in authority, who were in the secret, if they brought suitable presents, not forgetting himself. And with expressions of astonishment and great deference, the presents were promised.

All this occurred, of course, without the cognizance of Joseph, who had passed on in the litter, after which Kiri Banda came chuckling and grunting.

At Jambugama great preparations had been made. Irene said she had never seen anything so beautiful as the arch of bamboos and all sorts of leaves and fruit which had been erected at the entrance of the headman's house, standing in the midst of a clump of mango trees, which were covered with light and dark-green foliage. And Kumari pointed with delight to the jambu tree, which was crowded with beautiful little rosy apples, and said it was the best time in all the year to come home.

The younger members of the family were brought forward and introduced by Kumari. Almost before the guests were within the house and at the door, a large myna-bird came hopping out to meet them, poising its sharp head above its yellow collar with a perky solemnity, as it uttered a welcome in a variety of inconsequent expressions beginning with 'Live long, my lord!' and ending with 'What can do?' much to the amusement of the new-comers. He had a large vocabulary for a myna, but the arrangement was often faulty, as is not seldom the case with bipeds that are not feathered.

Special rooms of palm-leaves had been erected for the guests at little cost, which form an excellent shelter in the dry weather. And a hearty, respectful welcome was given them by Kumari's father and mother, the former leading them to two couches which had been covered with white cloths.

On retiring that night, the father and daughter sang together a sweet Greek hymn, into which the twenty-third psalm had been rendered, and that finished, Joseph said, 'Let us pray together the prayer of the Gospels—"Our Father."'

CHAPTER VII.

THE NEW RELIGION.

> I disbelieve in Christian pagans, much
> As you in women-fishes. If we mix
> Two colours, we lose both, and make a third
> Distinct from either.—E. B. BROWNING.

ALYPIUS and the Jewess had not been idle. The shrine of the 'Reconciler' had been made ready, not in the place originally intended, but in a house of imposing appearance, not far from the astrologer's Hall of Mystery. It was agreed that this was necessary, to admit of frequent visits on the part of the astrologer.

The building had been undergoing elaborate preparations, under the supervision of the three persons most deeply interested. At last the opening ceremony was announced, and it was arranged that, previously to the opening of the shrine to the public, there should be a select gathering of distinguished persons, to secure whose attachment to the new society was most desirable, called together in the hall for the purpose of friendly discussion, and in order to produce as favourable an impression to begin with as possible.

It was the night before the opening, and if all who came to the hall were favourable to the new movement, the 'Reconciler' would not languish for want of distinguished patronage. Prince Detu was there, and with him two of the three chief Adigars (the king's ministers), Dharma Sen, the Indian visitor who has been already introduced to the reader, the Princess of Kalinga, Anula, and some ladies of the court, whose influence Leah had made a great point of trying to secure. At the period of which we are writing, ladies mingled much more freely in such assemblies than they do now, and then, as now, the priests were not so punctilious with regard to avoiding the presence of women as they were commanded to be by the precepts of Gautama. Among the priests who were attending the conference were the high priest of Thuparama and Abhayo Thero.

The lead was taken, of course, by Alypius; the Jewess sitting by him as he spoke, apparently absorbed in the profoundest meditation. Alypius, speaking in Sinhalese, addressed a few words of welcome to the 'Guests of the "Reconciler,"' as he called them. He spoke with great fluency and ease. Nobody could come in contact in any way with the young Greek merchant without being impressed with the fact that here was a man with talents of no mean order, and on this occasion the talent for persuasive speech, and that in a foreign tongue, was conspicuous in the address with which Alypius introduced the subject.

He said that he had been impressed, during his long residence in the great metropolis of the Sinhalese kingdom, with nothing so much as the religious differences represented amongst the natives of the land, and the strangers who had been attracted to it from East and West, and the great kingdoms in the North (here he bowed to the Indian visitors), by the riches and glories of the city and the holiness of its shrines. Could they deny that religious differences had led to horrible wars in the past, and were still often the bane of existence? Some of his friends present, of the mercantile community, would remember how all Alexandria and the churches of the West had been split into factions, while a terrible and bloody strife pervaded all classes of society with reference to the exact position occupied by the Christ in the Christian Trinity. In the palaces of the nobles and in the lowest taverns, men fought over religious terms, the meanings of which were rarely understood, and when understood were found to be practically of the same import.

'It is a grateful and pleasing fact,' he went on to say, 'that the danger of such religious conflicts is not so great where we live under the tolerating influence of a merciful creed like that of the holy Gautama, and where those who occupy the highest positions are devoted to philosophical culture and the refinements of art.' (Here, a glance of admiration at the prince Detu, who occupied a prominent position in the conference.) 'We who have seen something of religious intolerance in the great cities of the West cannot but rejoice in the mercy and the calm, beautiful spirit of charity which characterises the followers of the mighty son of Suddhodana.'

'Maha Sen?' was suggested in a low voice from the back of the hall.

Faces were turned in the direction from which the voice came suggesting the name of the royal persecutor, but the speaker could not be identified, and few, if any, would think of connecting it with Kiri Banda, who might be seen seated on a mat, with his great black head resting against the wall, apparently in a profound sleep.

The Greek continued, without heeding the interruption:—' I have made the system unfolded by the holy, all-wise Buddha my study day and night, and I can see in that system so eloquently expounded from time to time by some of my reverend friends here' (waving his hand in the direction of Thuparama and Abhayo, who sat on the raised seats reserved for the priests), great truths, which need only to be popularly represented to ensure universal acceptance. I have said that Buddhism is tolerant. Its doctrines, properly understood, are the heritage not of one nation or race, of one continent or island, but, like the great sea, it was meant to embrace them all, by the all-seeing mind which under the sacred Bo obtained the vision of the universe. In the Tri-pitaka,[1] reverend sirs, you have the true wealth of the universe, and we of the West come to you, who are the guardians of these precious caskets of Divine Gems, saying : " Open to us, that our eyes may be blessed, and our spirits rejoice in their lustre ! "

'But in coming thus as suppliants we do not come empty-handed, though freely confessing that the jewels which we bring from the West become pale in the illumination which floods upon us with the opening of the " three caskets." Neither do we come as strangers to the truths which you teach. Unconsciously, in listening to the voices of the divine Plato, of Philo-Judaeus, and of some of our Christian teachers, we have

[1] The three 'caskets' or collections which form the Buddhist scriptures.

walked in the " eight-fold path " of the glorious Buddhas, and the gems of doctrine which we bring you ' (a gruff whisper of, ' How much apiece ? ' came from the back of the hall, where Kiri Banda was serenely sleeping, with his head against the wall), ' though not so precious and brilliant as those in the Tri-pitaka, are of the same nature, and may be of vast service in helping men to understand and apply the precious contents of the sacred caskets. Why should not the gems from East and West be brought together in one magnificent crown of pure gold, to illustrate the all-embracing charity of Buddhism and the unity of the true religion ?

'We are here to-day with that object in view—to honour the faith so worthily represented by the reverend gentlemen before me, to put an end to the strife of creeds, to turn our backs on a divided, unholy past, and to say that the time is come when we should look rather at the resemblances between our religious beliefs than at the differences, and seek for common ground on which we can worship together in one great brotherhood. The only process by which this grand object can be attained is that which is often sneered at by those whose eyes are blinded by prejudice ; it is eclecticism. I am confident that the mention of that word will not meet with disparaging treatment at the hands of so intellectual and sympathetic an assembly as this. But in the selection and amalgamation which we propose, the necessary reforms must not be forgotten, we must rise to the higher Buddhism, which means the highest religious life of the ages. And in this we are powerless, as we have been told again and again by the learned priest before me, the Mihintala Thero, unless we realise the communion and guidance of those adepts who, having passed through many births, victorious over sin and the flesh, and having overcome all bodily restraints, are occupying to-day the thrones of intellectual dominion.

'It is true that we see them not, and are unconscious of their presence; but we may be sure that they frequently visit, as of old, the holy places which are the landmarks in the sacred history of this wonderful city. But more attractive than the holiest shrine for the "great ones" is that heart in which dwells the æthereal essence which is the very nature of the gods, and constitutes their kinship. But in how few do we find this sympathetic essence, so necessary to this high fellowship! How rarely do we meet with these "revealers" of our race! It is my high privilege tonight to introduce you to one in whom dwells the divine essence to which I have referred, and who, even now, while I have been attempting in my poor way to explain our position, has, for aught we know, been engaged in converse with those great minds compared with which the finest intellects in this learned and intellectual community are but as babes in swaddling clothes.

'It is my privilege to introduce you to one of the great initiated, one who lives in the midst of what are to us the invisible mysteries. The marvels of which the sacred books of all religions speak are made clear to her in the æthereal sphere in which she moves.' (A curious cough came from the back of the hall, but Kari Banda slept on in undisturbed serenity.) 'Through her, we may bring the wisdom that exists in the society of the gods down to our help. This,' pointing to Leah, 'is the lady of whom I speak; in her the dual life is most strikingly developed and distinguished, and through her the gods will commune with men. She is most anxious to place the divine gifts which she possesses at your service, that you may get nearer the sacred mysteries which lie behind the letter of the pitakas and of all sacred scriptures. She is especially under the controlling influence of a great mind, who is perhaps the most perfect adept in existence, whether in the human body or out of it, and who, through this his handmaid, has signified his willingness to preside at this shrine. She has lived a varied life, has in her time devoted herself to various religious systems. She has left the creeds of the West, tainted as they are with murder and rapine, cursed with the dark shadow thrown over the nations by the imagination of a personal god. She has wandered through all inhabited lands, and could find no resting-place, no place which should be so suitable for the establishment of the new faith, for the revelation of the "Great Minds," as this great city of hallowed associations nurtured in the faith of the gentle and wise prince of the Sakyas.

'You would ask "who is this great mind of which I speak?" His name is to be withheld until you have witnessed the marvellous manifestations of his presence and power which will be unfolded to his disciples. For the present he is to be known as "the Reconciler." I am authorised to say that he knows each one of you, and is anxious that through you the wisdom of that higher sphere may be made available to the world. He, "the Reconciler," has this day declared that he has watched, for instance, the doubts and aspirations of the Mihintala Thero, knows all his associations, and has predicted that his mighty intellect will take the lead in inaugurating the new era of religious life and blessedness.

'You, reverend gentlemen, who have made the sacred books your daily study, will know that this is not foreign to true Buddhism. If there is anything in it that is not in accordance with the precepts of the Tathagato, we are prepared to wipe it out, that there may be no enmity or strife in the shrine of the "Reconciler." Welcome to Sarana, the house of refuge which is to shelter those who would flee from the religious animosities of mankind!'

At the conclusion of the Greek's speech the conversation began; questions were asked. Some of the priests were doubtful whether it was consistent with Buddhism for a lady to occupy the position given in the new system to the Jewess. But they were easily silenced by references to Buddhist history, and the mystery of the dual life was held to be sufficient to overcome any doubt of that kind. The merchants present, mostly from Alexandria, said but little, and looked as if the speech of Alypius, which had evidently made a deep impression on the native part of the audience, contained matter not altogether new to them.

Anula, who could understand by this time much of what had been said, began to wonder whether this was not after all the true way to that higher Buddhism which had been the dream of her life.

Abhayo Thero sat unmoved during the conversation with his arms folded, looking the old, far-off look of the meditating Buddha. At last the appeal was made to all present to enrol themselves as disciples of the 'Reconciler.' They were asked not to renounce the religions which they professed, but rather to take on this new-old faith which would make them pure and tranquil. They were to pledge themselves to show no enmity whatever to any religion. Offerings to the shrine were, of course, expected and asked.

Then, when the conditions had been read, Abhayo Thero drew himself up to his full height, and held out his hand, to secure the attention of the assembly. It was a moment of suspense. All were anxious to learn what the powerful priest would say of the new religion, especially as it had been so publicly announced that he was in high favour with the invisible 'Reconciler' himself. Slowly but earnestly he spoke:—'This is the most important subject that can occupy the mind of man. The rise and fall of dynasties and kingdoms cannot approach it in importance' (an approving smile from Alypius), 'and therefore we must not hastily accept such untried propositions as those which have been placed before us to-night' (a dark shade came over the Greek's face). 'There were certain signs by which men might know the true Buddha. Let us look for the signs that the "Reconciler" is what is claimed for him. It is said, so I have heard, that the highest authority in one of the world's great religions advised His followers to apply in all charity one great test to the works of all men. "By their fruits ye shall know them." Let us try this new faith by its fruits, and then if it is worthy and its claims are proved, let us accept it thankfully. But be assured of this, that the revelation, if worthy, will come to us in unswerving truth, in purity of life and aim, and with clean hands. The position offered me is no temptation. For me, the true Sarana is not here.'

The Greek rose, with a smile which covered suppressed passion, and declared that, in spite of what had just been said, he did not despair of seeing the prediction of the 'Reconciler' fulfilled. But he could explain the Thero's present antipathy to the new faith. He had received it from his Christian associations. He had quoted the very words of the Christian Scriptures. There was nothing that was so antagonistic to Buddhism as Christianity, with its lawless immoralities and bloodshed, and its worship of three Gods, a religion of childishness, which justly called for the contempt of the commanding philosophic intellect which pervaded the followers of Gautama. He went on to show what failures his own experiences of the Christian religion had been—experiences which were readily accepted by those present as correct representations of the Christian faith,—and concluded by asking whether they were to be deterred by arguments drawn from such foul sources as those.

The Thero held out his hand without rising, and said: 'My Christian associations, as the speaker knows, have been with pure-minded and honest friends, and their experiences of the Christian faith are in favourable contrast to his. Though not a Christian' ('Not just yet,' sneered Alypius), 'I cannot hear the faith of such friends defamed without protest, and this by one who has laid on you, as disciples of the "Reconciler," the solemn condition that you shall speak evil of no man's creed.'

There was a moment of indecision. But the Greek's attack on Christianity, with the hint as to the Thero's heretical associations, carried the day. Then the prince Detu stood up and repeated the formula of acceptance, and was enrolled. He was followed by one and another, until all had been enrolled except two, Abhayo and Anula, while Kiri Banda still sat with his great black head reclining against the wall, to all appearances in a deep sleep.

CHAPTER VIII.

THE BURNT HAND.

> . . . Truly these burnings,
> As Thirlby says, are profitless to the burners,
> And help the other side.—TENNYSON'S *Queen Mary.*

LIFE in Jambugama afforded the most striking contrast to the life of the great city. The village was not large; there were not many large villages in the kingdom, but they straggled out thinly to an almost indefinite length, and it was sometimes difficult to say where one village ended and the next began. It depended almost entirely on the rice-fields, as it does in the interior of Ceylon to-day. There were exceptions, as there are now. A noted pansala might cause a village to rise in its vicinity. And as the pansala was generally on an eminence, a beautiful picture was produced by the white dagoba on the summit, and by the houses of the villagers which clustered around the hill-side under the dark trees, down to where the sea of golden grain seemed to strike on the foot of the hill.

Such a village was Jambugama. Its inhabitants lived a quiet, restful life, and were rarely excited about anything, unless the peace of the village was disturbed by an invasion of robber-hordes from the hill-country, and such visits had of late been very rare indeed, and save for the 'new year' and other festivals there was little to break the monotony of daily existence. Kiri Banda voted it slow, terribly slow, after the life of the city. Two or three days were sufficient for him, he had said; and when these had passed he had gone back again to Anuradhapura, where we have seen him sleeping in the hall of the 'Reconciler.'

There were two persons, however, in Jambugama who had no sympathy with Kiri Banda's city preferences. To Joseph and his daughter it was a time of great peace. But their stay in the village was, for the simple folk by whom they were surrounded, a continuous and unwonted excitement. Foreigners had visited the village but rarely, and none had come to reside. And about these two distinguished foreigners the most exaggerated rumours had spread, and for some days after their arrival the house of Sikki Banda was besieged by the villagers who had come to pay their respects and to look on 'the beautiful white lady,' as they called Irene, and her venerable father. Nor did they come emptyhanded. Whatever may have been or may be the defects of the Sinhalese villager, want of hospitality and of kindness to strangers was not, and is not, found amongst them.

The people were inquisitive—courteously so—and the strangers were plied with numerous questions daily, which afforded them much quiet amusement. On the other hand, the visitors were delighted with the opportunities afforded of studying native character as it appeared in country life, so different from the character developed in the city. And there was much to be learnt. A new world seemed to Irene to be opening to her vision, while to Joseph it recalled his childhood in the old Syrian village home.

They were sitting one morning after they had sung and prayed together, and had partaken of the light morning meal, in what was really a pretty room made of poles and plaited palm leaves, and were talking of these new experiences, when Irene said: 'It seems wonderful to me now that I could live patiently in the city in ignorance of all the various beauty of this simple country-life, and of what constitutes the existence of the natives of the land. It is like living in a new world to me. Why, it is possible for people to live in Anuradhapura, and yet to know just as little of the country and the real life of the people as if they were living in Alexandria.'

'It is undoubtedly true, my child; and I am beginning to attach blame to myself for living in a similar condition of blindness. There is so much of selfishness and self-conceit in us; we hedge ourselves round with it, and despise the world beyond our own little community. And that, together with a pride of race—our connection with the mighty civilisation of the West—has kept us from knowing the true life of the people.'

'I am certain that our merchants when they go home grossly misrepresent the native life, or at any rate give only one-sided views of the native character. They of course see the worst side in trade. And they do not hesitate to pronounce judgment on the entire nation from the specimens they meet with in gem-dealing. I wonder how many of them could pass an examination in the historical traditions of the country or in the religion of the people and their customs! And yet I am told that when they go back to Alexandria they pose as authorities, and even take their places in the Academy as such.'

'Do not speak too harshly of them, child; it comes of thinking that our own community is the only one worth knowing and worth caring for. We have been much the same, and perhaps should continue to be but for such experiences as these. We have looked, for instance, on our little church (which may God have in His keeping!) as if it were for the foreign community only. Its services have been maintained in a language which is not that of the people. And the whole system, as far as we are concerned, is established on the foundation that the souls of the few merchants are of far greater value than the vast population inhabiting the great city. May the all-merciful God forgive me my blindness in this matter!'

'And yet, dear father,' said Irene, looking lovingly into his tear-filled eyes and stroking the old man's hand—'and yet you have not been indifferent. You have learnt the language of the people, and you have had me taught; and I remember that when Alypius was denouncing the nation so fiercely one day as a nation of deceivers and thieves, because of the way in which he had been over-reached in a bargain, you told him it was unfair to speak thus, and asked him to remember the number of times he had profited by their ignorance in gem-dealing, and how he had benefited by their cheap labour.'

'It is small comfort, child, to know that, when one feels that he has not done his duty to his fellow-men. We have not been *neighbours*, in the sense of that touching story in the holy Gospel, to those who lived

with us, who served us, who traded with us; we have
kept our good things, and have dared even to keep the
good things of God to ourselves. This movement on
behalf of a new all-embracing faith is a reproach to me
—a reproach to the Church of Jesus, as it stands in
Anuradhapara. I like not the spirit of compromise
which characterises the promoters of this scheme, nor
the ease with which cherished beliefs are forsaken; but
it appears to break down the pride of race, and in so
far as it does that, and advances the brotherhood of man
irrespective of nationality or class, it will undoubtedly
be acting in the spirit of true Christianity. And it
may be that my partner Alypius and his coadjutors
are moved in this matter by what they have learnt
from the Christian Scriptures. It would please me
much if thou couldest look more favourably on our
friend, my daughter. Beware of prejudice!'

'I cannot help it, my father. It may be prejudice,
but there is something which will keep telling me that
all his talk about universal charity is superficial. I
mistrust his motives. But let us not talk of him now.
I wonder how Thomas is getting on! Imagine him
poring over his manuscript. The servant has just
told him that the morning meal is spoiled because of
a chatty being broken, and he says quietly without
looking up: "Never mind; it will only make the
appetite keener for the next meal. Go, child, thou art
forgiven." Here the servant comes again. "Master,
look, the young lady's flowers are dead, what shall I
do?" And he replies with profound delight as if he
had suddenly found a complete remedy: "Go, child,
and put in others!"'

'Ah,' said Joseph, patting her playfully on the

back, 'my little one imagines that none can manage for the old people like herself.'

'Now, father, what does Thomas know of native life, or of life in our own community, for that matter? He seems, when he is not engaged in his sacred duties, to be living in a dream. We have known him for years, but he takes little interest in what surrounds us, except that he sits with you on the top of the house occasionally to watch a procession, and I have noticed that he wakes up a little when Abhayo Thero comes.'

'My child, I have told you before that our friend has passed through great tribulation, but I have not told you of the nature of his trials. It may be well, however, that you should know, and I think he would not object to your knowing; only remember that he does not like to have a word said concerning it in his presence.

'Thou hast noticed that he appears to have but one hand—his left. The right is always kept carefully concealed in his robe.'

'"Appears"?' said Irene, in amazement, 'why, has he two hands then? I remember asking him about his hand one day, and he replied that it was once fearfully injured, so that it was not of much service to him after. And I thought it had probably been taken off after the injury. But he looked so pained when I spoke to him that I did not like to question him further. That explains what I have often wondered at, the ability with which he manages for himself. And even when he is confined to the use of his left hand he seems to have no difficulty. He handles the roll of the sacred manuscript as well with his left hand as other people can with both hands.'

'There is no reason why he should not tell the sad story connected with it; it reflects the greatest honour on himself; but there were disgraceful associations, in which others, who were at one time dear to him, were concerned, and it is his anxiety to say no word to the discredit of these who were so cruel—to forget if he can that part of a terrible past, and prevent any reference to it. Remarks are occasionally made now, but a sight of the hand might lead to identification. And this he would dread. Thomas was not brought up for the Christian ministry, and indeed he was not a Christian in early life. He was the son of a wealthy Athenian who had married a Jewess and settled in Cæsarea. He was sent to Alexandria to study in the rhetoric schools, with a view to becoming an advocate. It was while there that he became impressed with the Christian faith. And during that same period his parents in Cæsarea had undergone the great change and embraced Christianity. On his return to his father's house after having finished his course of study, it was a great delight to his parents to find that no difference of faith was likely to disturb the family unity, and it was not long before he made a public profession of his belief in Christ.

'There was only one obstacle to this act, and that was his betrothal to a young Jewess named Athaliah, who at first was angry at the change, and resisted all attempts at conversion, and then—as we know now—for the sake of the family wealth, she consented not only to his becoming a Christian, but also to becoming a nominal Christian herself. She was, it seems—I never saw her—a fascinating person, especially in conversation,

and her consent, though reluctantly given, called out a
stronger affection than ever on the part of Theodorus.
That was his name then—a name which he renounced on
taking upon himself the Christian vows. He became
devotedly attached to her, and for some time after his
marriage they appeared to be of one mind with regard
to the Christian faith.'

'Thomas married!' said Irene. 'I always thought
him the severest of old bachelors. Why, he shuns the
society of women as much as any orthodox Buddhist
priest would; the priest in the pansala above us, for
instance, who held his fan before his eyes, that he
might not see us when he met me yesterday with
Kumari.'

'A Christian pastor of great influence in the city,
who was well acquainted with the family of our friend,
thought it his duty to warn him against certain associations which the young wife had begun to form without
her husband's knowledge, with persons who had been
carried away by the Neo-Platonist enthusiasm. It
might be nothing further, he said, than a desire to be
acquainted with the mysteries which the leaders of this
sect professed to unravel, but it was full of danger to
a Christian household. The words of his friend and
pastor were not kindly received by Thomas, who
naturally resented any imputation cast on his wife.
His parents also called his attention to the frequent visits
paid her by the crafty and designing man who was the
leader of this sect in Cæsarea.

'But enough of this. The persecution under
Galerius came on. The pastor, forewarned, carried the
greater part of his flock away to a place of security in
the desert, and would have taken the household of

Thomas, but his wife laughed at their fears, and declared that she at least would remain. Her husband determined to remain with her.

'When the persecution broke out, it was found that the Neo-Platonists were in league with the Pagans against the Christians. And there was fearful treachery in the house of Thomas. He was imprisoned on information furnished by his wife. He still would not believe in her treachery until he was brought before the judges, when in the open court he found that the chief witness against him was the wife whom he had so fondly loved, while a prominent place in the court was given to the Neo-Platonist who had so grossly abused his hospitality. He said that he was so painfully shocked, that for a time he could scarcely answer the question of the judge asking him if he would deny the Nazarene. Those in the court took it at first for wavering. Recovering himself, he declared manfully that he would rather die than deny the Christ.

'In the court there was a small statue of the Olympian Jupiter, and before it a brazier full of burning coals. Our dear friend was condemned, as many of the brethren have been, to have his hand held in the fire, and after that to be taken back to prison. Boldly —so I was told afterwards by one who had witnessed it —setting aside those who would have held him, he bared his arm and put his hand into the midst of the flame, lifting his eyes towards heaven in prayer. It must have been a time of excruciating torture, though he says that such was the state of his feeling at the time that he scarcely realised it. It was after a brief interval, when he had, by permission of the court, withdrawn the hand, scorched and blackened all over, that the intense suffering began. And then, as he was being marched off to the prison, he saw a look of wicked triumph pass between the traitress and her cruel friend, and he could not speak, but simply held out towards them his burnt hand.

'By some means he managed with much difficulty to escape from prison to the retreat of the Christians. There he found that during the rough journey his mother had died. And there, while he was being nursed by tender hands, news came of the doings of the wicked woman who had been his wife.

'When the edict of toleration was enforced, most of the exiles came back to Cæsarea. There were two who remained behind—Thomas and his father. They took on themselves vows of poverty, and for a long time lived in caves, although they might have gone back to the city, and have lived in the enjoyment of what property remained to them unmolested, for the wicked woman had left Cæsarea and gone, none knew whither. After a time they wandered into Africa, and it was there in the desert, about three days' journey from Alexandria, that I met with Thomas.

'We had come from Antioch, exiles. I had left your mother in the city with some friends, having obtained permission from the authorities to visit a holy saint whom I had known many years before, who was living the life of a recluse in the desert. On the third day, when I should have reached my destination, I missed my way, and was glad to have an opportunity of making inquiry at a cave where some hermits appeared to be residing. It was a day and scene that I shall never forget.

'A young man—but with an aged look, I could

hardly tell then whether he was young or old—came to the mouth of the cave at my approach. He was clad in the rudest garments, but more fully than is usual with these dwellers in caves. He appeared to have only one arm, and looked inexpressibly sad. In answer to my inquiry, he said that he knew the brother I was in search of, but it was too late to go further, and he pointed with his left hand to the shadows lengthening on the plain below. "It is a poor hospitality I can offer thee," he said. "I am alone with the dead, but it is the dead in Christ, and therefore thou wilt have no need of fear." He pointed to a corpse lying within on a mat on the floor of the cave, and said simply, "My father was taken to the Saviour last night."

'Nothing could be more peaceful or beautiful than death as it appeared to me that evening. The son and I watched by the dead through the night, and conversed together. Confidence begat confidence, and at last he told me his story, the story which has just been told thee, little one! He talked until daybreak; and the first light of the morning sun streamed into the cave revealing a burnt and withered hand which rested lovingly on the forehead of the dead.'

'Oh, father!' said Irene, bursting into tears; 'and I have been so foolish and often so fretful with him. God forgive me, and may God bless him!'

'Amen!' said Joseph. 'There is no need, my child, to talk of what followed, of how we buried the dead, and found the old friend of whom I had been in search, or to say anything further of the new friendship so strangely formed. As thou knowest, we had not been long here before we built the little church, and then thy mother died. Some friends returning homeward conveyed a pressing invitation to Thomas to go to Antioch for ordination, and join us here to be our pastor in this heathen city.'

At this point Kumari came running in excitedly, saying with much incoherence: 'Does the lady know that to-morrow is the baby's naming day? And we are going to have such fun, and the boys will stay home from the pansala,[1] and there will be *kiribat*, and lots of sweetmeats, and one of the dogs is dead, and to-morrow is a lucky day, and other visitors are coming. Shall I tell you who they are?'

'Well, that is a large mouthful for a little maid like thee,' said Irene. 'Pray tell us, for we are curious!'

'The clever Indian lady who came with the princess and the sacred relic. Anula is her name. She is visiting the most sacred spots in the country, and you know our hill is a very holy place, and very famous—though you may not think so—and this lady is coming on a pilgrimage, and she will stay here with her maidens for some days. She is very beautiful—I saw her once—but not so beautiful as a lady that I know.'

'Oh, you silly little thing,' said Irene, 'stop your chatter instantly;' but she was pleased nevertheless.

'How readily,' said Joseph, 'are our thoughts turned from things that are profoundly mysterious or

[1] Provision is made in the pansalas for the education of boys, a duty which has been almost universally neglected in modern times by the priests, who have misappropriated valuable endowments given for that purpose. No provision is made, of course, for the education of the girls.

sorrowful to the gayest and most superficial. It is good that the mind can be so easily turned. It is often one of God's ways of helping and comforting men. Well, little maid, we will join thee in looking forward to a happy morrow.'

A CEYLON DAGOBA.

CHAPTER IX.

THE PANSALA.

'Listen, O king,' he said. 'In the deepest shades of the forest there lives a hermit named Vibhandaka. Long ago, he left the city, his heart full of bitterness, because amongst men he had found crime and folly.'—RAMAYANA.

It was the day before the beginning of the *Wass*, the period of the year known as the 'Buddhist Lent.' It has very little in common with the Lenten fast observed in the Roman Catholic Church. Indeed, in some respects, it is strikingly the reverse. It is rather a feast than a fast, 'a feast of fat things' for the priests. *Priest* again is only a term of convenience, *Monk* would be the more fitting title. It is becoming fashionable now to invest the Buddhist system with the ecclesiastical terminology of Christianity. We have met with people occasionally, both Christians and Buddhists, in these latter days, who could see very little difference between Buddhism and Christianity. And on one occasion, at least, the writer remembers the fact of the Buddhist having a 'Lent' season advanced as evidence that he was 'not far from the kingdom!'

The Wass was ordered to be observed in India throughout the rainy season, during which time the priests were to go into Retreat, another inappropriate

I

term. They were not to go on long journeys or pilgrimages; and arrangements were to be made for the daily reading of the Buddhist Scriptures and preaching, and for the reception of offerings. In Ceylon it is often a time of great festivity. A favourite priest is invited to a village to conduct a 'mission,' and his coming is the signal for general holiday. He is received with great demonstration, with music and dancing. The Wass is characterised by more or less of holiday throughout, and the food offerings to the priesthood are especially liberal and varied.

Great preparations had been made in Jambugama, preparations which had been watched with great interest by our friends from the city.

Now, it would be easy and pleasant—for I must confess that I personally enjoy being with these friends in the midst of these village scenes—to make the people of Jambugama send the offering of betel-leaves[1] to Abhayo Thero, with an invitation to be the special preacher for the Wass. We should then be gathering our principal characters around us; and who knows what 'situations' might develop under such circumstances? But Abhayo Thero was not so honoured. In years gone by the betel-offerings at this time had come to him from all directions. This year there was a significant absence of such invitations, and the young monk felt it very keenly, although he had no difficulty in accounting for it.

The ominous whisper of 'unorthodoxy' had been growing in volume ever since his famous address in the new assembly hall. It was not that heresy itself was

[1] It would not be etiquette for a deputation to wait on a superior without an offering of betel-leaves.

regarded as such a fearful thing, but the whisper grew, as is the way of such whispers, into slander; and the most exaggerated and lying rumours were being circulated about the Thero. It was said that he had lost the royal favour, which was true; and this fact weighed far more than the charge of heresy with the multitude, although there were large numbers who would have wished, but scarcely dared to give expression to it, to have had the great preacher officiating in the city at such a time.

Even Detu had begun to avoid him. He appeared to be more than ever engaged in the workshops with Dharma Sen, the Indian visitor, who gave him, as he said, much assistance in stone-carving. And neither of them seemed now to care for the companionship of Abhayo. The loss of the royal favour was hard to bear, this was harder.

They, Dhama and the prince, had become frequent visitors to the shrine of the 'Reconciler,' and stories were afloat of wonderful doings there, and of miraculous manifestations brought about by Leah in the queen's palace, where she had now become a frequent visitor.

On this day, in our month of July, Abhayo was walking out by the Sacred Way to join his brethren on Mihintala in the Wass ceremonies. He passed the statues and the numerous shrines on the wayside unheeded. Processions were met, with priests escorted under white canopies, and offerings carried on trays covered with white cloth, and passed without observation. And the people in the procession would turn and watch the tall, striking figure hurrying along the holy street. The long walk had apparently not tired him. He was young, and accustomed to it, and he had also been occupied with his thoughts. He came to the foot of the wonderful stairway with its carved steps of solid stone; and after a few moments' conversation with a priest in charge of a small temple there, he ascended the sacred hill with nearly as much ease as he had walked down the famous street.

He had mounted nearly to the top of the third flight of stairs, when he turned by a path to the left under the stone aqueduct, and on between sculptured columns to the level space where the Bhojana Sālāwa or refectory stood, and where a Bana Maduwa (preaching place) had been prepared for the Wass. From this place a path leading around a part of the mountain over a precipice, which would be dangerous to a stranger, but which to Abhayo was evidently familiar ground, brought him to the rock-cells where the hermits dwelt.

In the front of one of them sat a venerable old man, whose shrivelled body was only partially covered by a monastic robe, the colour of which it would be difficult to describe. He shook with paralysis as he rested his hands on his staff, and looked, or appeared to look—for the aged eyes were not equal to distant vision—on the scene which spread out below.

You would have said that the light of life had left him, and that the faintest twilight was all that remained, had you seen him a few minutes ago; but now, with Abhayo's greeting, a remarkable change came over him, and his face became a sudden illumination of pleasure. He had been the young priest's tutor, and for him there was no joy like the company of his favourite pupil. The visitor's greeting was marked by profound respect and affection. Great respect is always paid to the aged members of the Buddhist priesthood by their juniors, but the relations between these two men were of no ordinary character. The old hermit had a reputation of extraordinary sanctity. He was, according to popular ideas, if it could be said of any one, in the last of the 'four paths.' But there was one obstacle to his attainment of Arhatship, in the old man's mind; there was one affection which he could not conquer, and that was his love for his 'boy,' as he sometimes called Abhayo. For often, as he sat there in the mouth of the cave, he would brood over the past, and it was pleasant to re-live the time when the young Samanera waited upon him—though he scarcely needed it then—so graciously and tenderly.

'How he did grow, to be sure!' the old man would mutter to himself; 'why, you could almost see him growing! And his mind would grow nearly as rapidly as his body. Nobody could repeat the Sutras like he. And the names Blessed of the One—why, he learnt them all in a few lessons! And how astonished the Theros were when his ordination to the Upasampada took place! Ah, that was a day to be remembered!'

Young monks would frequently come and listen to the reminiscences. The old man, barely heeding them, would go on with his life in the past. 'That was a day, to be sure! Such a congregation of Theros, and such a splendid procession of elephants! For was he not the friend and companion of the young prince? And the prince and the great nobles all came. He had his doubts then—my brave boy—and it was hard to get his consent, but he said at last that he "saw nothing better." Better, indeed! I should think not, than such an ordination as that. They said it was the finest the college had ever known. And I could have burst out laughing, but for the sacredness of the place, when they asked the question whether he was free from bodily infirmity. Why, he looked as if he belonged to another race. What an arm he had! I wish he was here to lift me with it now—I led him forward to the chief priest. How proud I was! They said it was comical to see a little fellow like me introducing a giant—I was old then, he had only seen twenty Wass seasons, and I three times that number—and it was not so long ago; but I feel much older now.

'Ah, I remember him when he was so small, and he used to write beautiful letters on the sand on the pansala floor. And one day he drew a caricature of me on the sanded floor, and the boys laughed. It was wrong! He saw that I was grieved, the little lad! And he came to where I was sitting, and rested his head on my shoulder and wept, so penitent was he! And I wept too, for I was beginning to get old, even then, and I loved him, you see. But what was I talking of? Oh yes, it was the ordination! How beautifully lighted the great hall was that night! And how grand he looked as he stood before them all, and said in that firm clear voice, three times, "I request Upasampada."

'But what have I to do with such thoughts as these now, and what have such affections as these to do with the holy ones? Oh, my son! My son! He is great, but I think sometimes that he is in trouble, and still wants his old tutor's guidance.

'Away, foolish thoughts! Ah, these are the demons that would tempt me from the "fourth way." And yet sometimes they do not seem evil things. The struggle is severe, and I am old now.

'Is that thee, my son? Of course it is! Thy appearance sent me back again into the old days—and not so very old either; but it must end before long, and I much fear I shall pass away without the blessed attainment for which I have been striving. Why, even that fear may be sinful. Dost think it is? I am glad thou art here. The moon is nearly at the full, and I have been wishing that I might sit to-night where the holy Mahindo breathed his last. As soon as the night comes, and it will not be long now—no, not long! Put thy arm around me, boy—what an arm it was, to be sure!—and help me there, that we may talk together in that sacred place.'

This recalling of the past was not unusual in such visits. Abhayo sat on a stone by the hermit's side, and tears filled his eyes at the thought of his old tutor's love for him, and as he compared that past of happiness with the present of doubt and trial. He said but little, and when the old man's talk had ended he reverently embraced him.

At last night came on and the moon rose. 'Ah, I thought so,' said the hermit; 'I have watched many moons from here. To-morrow is the full moon. I can tell by the light. And now the Wass begins. Thy arm, my son!'

Tenderly and strongly was the long right arm of the young Thero thrown around the hermit. Up the higher flights of steps they went, the old man scarcely walking, he was rather being carried. Abhayo humoured him as he said: 'Why, this is like returning youth. It does not oppress me at all; but I had forgotten for the moment that it is thy great arm after all. Ah, that was an arm!'

'But, venerable sir, thou art stronger and certainly younger than when I saw thee last. Here we are on the Bed of Mahindo. What a glorious night it is!'

Nothing could be finer than the moonlit scene which lay before them. The great white temples rising from the dark groves, and the white sheen on the Tissa Wewa and other great tanks, added strikingly to the impressiveness of the scene.

And there they sat and talked together, the strong arm still supporting the aged man. Under the influence of the night, but probably more because of the companionship of the loved pupil of other days, the hermit's mind grew clearer; and Abhayo soon found himself telling him of his troubles, and he opened out his heart to him as a son would to a father who was full of paternal affection for him. The loneliness which a man feels with the dropping away of old friends was coming over him, and he grasped the old withered body with a tender tightness, feeling that here at least was a heart that he might call home. He had many thoughts of the Syrian, and it must be confessed that he thought much of the Syrian's daughter, but he could not well follow them, and he had not visited Thomas since they had left.

Once or twice, in the course of the conversation, the hermit declared that he would leave the cave and go into the city, he would expose it all! And then he would pat Abhayo's arm playfully and say, 'Why, but for this I could not even sit up! How I wish I could help thee, lad; but alas! I shall never become the holy Arhat with such thoughts as these.'

'My beloved master, doest thou right to afflict thyself because of thy affections and desires? I am

free to confess that they are unworthily placed—they
are indeed! But I believe that in thee they are as
holy—nay, holier than the *Upeksha Bhawana*.[1] How
can it be right to crush the most blessed emotions of
our hearts, to destroy the noblest faculties that we
have?'

'Hush! This is perhaps the heresy of which they
talk. I know not. But still, I would help thee, lad.
Oh, my boy, my brave boy! What can I do for thee?
I would delay even the rest of Nirvana to do thee
service.'

'Do not think I would speak lightly, dear master,
of a faith which is so precious to thee, and has been so
precious to me. Thou art the most unselfish being
breathing, but the faith is selfish. "Save thyself," it
says,—"by any means and all means."'

'Say not so, my son! Now thou art speaking from
the bitterness of thy troubles. We are commanded to
do good to all living creatures. Kindness to all things
is enjoined on us.'

'True, my best of friends, but only for my own
merit, that the merit may outweigh the demerit in my
poor miserable Karma; and what is the end of it all—
death to the affections, indifference towards all? How
can that be true kindness? Ah, if we could pray, then
we might help each other. If we could but pray!'

'Pray, my son! What would that do for thee?
Is it not better to leave it all, to turn thy back on cities
and courts, for the undisturbed serenity to be found in
the life of the higher meditation?'

---

[1] The mode prescribed for the *meditation* of *equanimity*, in which
all sentient beings are regarded alike. This is the highest form of
meditation, and is necessary to Arhatship.

'What becomes of the others, of the multitudes from whom we separate ourselves? How can such a life help them, a life of solitary meditation without prayer?'

'To whom should we pray?'

'Ah, that, my oldest friend, is the difficulty. Where shall we go with our prayers? Where is the true Sarana? What if there be, after all, a Creator God, who made all these, this beautiful earth and that glorious moon? There is such a manifest purpose about them all, it cannot be that they came into existence of themselves. There must be a mind above all these glorious material forms. My dear old friend, there must be a God. To us He is unknown, but He may perchance hear men when they pray, and give them help; who knows?'

'Who knows?' echoed the hermit thoughtfully. 'Then some time, every day, will I send out from the side of this holy mountain into the great space around us a prayer for help and blessing on my boy. It can do no harm, and it may be that the unknown God will hear; who knows?'

The shout of worship rang out over Mihintala. The old man said: 'Child, thou art tired, strong as thou art. Help me back, and get to thy duties. The worship hour has come.'

Lightly and carefully Abhayo helped him back to the cave, reverently offered him the food which had been brought for him as a sick member of the order, and then left for the hall of refection.

On the next day the Wass ceremonies began. A preacher was brought down from the Maha Wihara in great state. In the procession an elephant bore, under a white canopy, a sacred relic; next came another elephant bearing the ola-books; and next, in a beautifully decorated palanquin, came the invited priest, in the order of the three Gems or Refuges (the Tun-Sarana), the Buddha, the Doctrine, and the Priesthood.

The principal duty of the day was to receive the offerings of the people, which function was performed in a temporary building made of poles and thatched leaves. Up to the priest the offerings were carried and laid on a temporary altar at which he stood. When the offertory was finished, the people fell on their knees in worship, and while they knelt the priestly benediction said in the Pali tongue :—

> May your desire and your happiness
> Soon be accomplished!
> May your hopes be fulfilled
> Like as the moon becomes round![1]

After which, with shouts of ' *Sâdhu! Sâdhu!* ' the people retired, leaving the priests to prepare the offerings for the principal meal.

It was then that a great trial befell Abhayo. His position in the monastery had always been one of great influence, though there were several who were his seniors. In the ordinary course of things it was his duty on this occasion to make the preliminary offering at the altar and divide the food for the priests. But it was intimated to him that, as this sacred office could not be performed by priests who are liable to censure, the duty was to be performed by another of the brethren. It was said kindly, but to Abhayo it was the clearest indication of the rising storm. He ate his food in solitude. He sat on in silence, wondering where it

[1] Dickson's translation of the Wass service.

would end. Should he fly? How he would like to see Joseph and—but no, he must remain, and as he sat he could hear the Wass preacher in the adjoining hall chanting the invocation, 'Praise to the Blessed One, the Holy One, the Author of all truth!'

Then the people followed, repeating as with one voice the three 'Refuges' and the first five precepts of the 'Sil.' And then he said to himself, 'How can I bear this? My brethren are deserting me. It will break that dear old man's heart to have me visited with the censure of my college. The people are rejoicing in "Sarana," are they? They have three Saranas, the Buddha, the Doctrine, and the Order. Oh, if I could but find rest in either!' Then he thought of Joseph, and of his advice on parting; and he said, 'I will go and see Thomas, the Christian presbyter.'

CHAPTER X.

PASTORAL.

> Near it the village of Senani reared
> Its roofs of grass, nestled amid the palms,
> Peaceful with simple folk and pastoral toils.
> EDWIN ARNOLD.

SEVERAL weeks had passed since Joseph and his daughter had arrived at Jambugama. They had at first intended staying only a few days. The dry season had lasted long. The messenger who came occasionally with business communications spoke of the heat in Anuradhapura as intense. But the village was comparatively cool, and our Syrian friends were more attached to country life than ever. It grew upon them with a daily increasing delight.

And I should like to say, if I may be permitted to put in a word here, that there are few experiences more charming now than a few weeks' residence, at the proper time of the year, in such a village in the interior of Ceylon. Nobody can be said to know the land who has not had such an experience and has not interested himself in the country people and their customs. There is, of course, in the modern Ceylon village (not very different from the ancient, we may be sure), as in most villages and cities, much that one is desirous to avoid, but there is also very much that is picturesque; and there are many scenes of quiet beauty, in which one may experience a restful delight. Chatting with the simple villagers, if you know their language, will form a never-failing source of interest, pleasure, and amusement. It offers a splendid field of study to the naturalist, and, taking it altogether, there are not many such opportunities for a holiday as a few weeks in such a village would afford. But let us get back to our story.

The jambus had ripened and gone—and what beauties they had been! How lovely they had looked as they crowded the trees with their little round apples, covered with that inviting rose-colour, spreading all over the smooth, polished surface! And how the village children rejoiced in the large quantities that fell from the trees! The mangoes had also ripened and gone. And what were all the delights of the city, with the processions, the elephants, and the bands of music, to the youngsters, compared with such a paradise as this in the time of the ripe mangoes?

The mango is a homely-looking fruit, not nearly so pretty as the jambu, but the beauty of the latter is outside, while the mango (when it is good) is all good and beautiful within its plain leathery coat.

Joseph tried to make a parable one day for the children out of the fruits, but without success. They were too much occupied with the fruits themselves to pay attention to parables. Kumari was in high glee at times, but she sometimes had a great deal of nursing to do, and she began asking her mistress about returning to the city.

The paddy had been gathered from most of the fields, but some of the farmers were late, and amongst them Sikki Banda. But even with him the harvest had begun. The lucky day for commencing had been ascertained from the village astrologer, and, after a preparatory ceremony, the first sickle was thrust in amongst the slender spears of rice corn, tipped with silver and russet gold.

Then the work went on with a will. The women worked in one part of a field and the men in another, and they sang, as they worked, such songs as would tend to prevent the fairies (the 'little people') from causing injury to the produce of the fields. They sang of offerings which they meant to present at the altar of Buddha, and to the gods; and they sang of the coming Buddha, in order to avert all bad omens.

One in each party would lead the song with the solo part, and the swish of the sickle kept up a rhythmic accompaniment; then all would fall into the chorus. And sometimes this choir-leader would extemporise and introduce a bit of fun with local and personal references, and a merry, hearty laugh would check the chorus. And when two parties would near each other in the reaping, the choruses would unite into a pleasant harmony of voices, though it must be confessed that much of the singing was like that of Chaucer's St. Eloyse, who 'entuned the service sweetly in her nose.'

Some of the reapers were mere children, and a beautiful sight it was to see their little bright laughing faces and dark figures in the midst of the standing corn. And how delighted they were, these youngsters, when a hare was started by the approach of the chorus, or a paddy-bird was frightened out of its nest and rose in the air with great flapping of wings and uttering shrill curses on the intruders! And they were pleased when the chorus had got on so far with their work as to reach the hillock in the middle of the field, where the big jak-tree grew and gave them such a grateful shade. That was much more to them than the glorious colour formed by the clusters of purple Bowitiya blossom, a little way off, surrounded by the corn that was so soon to fall. Purple and gold! There is nothing more beautiful in Nature than such a combination. Joseph pointed it out to Irene as they looked on, and watched the reapers from where they sat in the shade of large jak-trees at the foot of the hill.

Kumari's brothers were stationed about in little 'sentry-boxes' perched on high poles, where they had instructions to yell the most horrible cries that the voices of Sinhalese youth can compass, to frighten away birds and demons. At first it was glorious play to the boys, but like all play, when long continued, it gradually developed into work, and the cries, which at first seemed evolved from the frantic delight of young fiends, echoed lazily and not unpleasantly across the valley.

Kumari envied them their employment. She thought it much better fun than nursing baby. It was the same baby who was honoured with a sort of half introduction to the reader in a previous chapter, in which we got to the eve of the naming-day. He was nearly a year old, and it was time for him to begin eating rice. This is an important epoch in Sinhalese child-life. The astrologer had been consulted, the horoscope studied afresh, and a fortunate day selected for giving the *bat-nama* or 'rice-name.' Invitations were sent out to all the relatives and friends in the neighbourhood. And they are all generally in the same neighbourhood. Kiri Banda was a notorious exception. And there was a large assembly at the house of Sikki Banda. Kumari was very important, and took great pleasure in explaining to Irene what every part of the ceremony meant.

At the lucky hour, Sikki Banda's aged father came forward to where the mother stood with the most important personage in the ceremony, the baby-boy, in her arms; both of them—as indeed were most of the guests—richly dressed in robes and jewels. The old grandfather then took a little rice between his fingers and put it in the child's mouth and whispered the name into the ear of the infant, who did not appear to be profoundly impressed by the information thus mysteriously imparted; nor did he appear to relish the new style of food to which he had been treated with so much ceremony. The name was only to be used in the child's infancy.

This was followed by an elaborate entertainment. First the men sat down together, and after them the women, and a delicious repast was served to each on a piece of fresh plantain-leaf.

On that same day too, as Kumari had said, Anula, the Indian lady, had arrived. She had been well escorted, as suited her condition. And now the Wass had begun, and she had stayed on in the village, partly for religious observances and partly because a strong attachment had grown up between herself and the daughter of the Syrian.

The Sinhalese tongue was to her an easy acquisition, from the extensive knowledge which she already possessed of the languages (Sanskrit and Pali) from which it was derived, and which made her language so different

K

from the talk of the villagers that Kumari called her 'A very deep lady.'

And, after a time, she conversed freely with Joseph himself. We have already said that the women had much greater freedom in those ancient days in Eastern lands than they possess now. Without father and mother, Joseph regarded her with a somewhat paternal interest; and on her part she thought that, but for the difference of religion and race, she could look up to him as to a father.

The three often talked together of those matters which lay nearest to the heart of each, for they were all ardent disciples, the one of the Buddha, and the other two of the Christ. They conversed on these topics with great gentleness and forbearance. Not a word of harshness or ridicule was used on either side. It was a matter that was too serious for ridicule, Joseph had said; and the differences ought to move to compassion rather than unkindness. And this forbearance and tenderness had great weight with the thoughtful Indian girl, for she knew something of the terrible controversy raging between the Brahmanists and Buddhists in her own land, and she would tell of the ridicule which had been heaped upon her friends professing the faith of Gautama, and of the fierce persecution which was driving them from some parts of North and Central India.

They had been interested greatly in her description of the inauguration of the new faith of the 'Reconciler' at Anuradhapura. She laughed a bright rippling laugh, which illuminated her beautiful face, as she spoke of the interruptions which occurred in the course of Alypius's opening address, and tried to mimic the appearance of Leah. And then she would excuse herself and say: 'Perhaps I ought not to laugh. But this is not a true faith; at any rate, it is not true Buddhism. My studies have made that clear to me; and, as the Mihintala Thero intimated, it conceded too much to be a true faith of any kind. The Jewess looked as if she were in a trance all the time until the collection was made, and then I noticed that she looked particularly alive.'

'Ah, thou art not one of the initiated!' Irene ventured to say, with a touch of irony.

'No; there were only three in all the assembly who were not enrolled—the Mihintala Thero, myself, and a funny little Sinhalese man, who slept through it all with his great black head resting against a wall.'

'Ah,' replied Irene, clapping her hands, 'I know him; that is Kiri Banda! He is our host's brother, and is in the service of the royal astrologer—a sort of general factotum. He is such a droll fellow! And why didst thou not join them, my friend? Was it because of what the Thero said?' This with a little look of arch interrogation.

'It did not appear to me consistent with the faith of the Blessed One. It seemed to degrade it altogether. Therefore, I resolved to wait and see if it should prove worthy. That was the Thero's advice, and I mean to follow it. I have since been alternately scolded and laughed at, because of my excessive caution, by Dharma Sen and other of my friends; and shortly after the great meeting I had a visit from Leah—my princess is much taken with her, and so is the queen, as well as other ladies of high rank—and she, Leah, told me that a "certain high personage" was deeply grieved with me for abstaining from the enrolment, and she evidently thought it would make an impression. I have had hints in that direction before. She seemed surprised at the slight effect it had on me. And I said that my faith was more to me than that, and that my religious belief did not sit so lightly on me as it appeared to with some. But she is a fascinating woman, this Leah. Dost thou know her? She is of thy nation, and was of thy religion, I think.'

'Not exactly of our nation, and only nominally of our religion; but there are many Jews and Jewesses in the city. I think my father knows her, but his acquaintance is only of the slightest. She must be an extraordinary person.'

'Undoubtedly; but it may be my excessive caution, I do not think she is to be trusted. Just now, the city is full of her praises. Popular favour is altogether, or nearly so, on the side of the "adepts," as they are called, though, I believe, the Greek does not profess to be an "adept" himself; he only claims it for the "cofounder," as he styles the Jewess. And she, if rumour is to be credited, does many marvellous things. A golden and jewelled ornament which had long ago been lost by the queen was found in a most unlikely place by her agency. Epistles written on the ola leaf have come in the most mysterious way suddenly, as if from the skies, or from the roofs of houses, addressed to most distinguished persons, from the "Reconciler" and other great spirits; and the letters have had reference to conversations which were being held at the time. There are glaring inconsistencies in the woman's character, but that is all explained by the "dual nature" which she claims for herself. In the one nature she permits herself great freedom, not to say license; in the other she is all that is pure and good. It is true that our Arhats and Rishis have produced wonderful manifestations, but these people are not of that class. No, indeed, anything but that!'

This was a little talk between the two. Here Irene's father joined them, and described the developments of Neo-Platonism and Gnosticism in the West; and they had no difficulty in identifying some of the leading features of those systems with the new religion of the 'Reconciler' recently propounded in Anuradhapura.

The reaping lasted but a few days, and this was followed by the drying and threshing. A threshing-floor was got ready in a large field, another fortunate day ascertained and another ceremony performed. The buffaloes were roused from two or three big pools, in which for days they had been wallowing with a look expressive of the utmost content with their mud bath; it must be allowed, however, that the buffalo's face is not capable of a great variety of expression. And now they were made to go through the monotonous round of treading out the corn.

The bringing in of the bundles was almost as great a delight to the young people as the reaping. One day—towards the cool of the evening—our little party, accompanied by Kumari, went out to watch the proceedings. They sat under a clump of trees which covered a slight eminence, from which all the operations on the field were visible. Irene was anxious to take some part in the harvesting, and throwing her light veil over her head, she went across the field picking up scattered corn, the gleanings that were left. Joseph looked at her dreamily and said: 'Yes, it is a picture of the old days, and so might Ruth have gone into the corn-fields of Boaz.'

Anula and Kumari sat and watched, the former looking on with thoughtful admiration at the beautiful picture presented by the graceful, curving figure of the Syrian girl, while Kumari was compelled, much against her inclination, to remain with the baby.

And when Irene returned laden with a small sheaf of rice-corn and various flowers of the field, blue and red, with the starlike white of the jasmine, the other girls set to work to weave the gleanings into a coronet, with which they crowned her, and that done, Kumari made a wreath with no little art, and threw it round her mistress's neck, Joseph regarding her the while with much paternal pride. So might Ruth have been crowned, and so might she have looked, when made by the husbandman's favour the queen of the field.

And, as the queen, Irene was to hold a mimic court, the girls professed to make obeisance, and Joseph was told laughingly that he must do the same. And baby was made to bend his little fat naked body and do *pujah* with closed hands to the newly-made queen. The pets were brought forward also to show their loyalty. The buffalo with the broken horn thought that her milking-time was come, and came slowly at the call of Kumari, who explained the situation to her, while she scratched the great rough, broad head. The dogs came around, wondering what new sensation was being provided for them, and whether it would mean a scrap of anything to eat. The myna, much to the amusement of all, sprang on to Irene's shoulder with a great show of profound and affectionate loyalty, but having all the time an evident liking for the ears of corn in Irene's crown, uttering phrases in which religious and profane expressions mingled indifferently.

Then all the family of Sikki Banda gathered around. And the people engaged on the threshing-floor stopped their curious chatter, in the language peculiar to threshing-floors, and paused to gaze with the faintest of smiles, and expressions of admiration, at the group under the trees.

When the homage was over, the queen and her courtiers still remained chatting together in the same spot, and, as Irene said, nothing could be more beautiful. The birds had not gone to rest, but were singing in the trees, with all the energy imparted by the cool evening, to make up for the long period of songlessness during the heat of the day. Dove cooed soothingly in response to dove, and underneath it all was the music of the running stream which, when it was required, irrigated the rice-fields.

Joseph talked of the Saviour in the fields of corn, and described the appearance of those fields. Then Anula brought forward incidents from the story of the Buddha which were of a pastoral character, and she dwelt fondly upon the love and compassion of the Teacher for the animal world.

Joseph thought it a beautiful trait in the Buddha's life and doctrine, but it was wanting in discrimination. 'Why, in that region of the higher life to which the Buddha had attained, it would be as great a sin to crush that gorgeous butterfly yonder on the corn as to slay our queen of the fields! It was not Gautama's teaching alone; he derived it from other and older masters, and I suppose it is the logical outcome of the transmigration theories. But it is an estimate of life which is absolutely unworkable. It sets a low comparative value on humanity, and helps to prevent men from rising to the heights of noble manhood, and realising their true position in the universe of God. Jesus of Nazareth has shown us how to be true men.'

'According to its Karma,' said Anula, 'life rises from the lower forms to the higher. Surely there is no inconsistency in that?'

'Perhaps not, theoretically, but there is a glaring inconsistency in those laws of Karma which may, for one slight offence offered to the priesthood, degrade the loftiest intellect and a godlike manhood down to the state of the most loathsome insect. But let us avoid controversy if we can, and give ourselves up to the quiet delight of the evening.'

'We can happily talk of these things without being controversial. Was Jesus of Nazareth kind to animals? I have heard that in that respect He was not like our glorious Buddha.'

'He was as kind and compassionate to the creatures of the lower creation, my child, as the Buddha; but, as God, He estimated their life at its true value. I have always regarded the estimate placed on such life by the Buddha as one of the greatest infirmities of a noble mind. What can we say, for instance, of the story in which he offers himself to the starving tiger? Admitting its authenticity, what profound ignorance does it show of the true value of his own life! and what a want of consistency in the encouragement offered to cruelty in the tiger! With such examples and under this system, self-murder and homicide become less heinous than the slaying of serpents.

'The Christ declares man to be of greater value than the birds, but in one of the most touching of His parables He shows with what tenderness He regarded the dumb animal life which surrounded Him. And on another occasion, in speaking of the Providence of God, He said: "Not a sparrow falleth to the ground without your Heavenly Father's notice."'

'What is the parable you refer to? I should like to hear it.'

And Joseph told the Story of the Lost Sheep and the Good Shepherd; and none could fail to be impressed with the manner in which the old man told that marvellously beautiful illustration of the Redeemer's loving-kindness and compassion.

When he had finished, Irene broke in with the remark, 'And He was so fond of children! I shouldn't like a Saviour who was not fond of children.'

This remark was not intended to imply that the Buddha was devoid of that quality, but it set Anula thinking and trying to remember, without success, some incident in the life of Sakya Muni which would illustrate a love of the little ones.

After a little pause, Joseph said: 'What could be more appropriate now, or fit in more suitably with the spirit of the evening hour, than sweet music? Sing for us, my daughter, sing the song of the Son of Man!' They had during their stay in the village put the great story into Sinhalese verse, to be sung to a metre which Joseph had learnt in the old days at Antioch.

It has not been referred to before in this narrative, but the Syrian girl had in her voice a precious gift with which she had frequently cheered the exiles in the city home. And now, as she stood and sang the opening stanza, still crowned with the corn and the flowers, Anula thought she had never heard or seen anything so sweet in all her life.

It was not mechanical; every word was full of the soul-breath as well as the breath of the body. She sang of the little child in Bethlehem, of the carpenter's house at Nazareth where the King of kings lived and worked, of the temptation in the desert, of how the Holy One healed the sick, fed the hungry, and brought a mighty comfort to all. Then the bereaved home in Bethany was the theme, and the singer looked as if she could really see the Living One standing in the house of death. On the voice went to the festival where the grateful anointing took place; and the Syrian girl looked, as she sang, as if she could have clasped the hands of that other Syrian girl in the Bethany story. Down the voice went into the garden of the agony with the cry, 'If Thou wilt, let this cup pass from Me!' Tears filled the singer's eyes, Anula could scarcely control her sobs, and Joseph leant his face on his hands, while the children looked up at Irene, their great eyes filled with awe.

On the voice went to the cross with the bitter wail, 'My God! My God! why hast Thou forsaken Me?' Then a pause of deep silence, as if it had gone down into the abode of the dead, to rise again in a glorious burst of melody, which made smiles replace the tears in the joyous cry, 'He is risen! He is risen!' Then the song finished, and the little audience listened, speechless, as if to hear more. The doves cooed again soothingly in the trees, and the little stream made music as it ran underneath.

'Oh, father,' said Irene at last, 'let us remain here! What are riches to us? God is so near us here, let us stay! And she looked as if she had seen a vision of God.

'That is like the holy Apostle Peter in the Gospel-story, and thou would say with him, "Let us build three tabernacles." I would willingly remain, but——'

'May peace be with thee, Joseph, and with these fair ladies!' It was the Greek Alypius who stood before them, bowing.

During the singing he had approached them unobserved. 'Can this be Irene, or is it Ceres, as the Romans call our Demeter, come to extend her rule over this portion of the earth? Nay, but it was a Christian song which I heard but now in a voice which, Orpheus-like, might tame the wildest of beasts. Joseph, I bring thee important tidings from the city, where thy presence is immediately required.'

CHAPTER XI.

THE NEW FRIEND AND THE OLD.

They stood aloof, the scars remaining,
Like cliffs which had been rent asunder.
     COLERIDGE, *Christabel.*

ABHAYO THERO, when he had made up his mind to a thing, was soon on his way to its fulfilment. He had no sooner determined on paying a visit to the Christian presbyter than he proceeded to carry it into effect. It had been practically conceded to him long ago, that he was not expected to be bound by the ordinary restrictions of the brotherhood. His rank and influence were great, and, although not sufficient to prevent the enforcement of some of the strictest rules of the 'order,' yet the 'brethren' were ready to make allowances for his erratic character, and long walks from his monastery even during the Wass season, when the monks are all supposed to be in residence, were not regarded in him as grave offences. The liability of censure, to which he was now subject, made it necessary for him to give information to the senior brother as to his movements. On other occasions this had not been necessary for him, and this new experience of a limit on his liberty was painfully galling to such a nature as his.

It was not that there would be any difficulty; he knew the sympathetic, kindly nature of the old man who presided over the monastery. The senior, in common with most of the brethren, had the highest respect for Abhayo's talents and acquirements, and they had winked at some heretical tendencies, which, so far as they could see, did in no way identify him with the Buddhist factions with which they were at enmity. But now hints that an investigation should be made had reached them from quarters which they could neither afford to despise nor ignore. This was explained to Abhayo by the head of the establishment in the kindest way, half apologising for the manner in which he had been treated at refection, but earnestly urging him to keep to the orthodox lines.

After promising that he would be ready when wanted, and that he would not go beyond the city boundaries, the young Thero was soon in the Sacred Way again, walking with his long stride and swinging gait towards the heart of the city. And as he walked the night came on.

He had no retinue, and rarely took a servant with him on his walks, as did other monks; and nobody who knew him thought it at all strange to see him journeying alone on such a night as this, when the full moon gives opportunity for cool and comfortable travel.

The walk was doing him good. He had lived much in the open air, and had frequently realised the effect which a walk under a clear, moonlit sky had in quieting such little worries and troubles as occasionally arose in the life of the monastery. And to-night he felt as if lifted into communion with the skies. He could almost imagine that it was another than himself, walking along between the gilded shrines, statues, and small white dagobas.

It was late before he reached the house of Joseph in the foreign quarter. Thomas, who was on the roof, enjoying the cool night, knew, as soon as the unexpected visitor was announced, that such a visit, at such a time, would not be made without some important reason; and his first thoughts were of his dear friends, Joseph and Irene. It was a great relief to know that the visitor brought no ill news of them, and it was a happiness to realise that he was called upon to minister to a mind diseased, and to such a mind as that of Abhayo.

Thomas was not a proficient talker in Sinhalese, but he had long made the language of the Damilos a study, assisted by the linguistic abilities of Joseph and Irene, which were of no mean order, in the hope that he might be useful to the large numbers of that people dwelling in the city, when the time should come for him to break through the comparative seclusion of his present habits. His vocabulary was large, and the difficulties of idiom did not interfere much with the success of such a conversation as that which he now entered upon with the Buddhist priest, who understood the language of the Damilos almost as well as his own, and who did his utmost to make his part in the conversation intelligible to his auditor.

They sat together on the flat roof, and talked for hours of the Buddha and the Christ, for, talk as they would about systems, they invariably found themselves coming to these great central personalities for the illustrations which they needed.

Abhayo propounded the anxious question whether it was not possible to amalgamate the two systems of faith. Was it not possible for a good Christian to hold such liberal views of Buddhism as would recognise in the teaching of Gautama a divine revelation for the nations of the East hitherto unvisited by the light of the Gospel of Christ? Was it not, after all, very much a matter of race and locality?

From many of his conversations with Joseph, he said, he had gathered that Christianity was evolved out of Judaism, just as Buddhism was evidently a development of old Hindu faiths and philosophies.

Here the Syrian pastor observed that this was not a correct deduction, as he would know if he would make a careful comparison of the Old and New Testament scriptures. It would make it altogether a growth of the human mind, and not a revelation, and that was one of the chief distinctions between the two faiths.

'The one,' he said, 'is of the earth, earthy; the other is the Lord from heaven! I have heard you admit in conversations with my friend, that the great power of deliverance was not to be found in man himself. The lower must be lifted by the higher, and the leverage must be higher than the thing to be lifted. It is at this point of confessed helplessness that Christianity comes with the power of God to the rescue of a fallen race.'

'It is true,' replied Abhayo; 'wherever one turns in Buddhism it is "self," "self," "self-work," "suffer," "work," with no outside help. I did not think it was possible to put the Christ and the Buddha together, but it ought not to be impossible that there should be a larger tolerance on both sides.'

'Mercy there is, and toleration there may be, but amalgamation there cannot be; if there can be no fellowship between the Christ and the Buddha, there can be no amalgamation of their doctrines, and no true union between their followers. How is it possible that there can be union between Christianity and a faith or philosophy which denies the existence of God and of the immortal soul?'

'But all Buddhists do not do that.'

'Then I should say, from what I have gathered from yourself and others well versed in the Buddhist system, that they were not true disciples of Gautama.'

'I have watched,' said Abhayo, 'the lives of some Christian traders in Anuradhapura, and have found them not at all holier in life or more upright in their business dealings than many of our own faith. And that has sometimes made me think that faith after all was perhaps a matter of race and climate.'

'It is natural to look at the lives of the professors of a faith,' said the Christian pastor, 'as affording a standard whereby to judge of the faith itself, and that makes the Christian name a fearful responsibility in such a life as ours; but why go to the worst for examples—you who have seen so much of the life of our dear friends in whose house we are now met? The general influence of a faith on mankind or on masses of people may form a proper ground for deduction in such a matter as this, but not such instances as you have hinted at, where the profession of attachment was only nominal. In Christianity, as in Buddhism, it is one thing to be called a disciple, and another thing to be one.'

'Forgive me!' broke in the priest, 'but such thoughts will come to us all, and my doubts are manifold and strong.'

'Truth is not, and never can be, a matter of race or climate. It is unchangeable in all ages, places, and climes. Interpretations may be various, and the lives of those professing to be guided by its light may be inconsistent, but the Truth will always remain the same, and forms the one divine standard for all times and places. The Christ claimed to be the Truth, and in doing so challenged the application of the tests by which men seek to discover Truth. I would speak with admiration and reverence for much of Gautama's teaching, but is there not in it much that will not stand the application of the Truth standard? Why be satisfied with fragments of a statue covered with the soil of earth when the Living Truth Himself may be ours? Why blunder on with broken lights, when we may go to Him who is the Light of the world?'

'Ah—and how may we reach Him?'

'By prayer. He is with us now, and I believe it is His Holy Spirit which has led thee here.'

'If I could but see Him!' said the priest, 'then the light might come.'

Then Thomas, standing up with his hand lifted towards the glorious sky, prayed with an earnestness and power which Abhayo felt to be real, and to betoken an intercourse which was not infrequent, that God would open the eyes of his friend and pour into his soul the divine light which would enable him to recognise in Jesus the Truth, the Saviour of the world.

The priest was deeply impressed, and felt as if he could realise the divine presence in the inspiration of that moment. He then began to speak of the difficulties which he was beginning to encounter and of the hardships of his position, and from this they went on to speak of persecution. And Abhayo spoke as if it was easy for his new teacher to talk of how he should behave in the midst of troubles which he had not to endure himself. He thought the Syrian did not sufficiently realise what persecutions would follow on a declaration of attachment to the Christian faith to such as himself.

It was then that Thomas told him his story, without mentioning his cruel wife; and we may judge with what feeling of sympathy the listener followed the narrative, and with what surprise he saw the speaker draw out from within the folds of his robe the scorched and withered hand, which testified to sufferings on account of conviction and faith such as he had not yet been called on to endure.

After a brief rest, as soon as the sun had risen, Abhayo left the house with many expressions of thanks on his part, and with many exhortations to steadfastness and courage on the part of Thomas. He had ascertained that Joseph and Irene were so much in love with the life of their country retreat that their absence might be indefinitely prolonged. It had made him sad to receive such information, for he had looked forward with great hope to their return, but he was thankful to find in their absence such a helper and guide as their friend and pastor.

He had turned down into the street leading to the Maha Wihara, thinking of what was before him in the course of life which he now felt bound to pursue, and especially of the attitude which was being taken towards him by his friends, when his thoughts naturally dwelt on his friend the artist-prince, and he said, 'I will return and see him at once as soon as I have attended to a duty at the Brazen Palace; he is sure to be in his studio now, for he loves the early morning for such work.'

He returned by the great North and South Street,

in which at that early hour the scavengers were busily engaged in finishing the duties assigned to them before the traffic of the day should fill this great artery of the city. Passing beneath the gallery on which the palace of the tooth-relic had recently been built, and where graceful columns with elegant capitals surrounded the Thuparama Dagoba, he turned to the left by a street which led close by the banks of the Abhaya-Wewa and the Viyan-kulam Tanks on beyond the Lankaramaya Dagoba, past the royal palace, into the deep cool shade of the mighty mountain of masonry which formed the Jetawanarama Dagoba, and on to the house which was set apart to Prince Detu.

It was familiar ground to Abhayo, and he entered the palace-yard, enclosed by mighty granite monoliths, without being deeply impressed by the surroundings. His travels in India had made him acquainted with buildings of greater architectural beauty and magnificence, but as he passed through the corridors, with the numerous pillars of elegantly carved woodwork in the light of the early morning, there was a sad reflection in his mind that perhaps this was the last time that he would be permitted to enter the prince's house on the old friendly footing. His friendship with Detu had been very dear to him, not simply on account of his high rank and great influence, but because of his unusual ability and affectionate disposition, and there had been between them the strong attachment which in those days always existed between tutor and pupil. Though not much the prince's senior, Abhayo had always regarded his royal friend with something like a fatherly interest and affection. He knew how easily he could be led by anything which presented the slightest show of reason, and was fully aware of the dangers to which his friend's want of firmness made him liable in his exalted position. This made him fear for the future.

And he more than half dreaded the approaching interview, as he thought of the coldness which the prince had recently shown him and of the influence which the authorities at the hall of the 'Reconciler' had obtained over him. He had hoped great things from Dharma Sen, the friend from India; but he too was easily impressed, and had apparently been only too glad to cast in his lot with a movement which promised such great things in support of the Buddhist faith. Abhayo knew that the prince had been no bigot, but he also knew that he was devotedly attached to the faith of his fathers, and he thought it not unlikely that he might degenerate into a bigotry as zealous and unreasoning as that of some of his ancestors, notwithstanding the loud profession of liberal principles and charity which characterised the disciples of the 'Reconciler.'

Thoughts like these had occupied his mind in the morning walk. The sights of the journey had scarcely attracted his attention. The hundreds of yellow-robed priests and their attendants stirring about the Maha Wihara like bees coming forth from a hive to engage in their morning duties, and setting out from the Brazen Palace with the alms-bowls slung from their shoulders, to make the morning collection, received no more than a passing thought, and many of them looked significantly at each other as his well-known figure went by with the usual rapid stride.

The prince would see him, an attendant said, and led the way to the workshop or studio. Detu was absorbed in what he spoke of as the great work of his life—a statue of Gautama the Vanquisher, which should surpass anything of the kind ever seen in Anuradhapura. He was not alone, as Abhayo had expected to find him. Dharma Sen was there, giving advice with regard to the work, and a few of the highborn youths of the city were carefully employing their tools on it under the direction of the artist-prince.

After addressing the visitor in the usual reverential form, Detu proceeded with his work, while Dharma Sen gave the priest a cold salutation and said: 'The Thero has little sympathy, I presume, with such pursuits as this, with a result which will command the worship of the populace. If I remember rightly, I have heard our orator condemn the worship of such statues as unworthy of the disciples of him who conquered "the five deadly sins."'

A look of displeasure crossed the face of Detu, but he continued apparently absorbed in the movements of his pupils, afraid lest a false stroke should spoil this triumph of his art. Abhayo replied: 'Thou knowest the words of the Vanquisher: if thou canst find anything in them to countenance this universal imageworship, I will most willingly concede the point in favour of this beautiful creation of genius.'

A smile of satisfaction played across the refined features of the prince, and he cast a grateful look for a moment at his old friend, and said: 'It is my ambition to realise what the presence of the Blessed One must have been, and to help others to realise it by this representation.'

'And right nobly and beautifully is the work done, my prince; but none the less effectually will it help forward or downward that degeneration which shows itself in the worship of the representation instead of the thing represented. The human mind is too lazy, too well satisfied to stop at the symbol, to search behind for the being or the truth symbolised.'

'I remember now thou wouldest have dissuaded me in the same way, for the same reason, when I made the golden statue of Mahindo.'

'Let not our controversy prevent my admiration of the workmanship. It is by far the most delicate and beautiful production of thy studio. I can admire, though I cannot worship.'

'Of course,' replied the prince, 'none can worship till the ceremony of the dedication and the "giving of the eye."[1] The king, who came yesterday to see the progress of the work, was so pleased with it that he has sent two of the richest and brightest jewels in his possession to be fixed as eyes in the head of the statue, and one of them is the great flawless sapphire, the miraculous stone of which you have doubtless heard. We are engaged now in preparing, as you see, for placing the royal gift. There is the jewel, lying before you!'

It was the first time Abhayo had seen it. After a slight exclamation in admiration of its dazzling beauty, he went on: 'That of itself is evidence of the degeneration of which I speak. The ceremony of the "eye-making" would be unnecessary if the statue were meant to be simply an aid to reflection. But I came to have a talk, if possible, with my old friend and pupil alone. Could we converse in some more private place?'

Dharma Sen and the pupils took the hint and

[1] The painting of the eyes of images intended for worship is always attended with great ceremony.

retired, but the prince went out after them to call them back, thus leaving Abhayo, for a minute or two, alone in the studio. Detu set the student-carvers at work on parts of the statue which required less attention and less delicate manipulation, and with a word to Dharma Sen walked away with the priest through a grove of ironwood trees, shady and cool, where the dark foliage canopied many a work of art. They conversed walking slowly through the grove to the baths, which were not likely to be frequented at that hour. And there they paced to and fro in earnest conversation on the upper terraces until they were tired, when they went down by the beautifully carved stairs to a shady gallery below, where they sat down, the prince seating himself punctiliously a step lower than the priest.

There are baths which are still the most perfect of the remains found in the ruined city. They are of large proportions and are lined with granite, in some places exquisitely carved. Nobody can visit them, even now, without realising that the baths were an important feature in the old city, on which some of its best work in stone was lavished.

On the occasion of which we are now writing, they formed a delightful retreat. Every arrangement which could contribute to coolness and shade had been provided, and in the neighbourhood were growing trees whose fragrant blossoms threw a delicious perfume into the great stone tanks. As the day got hot, those who had the privilege of access would come out to revel in the luxurious coolness which the place afforded.

It was a favourite resort of Detu, and was secured to his sole use for certain hours of the day. He and his quondam tutor were now evidently engaged in the most animated conversation. They at last got so excited that both rose from their seats, in order that each might speak with the greater liberty.

'What say the sages?' the prince asked, in a tone of passionate entreaty. '"Do not walk in the path of the wicked law! Do not go after the false teacher!" We all know of thy doubts, and of the strange thoughts which have disturbed thy mind; but stay, I beseech thee, and think seriously ere thou takest such a step as this. Think of all that it will mean for one filling such a position as thine.'

'I may delay for a while, though it is a question whether that would not be sinful, with my present convictions; but my doubts are still many. I may wait a little longer for a fuller light, but no thought of or care for self shall hinder me when that true light comes. What saith the holy Sage? "Cut out the love of self like the ripened lotus, with thy hand! Keep the road of peace. Nirvana has been revealed by the Buddha!" But why should we seek Nirvana? Life and immortality have been brought to light in the words of Jesus of Nazareth!'

'What if this Jesus be after all but a phantom of the imagination? I have heard of heretics who have said that of the incomparable Buddha.'

'No. The evidence against it is too strong. And those who know Him and follow Him say that He is to them a real, living, personal Friend. And you cannot associate with them without being impressed with the reality of their faith. They call Jesus their Sarana, their only Refuge.'

'This must be a deceit of Mara; the "eight-fold path" is the only true way. And there can be no permanent refuge but in the Buddha, the Doctrine, and the Order. Cast it behind thee, I pray, and go into a retreat, which shall give time for calmer thought, or on a pilgrimage to the Mount of the Holy Footprint, or some other sacred place hallowed by the presence of the Buddha.'

The priest shook his head, and then with a look of affectionate earnestness besought his friend to beware of the sophistries which came from the hall of the 'Reconciler.' He expressed himself strongly with reference to the performances there, which were now becoming notorious.

This was a turn in the conversation which to the prince was not pleasant. He could not see, he said, why, if the Thero held such views as he had just stated, he should not make himself at home there. It was a religion of great charity which the 'Reconcilers' taught; and he proceeded to speak in the harshest terms of his old friend and those who had seduced him from the right way, hinting that the toleration hitherto extended to them could not be expected to be continued long. It was impossible that their friendship could continue, with such views as Abhayo was holding.

They returned between the ironwood and fig trees to the workshop, where the priest went on, while Detu went in with a look of great displeasure on his face.

Abhayo went out between the carved pillars, scarce knowing whither he went. 'This is the mission of the "Reconcilers,"' he said to himself, 'to break up old friendships and spread hate instead of the charity of which they talk so much. This is the beginning of the end. "In this world tribulation," Thomas said. The light is coming. I feel stronger already for the step taken and the determination arrived at; but I have lost my friend. Is the ground firm, after all? Now faith, now unbelief, where am I? Now Sarana, then Asarana (no refuge)! What can I do?'

'That is exactly what my brother's old myna is always saying, my lord.' It was Kiri Banda ascending the steps leading to the platform on which that part of the palace stood, while the priest was coming down, unobservant of the little man who was puffing and breathing heavily as he made the slight ascent.

'What does it say?' asked the Thero.

'Why, it says just what the reverend sir has just repeated. It picked it up from some of the boys who got the words at the pansala. And the venerable foreign gentleman who is staying at Jambugama now says that there are many men who talk about Sarana just as glibly as the myna, and who know just as little of it.'

'When do the foreign lady and gentleman leave thy brother's house?'

'That I cannot say. They like it there; and that is more than I do. Give me the city, with all its multitudes of people and its wonderful sights. But there are two ladies there now. The clever Indian lady is there also, and from what I can gather they have long discourses about religion.'

'How did you get to know this?'

'Well, my lord,' said Kiri Banda, 'at the hall of the "Reconciler," at Sarana, we are supposed to know everything. That Jewess is a wonderful woman. That invisible body of hers may be here now, for aught I know, listening to my talk. There is no saying where a woman like that will be. So I must have a care. But I may say that our people take a great interest in the Mihintala Thero. They know, for instance, that he spent all last night with the one-armed Christian priest. They are also uncommonly keen about getting information concerning the doings of the little foreign party at Jambugama. I hope they will not bring trouble to my brother's household. It is well known that "a foreigner to a village and a creeper to a tree are both alike." With my lord's permission, I will go and deliver my message; it is from the " Reconciler " to the prince. We are high in the royal favour now. But this is an unlucky day for somebody, I know; for nearly every dog I have seen in the streets to-day sneezed, and the lizards are all running from the south. That must mean more than calamity to a poor unknown fellow like me. There must be a public evil approaching, reverend sir, or bad days for some great personage.'

CHAPTER XII.

WITH THE 'RECONCILERS.'

Asleep and naked as an Indian lay,
An honest factor stole a gem away :
He pledged it to the knight ; the knight had wit,
So kept the diamond, and the rogue was bit.
POPE, *Sir Balaam.*

In order to understand the reason for the sudden visit of Alypius to our friends at Jambugama, it is necessary that we should spend a short time with the founders of the new 'Society of the Universal Brotherhood.' The faith was becoming popular with high and low alike ; with the low probably because it was popular with the high, and with the latter because it was declared to be a useful aid to Buddhism, and they were flattered with the unceasing flow of compliments paid to the faith of their fathers by the promoters of the new movement, who, from the West themselves, were ready at all times to declare that nothing good had come from the West but themselves ; that all wisdom was from the East, and especially that part of the East in which they happened to find themselves at the time.

There were a few who took the liberty of doubting the sincerity of this constant depreciation of everything which had not its origin in Buddhism ; but to the majority of the people it was very pleasant, and as there were very few who had travelled and seen anything of the big world among them, they had but little difficulty in accepting without reserve the statements made by the Reconcilers. The love of the marvellous was as fully satisfied as the love of self. Exaggerated rumours of the wonderful performances of the Jewess were in circulation, and received amongst the people as evidences of the mysterious power and authority of the Universal Brotherhood Society.

Alypius walked about the city on the best of terms with priests and nobles, greeting all with the universally brotherly smile, while Leah seldom made an appearance, except at the shrine or at the queen's palace where she had managed to secure a hearty welcome. The other member of the triumvirate, the astrologer, was not often seen in public, although it was rumoured that he had fully regained his old position in the royal favour.

Inquisitive people—and there were many such in Anuradhapura—noticed that the astrologer's residence had apparently become at night the scene of unusual activity. There was more than the ordinary flashing of strange lights in the Hall of Mystery, which, as we have seen, formed the topmost story of the deserted monastery which had been converted into the astrologer's dwelling. There were sounds as of men working. There were also frequent visitors who came and went in a mysterious way, concerning whom, if questions were put to Kiri Banda, his invariable reply was that they were the gods and demons, the inhabitants of other worlds, who had come to hold converse with his master; a reply which perfectly satisfied the inquiring minds of his friends, as they had no desire for investigating such subjects in so uncanny a neighbourhood.

It might have been noticed, too—although it probably was not—that often the ghostly visitors carried away with them small burdens which they had not brought with them on coming to the astrologer's, and that these visits were followed by sounds as of considerable preparations which were being made in the hall of the Reconciler. But nobody carried inquisitiveness so far as to connect the activity at the astrologer's with the corresponding activity in the headquarters of the Universal Brotherhood Society.

'Did the prince read the message sent by the "Reconciler"?'

This question was addressed by the Jewess, who lay on a couch in a private apartment connected with the shrine, to Kiri Banda, who had just returned from the errand on which we have seen him employed.

'Without a doubt, noble lady, and with much agitation too.'

'And didst thou see the Mihintala Thero?'

'He was leaving the palace as I entered.'

'So much the better for our purpose—I mean that it was a strange coincidence that he should have been there at that very time. I am only a humble medium, the channel through which the great spirits operate, and know not what may pass through my agency, but the Reconciler must have known exactly what would happen.' This was said as if to herself, then turning in another tone to Kiri Banda, she exclaimed: 'There you are as usual, you will go to sleep again in another minute. Wake up, wretch! and let me know what the prince said and how he looked.'

'I have said that he looked agitated; that is a mild way of expressing it. If it had not been Prince Detu, the meekest of men, I should have said that the look meant murder. What he said was: "How true!"—they were his very words. But just then he became more excited than ever.'

'And what then?'

'And it was then that it was discovered that the glorious sapphire was lost which was given by the king to the great image of the Vanquisher, which, it is said, is finished, all but the painting of the eye reserved for the great ceremony; and then, of course, the prince could think of nothing but that.'

'Was there no one there with the prince?'

'None but the students and the Indian nobleman, who declared that the only person who had been alone with the sapphire was Abhayo Thero. I stood, of course, at a respectful distance from the group which gathered around the statue in earnest conversation, but I thought I heard one of the students say something about the Thero reaching his hand to the head of the image, as if to discover its comparative height. It was the same noble student who is one of the most devoted disciples of the Reconciler.'

'Now a pest on thy slow tongue! Why couldest thou not have said that before? That is a serious loss. It will perhaps be found again by now: nobody can have stolen it. Leave me now, stupid dog!'

Kiri Banda passed out, muttering to himself: 'Dog, am I? But dogs can bark, and sometimes they bite! We shall see.'

It was not long before a messenger arrived commanding the attendance of the Jewess at the queen's palace. Leah was evidently expecting such a command, for, instead of resting, according to the intimation she had given to Kiri Banda, she began at once to make elaborate toilet preparations, which were scarcely finished when the messenger arrived.

The bearer of the royal command was dismissed with the reply that Leah the queen's servant would be at the palace immediately; but for all that she showed no particular hurry. Other arrivals came who claimed her attention, and among them one of Prince Detu's pupils. The conference was evidently an exciting one, and it was some time before Leah could set forth on her visit to the palace.

She started at last, accompanied by several attendants, for an increase of means enabled her, when she did go out, to go abroad with much greater ceremony than formerly, and in a style more in keeping with the mysterious authority which she claimed. As she passed through the same streets, which have been already described, it is not necessary to say anything here about the various sights which presented themselves to her in the course of this short walk, except that, as it was now the afternoon, some of the streets were crowded with pilgrims and with those that buy and sell.

All this, however, had apparently but little interest for the Jewess, who walked through the busiest portions of the city as though she saw not, and on this occasion the dreaminess which characterised her movements was not assumed. Her thoughts were sufficiently interesting to outweigh any excitement provided in the streets.

Little if any notice was taken of the entrance to

the royal enclosure in which was the residence of Sri Meghawarna's chief queen. It had become familiar ground to Leah, but she had never concerned herself much with regard to architecture or works of art of any kind. She had often said that no study was of any interest to her but that of human nature, and in that study she claimed to be proficient. The gateway with its mystic carving attracted no attention, any more than did the pillars covered with white and gold on which the roof of the queen's pavilion rested. And as she sat in the audience hall waiting for the queen, she was not at all impressed with the view which presented itself of the royal gardens, that, with their dark foliage surrounding a shrine, overlaid with gilding, made a striking and beautiful contrast to the white columns and carved stonework of the buildings in the neighbourhood. Her one thought just then was a vexed one of impatience at being kept waiting, and at what she called 'the stupid etiquette of these people.'

But she was gracious enough, not to say obsequious, when the queen appeared with her retinue coming from the direction of the baths. Anybody less preoccupied than Leah would have felt deeply impressed with the scene thus presented, as the royal party came up through the gardens, some of them strikingly handsome, and all elegantly attired in loose flowing costumes as unlike as possible that which is worn by the Sinhalese ladies of the present day in the maritime provinces.

They were soon engaged in one absorbing topic of conversation—the loss of the great sapphire from the sculpture of the new Buddha.

'This was to be the prince's great life-work,' said

the queen, 'and his disappointment is very great. For although the skill shown in the sculpture cannot be affected by the loss, yet such a splendid gem would have wonderfully increased its value with the multitude. We have sent for thee, O wise woman, to tell us, if thou canst, where this precious jewel can be found.'

'Has a diligent search been made for it?' asked Leah.

'The prince's studio has been searched in every part, for he himself is unwilling to believe the suspicion which has somehow become connected with a visit paid to him early this morning. But you in your wisdom will know all about that.'

'It is a common mistake, great queen,' said Leah, 'to suppose that we who are the Reconciler's servants are acquainted with the master's mind. We simply do his bidding. His messages pass direct to those for whom they are intended. And when a revelation is made through us, we are only the passive instruments for its conveyance. Our minds are a blank when it enters and also when it leaves.' All this was said with difficulty, for Leah was not fluent in conversation in the native languages, and sometimes, as at present, she found her deficiency in this respect not unserviceable.

'The "supremely illustrious" monarch, who is an "ocean of wisdom and a mine of wealth," is exceedingly wrathful at the loss of the jewel, and at first he seemed inclined to imprison all who might possibly have been implicated, from their being in the neighbourhood at the time of the loss, but on reflection it was considered that it would be better to make the investigation as secretly as possible. It is the royal will also that a substitute, though of an inferior character, shall be provided in place of the lost gem, that the disgraceful theft may be kept from the knowledge of the public as long as possible. The Mihintala Thero is suspected, partly from his well-known antipathy to image worship, and partly because he was the only visitor to the studio this morning. It is difficult to proceed against a priest directly. But, as he is now under ecclesiastical censure, and is pledged to appear in answer to a charge of heresy, there is no danger of his being absent when it becomes necessary to bring him forward. It may not, however, be the Thero, and many of us think it can hardly be likely. Is it possible, thinkest thou, that the foreigners of that religion which is called Christian could have had anything to do with it? They are dealers in gems.'

'That would be no sufficient reason for suspecting them, great lady,' said Leah, boldly, 'for I also have been a dealer in precious stones, and might be as justly suspected on that ground.'

'Then that is impossible,' returned the queen; 'but when the royal desire is laid before the shrine of the Reconciler, we shall doubtless obtain the information that we need. That proposition had great weight with his majesty in dissuading him from immediately imprisoning the suspected ones. But thou art so skilful in the magic arts that I thought it would be possible for me to be enlightened at once. The discovery of the jewel which was to form the eye of the "Vanquisher of the five deadly sins" would secure for me a wonderful increase of the royal favour, and it would not be worse for thee.' This was said in a low tone, inaudible to the ladies of the court. 'The finding of the ruby-studded bangles which I had lost so long ago was marvellous. This will certainly not be more difficult to such knowledge and skill as thine.'

'It might be done,' said the Jewess reflectively; 'but in that case the formal appeal to the Reconciler must be a last resort.'

It was promised that this should be arranged if possible, and that Leah, in the course of a day or two, should do her best to aid the queen in the discovery of the precious gem. Then the conversation became general gossip on such subjects as the king's health, which of late had not been good, of the comfort which had been derived latterly from the visits of the astrologer, of the household of Prince Detu (the prince's mother had died long before, and the chief queen now was as young as Detu himself). They talked of Detu's princess, of her appearance and her jewels, with great gusto. They talked also of the prince's son, who appeared to take but little interest in his father's art, and, although so young, had already begun to practise the healing skill, which had been derived in lessons received from the court physician. Then the gossip turned on Anula; on her beauty, with reference to which there were diverse opinions; on her learning, about which there was no doubt; on her firmness of character and her strong-mindedness, which had shown itself so strangely in refusing to be enrolled with the Reconcilers, which the queen thought was an evidence of unorthodox Buddhism, while one of the ladies said that, on the contrary, Anula had maintained in conversation with her on the subject, that the new movement was altogether inconsistent with the pure religion of the Buddhas.

Leah, of course, agreed with the queen, and urged some very specious reasons in support of that view.

Then the lady who had reported the conversation she had had with the object of their gossip said that she would like very much to know what Anula was about just then. She supposed that she was leaning over some old stone trying to decipher an inscription. On which Leah remarked that she thought she could satisfy her curiosity. Soon the whole of the party were beseeching her for a manifestation which would enable them through her to see Anula at that moment. And in response to this request it was not long before the Jewess was in a state of trance, in which her æthereal body had wandered off to Jambugama. She described in a vacant, dreamy manner, as if the body on the couch in the queen's pavilion were bereaved of the spirit, the rice-fields, the threshing-floors with the ever-circulating buffaloes, the fruit-trees and the house in which the Syrian father and daughter were lodged.

'Why, that is Jambugama exactly!' exclaimed one of the queen's attendants, the daughter of the chief of the district in which that village was situated.

Then the wandering spirit went on to describe the little party gathered together for conversation in the cool of the evening under the trees where we have already seen them, sketches of Joseph and Irene, of Anula and little Kumari. Two of the portraits at least were recognised at once. The conversation of the little party was then reported. It was on religious subjects, of course, and represented Joseph and Irene as earnestly seeking the conversion of Anula, while the latter was making concessions which would form a grave impeachment on her orthodoxy as a Buddhist.

'This is serious,' said the queen; 'we will recall her at once, and will know from her whether the conversation has been accurately reported.'

On recovering from her tranced state, Leah appeared much exhausted, professing the utmost astonishment at the descriptions given her of the pictures she had drawn and the conversations she had reported. In answer to numerous questions, she declared that she had never been near Jambugama, and that she knew nothing or next to nothing of the persons about whom she had been talking. As to the Christians, she never went near them if she could help it, because of the bad antagonistic spirit which they had shown to the compassionate, loving, healing faith of the conqueror of Mara.

'Wonderful woman!' the queen whispered to her. 'I am certain that thou couldest grant me my desire. As for these Christians, we will look to them at once.'

Refreshments were brought, betel was handed round, and the talk went on in whispers of awe with regard to the manifestation which they had just witnessed, and in discussions concerning Anula and the Christians.

It was a striking scene which presented itself in the pavilion in the cool of that evening—not that the evening was cool outside; still the air in the streets was as the air of a furnace when the fires are dying, but in the delightful shade of the royal gardens it was cool and fragrant.

The ladies were reclining on couches elaborately carved in wood and on mats spread on the cool floor, chewing betel and sipping at little cups containing cooling beverages, fanned by slaves, one of whom stood waving a gorgeously decorated talipot leaf over each group. Even Leah could hardly fail to be impressed by the picturesqueness of the scene, the gracefulness of form which characterised some of the party, and the colour-contrasts between the wealth of black hair which adorned each head, and the bright Indian fabrics in which all were attired.

The pavilion itself opened on two sides into the gardens through magnificent columns of stone, while at either end windows of pierced granite, which looked like delicate tracery, surrounded by carvings of the sacred lotus and the king of serpents, added not a little to the beauty of this part of the palace, which was used as a reception-room, and was regarded by the queen with some justifiable pride.

The dark shadow of a tower, lengthening over the palace grounds, gave the Jewess reasonable excuse for permission to leave, after which she was soon at the hall of the Reconciler in deep consultation with Alypius, in which conference it was decided that the time had come for putting an end to the Retreat at Jambugama.

CHAPTER XIII.

OMENS AND REFLECTIONS.

Like a beautiful flower full of colour, but without scent,
So are the fine but fruitless words of him who does not good deeds.
DHAMMAPADA.

WHATEVER was the purport of the news brought to Jambugama by Alypius, there was no doubt in Joseph's mind as to the advisability of an immediate return to the city. It was a sudden change from elation to depression for all three. Neither of them wished to leave the quiet life of the village in which they had found such great enjoyment. At first the proposal was met by various suggestions from the ladies. Could the matters—whatever they were—not be arranged by correspondence, or by sending instructions through Alypius? But Joseph shook his head sadly, and after a private conversation with the Greek decided that there was nothing for it but to prepare for a hurried departure. And when this decision was once taken, Irene began to see many reasons why they should go back, and even looked forward with delight to the duties which awaited her in the city, and especially to the pleasure of meeting Thomas.

Anula entered readily into the situation. She would have remained willingly for some time longer, but life in the village would not always be like what it had been during the last few days. She had got all the information she wanted about the ancient establishment to which generation after generation of the yellow-robed brethren had succeeded in the village monastery. She had become intensely attached to Irene, and was beginning to feel that this new attachment was interfering with her Buddhistic development, not because of any wavering in her devotion to the faith of her fathers, but because it brought out emotions which, however exalted, interfered with the upward progress of her Karma.

She had spoken of this to Irene one day, and had told her that it would soon be her duty to tear herself from her; on which the Syrian girl had burst into tears, denouncing in no measured terms a religion which could thus teach it to be the holiest duty to kill the purest and noblest affections of the heart.

To this outburst Anula had replied with tears, and then immediately reproached herself for being capable of such emotion. How far she was from that higher life of which she had constantly dreamed! She had given way to her humanity, which was her curse. Was it true that she, who, although not of the order, had lived for years as if she had been; who had so repeatedly kept the night-long vigil and so regularly fasted; who had even lived in the higher meditations, could so far be the victim of 'desire' as to give way like that on account of that pale-faced girl from the West who was not even a follower of Gautama?

There was nothing for it, she had said, but to go back as soon as possible to the sisterhood, where such exhibitions of emotion were impossible, and where, by heavy penance, she might in some measure redeem the past.

Then there rose up before her mind the commanding form of the Mihintala Thero. That image was not an infrequent visitor, but as often as it came it was instantly dismissed, and some slight penance resorted to, because the thought, though only momentary, could have been possible.

Much of her time had been occupied in reverie, which her friends thought natural to one of her character. While they imagined her to be meditating on the ills of existence, and the evil of desire, according to the regulation for the order, she was often analysing her own motives and investigating the thoughts and feelings of her own heart.

Life had become to her a constant battle with the purest affections, varied with doubts as to the righteousness of the conflict, followed by remorseful feeling on account of the doubts themselves. Even her affection for Irene did not seem to be all bad, in the analysis to which she subjected it, for she said to herself, 'It shows how I have conquered the affection which was once growing in me for Abhayo, when I can love this girl;' and then she would reproach herself for her readiness in finding excuses. 'It is all wrong,' she said to herself. 'There is nothing for it but to take the full vows and live with the holy sisters.'

Such had been her thoughts. The pleasant interlude in her life which she had enjoyed recently at Jambugama had thrown back her Karma for years, and she must make what atonement was possible. The opportunity for returning to the city had come, and she would at once make the preparations necessary for the complete renunciation required of the consecrated sisterhood.

Such was the determination she had arrived at when Alypius made a proposal to the little party, which he had not much difficulty in prevailing on them to accept. It was that Joseph should go back with him to the city, leaving Irene and Anula—if she would stay—at Jambugama for a week or two, in which time he thought the important business on which they were about to proceed would be concluded. The arrangement appeared to him all the more reasonable because it was probable that they might find it necessary to take a journey to the seaport. For the time Anula's new resolutions vanished. She would stay with Irene for a little longer. 'The conquest would be all the greater,' she said to herself, if she could accomplish it under such circumstances. It would also afford her such an opportunity for influencing her Syrian friend on behalf of the faith of the Buddhas as might never occur again. It was clearly her duty to stay, she said.

Irene was not at all willing to remain behind at first, but eventually consented, on her father's promising to return as soon as possible, and bring Thomas with him.

It was on the morning of the day before that fixed for the return to the city that this decision was arrived at. In the evening Anula went to the temple with a flower-offering. It was a duty which she had somewhat neglected of late. Joseph had submitted to be led away by the children into the fields to see the grain brought in, and Irene was left alone in the pretty leaf-thatched room where she and her father had spent most of their time together. She was sitting on a low couch bending over a leaf cut and prepared, on which she was busily engaged with a stylus in writing a letter to Thomas. 'He would like it better,' she said, 'than any verbal message.' She would not be long, she had told her father, and would follow him into the fields as soon as she had finished her letter.

Absorbed in her occupation, she had not noticed the approach of any one until a shadow was thrown across her writing materials, and, looking up, she saw Alypius standing in the arched doorway regarding her with undisguised admiration. 'I must have one word with you before I go,' he said, with a passionate earnestness so unusual to him that she hesitated to give expression to the displeasure which his appearance there at that time had caused her.

'May I not hope that the fair daughter of my partner has learnt in the midst of these sylvan scenes to think less unfavourably of one who is ready to give his life for her? The days have passed slowly and drearily in the city since you left.'

'And yet,' returned Irene, 'report says that you have been busily occupied, and you have not seemed anxious that I should return with my father.'

It was spoken like a girl would speak in such a situation; and Alypius, reading in it wrongly an unusual interest in his movements, clutched at it as to a straw of hope.

'You have heard,' he said, 'about the Reconciler, and about the new society formed in the city; but rumour has a lying tongue, remember. As to the object which we have set before us, can anything be more noble? I have thought that nothing would be

more agreeable to the mind and heart of her whom I
adore, and whose opinion I value above that of any
other human being. Can anything be more commend-
able than a life spent in devotion to such objects as
ours—the brotherhood of mankind, without respect of
persons, and the quelling of religious strife? What can
be more consistent with the true spirit of Christianity?
It may be immodest to say so, but to my mind the
lady Irene should only see in that additional reason
for favour.'

Irene had by this time discovered that the impression produced by her words on the mind of the young
Greek was favourable to his suit. Nothing could be
further from her desires, and she broke in at once on
his pleadings with an expression of haughty disdain,
standing as she spoke.

'It is not for an ignorant girl such as I am to
discuss your schemes for the reconciliation of religions;
neither can I talk with you about the associations
which you have formed, and the un-Christian attitude
which you have taken up. I will not say what I think
of it all, for that has little if any bearing on what I
have to say now. It would be foolish and useless for
us to go on talking in this strain. It is impossible,
Alypius. I cannot love you, and do not even respect
you, and can never be yours.'

'These are but hasty words,' replied he. 'Lying
tongues have been at work. I have been misrepre-
sented. You spoke of associations. It was Leah the
Jewess you referred to. Oh, if you did but know her,
no disparaging allusion would ever again pass your lips!'

'I have said that it would make no difference whatever, Alypius. Let us join my father.'

'Have you thought,' he hissed rather than said, 'what the influence would be on him—your father?'

'On him? Why such mystery about him? Ah! little do you know, after all, of the oneness of the life between us. How should you understand such as he is? Other fathers, I know, give their daughters as they will. He loves me too well. And my love for him is too great to let me listen to such talk as yours.'

'Or even the talk of enthusiastic young Buddhist priests?' sneered Alypius; to which she replied with nothing but a look of fiery scorn, and would have rushed past him, had not Anula entered at that moment on her return from the temple, thus compelling him to retire, but not before he had managed to give a dark hint to the effect that her father's safety and honour lay in some mysterious way in his power.

He was no sooner gone than she sank down on the couch, as if tired and faint. Anula was busy with the devotional exercises which she had resolved to rigorously impose on herself, in order to recover lost ground. But a glance at her friend scattered the exercises from her mind at once. It was the work of an instant to bring the water-gourd and give Irene a drink, which evidently refreshed her.

'What can be the matter? You look ill, or as if you had been tired with a long journey. Your eyes were fixed, as if on some object at a great distance. It was like Abhayo looks when— I mean that you appeared to be wandering away from yourself—but you are pale and faint. What is it, child? Did the Greek say anything to cause it? His looks were not pleasant, but, of course, I could not understand his words. Come, let us go out into the cool air.'

It was the best restorative that could be applied. They went out into the fields, where they found Joseph and Alypius with the children, the Greek talking with his partner as if nothing of importance had transpired in the house. And in the course of the evening he managed to whisper to Irene that she must forgive him for his foolish words with reference to her father. There was no foundation for them. They were the words of stupid passion, when he knew not what he was saying.

This was somewhat reassuring, but Irene could not help thinking of the many times when the visits of the young gem merchant had caused her father much uneasiness and trouble, and it was with difficulty that she could bring herself to let him return to the city without her.

The evening passed in talk, chiefly about the Reconciler and his following, in which Alypius argued persuasively and ably on behalf of the movement. The conversation was confined in great measure to the two men, the ladies saying but little. As it was carried on in the vernacular, Anula had little difficulty in understanding it.

'It is incomprehensible to me,' said the younger man, 'that there should be any opposition on the part of intelligent Christians to a work like this, which has for its aim the promotion of brotherliness and all good feeling between the various races of men. Concessions are needed, of course; they are concessions, however, not to the creed of a rude and savage people, but to a faith more ancient than our own, with a system of ethics which in many of its features closely resembles that of the Christian.'

'There you mistake, my friend,' said Joseph. 'I have talked much of the system with our friend the Mihintala Thero. And I think I can judge now of the resemblance on which the Reconcilers sometimes so fondly dwell.'

'But,' interrupted Alypius, 'is it fair to gather your interpretations of Buddhism from one who is so notoriously unorthodox? That the Thero is learned and enthusiastic we know full well, but he is scarcely an unbiassed authority with regard to Buddhism. And it is possible that he may not be free from that flexibility of speech which characterises his countrymen when there is a desirable object to be gained, and often even without the inspiration of such an object.'

Anula's eyes blazed on him fiercely. 'What shall we say then,' she asked, 'of that flexibility of the Christian Greek, who could denounce Christianity so readily in the hall of the Reconciler?'

'Ah!' replied the Greek, in his blandest manner, 'that was spoken in a moment of irritation. Our friends here' (waving his hand towards Joseph and his daughter, but evidently intending it especially for Irene) 'are acquainted with my unfortunate failing in that respect. My ungovernable temper is a source of continual repentance to me. I remember now that the lady Anula was present at the conference, and formed one of the only two who did not sign the roll. It ought to be gratifying in the highest degree to see one who is so distinguished a student of Buddhism and follower of Gautama inclined so favourably to the faith of the Nazarene.'

Anula looked her resentment at this construction put upon her words, but said nothing. 'Thou hast entirely misunderstood Abhayo Thero,' said Joseph. 'He would never knowingly be guilty of false representation. And his interest lay all in the other direction. But we were talking of comparisons between Buddhism and Christianity. I was saying that it is a mistake to speak of our faith as if it were modern, compared with the creed of Gautama. You forget that it is as old as the Jewish race, that it goes back to the time when the first promise of the Messiah was proclaimed to men. We are Jews by religion, but Jews who have accepted Jesus as the true Messiah. But what is the value of the age-argument? The demon-worshippers who, according to the songs that the Damilos sing, inhabited this land before the Sinhalese settled in it, may claim for their faith a much greater antiquity than Buddhism.'

'Now, my dear father,' said Irene, 'must not be tempted into speech-making. He must think of the morrow's journey, and take the needful preparatory rest.'

Joseph smiled, and continued: 'You talk also of resemblance between that Life which is the light of men, as the Holy Gospel says, and the life of Sakya Muni, but the comparisons are not so many nor so great as the contrasts. Think of the contrast between the childhood of the Christ and that of Gautama Bodisatwa; the carpenter's shop at Nazareth, and the palace of King Suddhodana. Other contrasts quite as striking might be easily mentioned. I have sometimes thought there were resemblances between the life of the Messiah as shadowed forth in the misconstructions put by Judaists on the glorious prophecies concerning Him, and I have thought that it is not impossible that the Jewish stories of the "coming One" had got mixed occasionally with the Buddhist legends, just as in centuries to come, it may be, as a result of the compromising spirit abroad now, men may find it difficult to distinguish between some features of Christianity and some aspects of Buddhism. Rumour says that the mixing process is going on even now in the hall of the Reconciler. Have a care, Alypius! Beware of concessions. I have the kindest feeling for the poor idolater, and for the man who trusts his hope to his asceticism, but remember that such compromises mean a derogation from the divine honours of our Redeemer. All that is good in Buddhism may already be found in Christianity, with much more without which we are helpless. The task is hopeless. They cannot be reconciled.'

The Greek moved uneasily under the words of the good old man. He thought of the dark and devious ways by which he was pursuing his ends, and for the time, in that society, he felt a loathing for himself and the hypocrisy of his life.

He made no reply, but Irene took up the conversation briefly: 'We were talking the other day about the Christ's love for children. Why, you remember that He took a little child and set him in the midst of His disciples, and said, "Of such is the kingdom of heaven." But the Buddha points to the old man crouching under the burden of years, worn out by much fasting and severe penance, with all desires, all affections conquered, having the vast knowledge which is said to belong to such an old age, as the truest representation of his kingdom. As I said the other day, I will follow the Saviour Who is the Friend of little children.'

'Irene is right,' said Joseph. 'There should be no

talk of resemblance between Christianity and Buddhism; at any rate, no building on them, while Jesus stands before us in the beautiful Gospel picture with the child in His arms, saying, "Of such is the kingdom of heaven;" and Gautama points to the old age of a life of terrible struggle after repeated transmigrations, as the nearest approach to the great object of all Buddhist aspirations, the birthless, lifeless hereafter. I once saw a monk in the Maha temple in Anuradhapura worn to a skeleton by his fasting and penance. I was told that he was one of the Arhats, that he had nearly reached the perfection of knowledge by his chastisement of the flesh, by the repression of desire and obedience to the precepts. He had arrived at a stage in which he could feel no pity and no affection for any living thing, and his chief occupation was gazing intently into the cells cut out of a huge block of granite. On this employment his whole being seemed concentrated. And of such is the dominion of the Buddhas. But let us not spend our last night here in controversy. Is there no message for our friend Thomas, child?'

'Would that I could go instead of sending a message,' replied Irene. 'I have a feeling as if we ought not to be separated, as if something unfortunate would happen while we are away from each other. What will you do,' she added playfully, 'without your little girl to make you the food that you love, and to sing to you, even though it be only for a week or two?'

'We shall see, we shall see, little one! Perhaps thou art not so necessary as all that.' And Joseph rested his hand lovingly on her head.

They retired early, and awoke next morning with the dawn. Alypius started first. Joseph was saying his farewell to Irene before stepping into the litter, when Sikki Banda came forward, imploring him not to venture on his journey on so unlucky a day; the lizards had chirped as he had never heard them before, and a woman had just crossed the path with a bundle of sticks. He knew her, and he would give her a good scolding for bringing such bad luck on the gentleman's journey. But that was not all—the villagers had heard the horrible cries of the devil-bird ringing through the night.

'I thank thee, friend,' said the old man, 'but I have a charm which is superior to all those evil omens. Remember, child,' turning to Irene cheerfully, ' only a fortnight at the longest.'

CHAPTER XIV.

WITH THE GOSSIPS AT THE GOLDSMITH'S.

> A country can be hedged about:
> But not the tongue.—SINHALESE PROVERB.

OF all the goldsmiths' shops in Anuradhapura—and they were numerous—that of Jotthiyo was perhaps the most popular. It was situated in a small street leading from the Great East and West Street to the Abhaya-Wewa, the oldest tank in the city. There were other goldsmiths in the same street, and though there was much rivalry amongst themselves, and desperate struggling to outvie each other in trade with a cunning for which the Eastern goldsmith is proverbial, yet Jotthiyo was acknowledged to have reached an eminence which placed him above the rest of his fraternity in an assured position which it was useless for them to attack.

He had a reputation for being exceedingly shrewd in his business. He would look at a stone with a glance which indicated the profoundest insight, and a movement of the head which appeared to speak volumes. His opinions, given in the briefest form, were seldom wrong. There were a few detractors belonging to his craft, who declared their belief that it was all because he was born under such a lucky star; but with the majority it was understood that the wisdom of the profession was concentrated in the brain which lay behind the eye of Jotthiyo. I say *the eye*, for he had but one, he had lost the other through the carelessness of a Wedarala (native doctor), who had operated on it in order to extract a tiny fragment which had been struck off from the wheel, and had stuck to the eye with great tenacity. But it was generally conceded that one eye was sufficient for a man like Jotthiyo, and that for keenness there was not a pair of eyes in all the city that could match his one.

He was a man of few words, and he encouraged the gift of silence in his workmen, and yet his shop was the gathering-place of the greatest gossips in the city. Perhaps it was because garrulous people love silent but wide-awake listeners; and it was partly due also to the fact that the one-eyed goldsmith's judgment on all doubtful points, and on the tendency of things generally, was regarded as authoritative and almost infallible.

The shop opened on to the street, as is the fashion of such shops in the East to-day. Anything more unlike a jeweller's shop in the West End of London could not well be conceived. There was no display of gold and precious stones, with the exception of what was in the hands of Jotthiyo and his workmen. But there was a strong box within, barred and clamped with iron, which was jealously guarded, day and night. In the inner room in which the box was kept the master slept; and it was so closely watched by day that theft was regarded as an impossibility.

The box was often opened, but always with due safeguards. It was never opened to gratify idle curiosity. When the clank and rattle of the iron was heard, the gossips in the shop knew that it meant business that there was a wedding festival to be held somewhere in the city, and the friends of the bride elect were borrowing a string of pearls and golden bangles, or the guardian of a temple was negotiating for the purchase of a little golden dagoba or a small image of Buddha.

There was a noise as of the clanking of iron and heavy creaking of hinges coming from the small inner room on the afternoon of the day to which this chapter refers. A visitor had been ushered into the inner room by Jotthiyo—a visitor who was evidently not a stranger.

'It is that man who does everything for the people at the hall of the Reconciler, Kiri Banda,' said one of the small party sitting in the shop on some of the little log-stools provided for the workmen. It was Jantu, the chief gossip, and he was speaking to one who had dropped in to-day for the first time.

'Does he come here often?' the stranger interrogated.

'Often enough. He is here, there, and everywhere, and yet he is never in a hurry, and seems to spend the most of his time in sleep.'

'I should like to have a chat with him about those Reconcilers. We'll draw him out a little presently.'

'That shows that you know precious little of Kiri Banda. He talks in proverbs and dark sayings, which may mean a great deal, or may mean very little. My belief is that he sees as much with his eyes shut as old Jotthiyo does with his "piercer," and that is saying a great deal; but it is very little that one can get out of him.'

'Is he the servant of the Jewess?'

'He seems to be now. He was the head-servant of the royal astrologer, but it is said that he was discharged from that office. Anyhow, he is at present in the service of the founders of the new religion.'

'They are very popular in the city now—are they not?'

'That you could ask such a question shows that you are a stranger in Anuradhapura. Where have you come from?'

'I come from Mahatotai. I have been much in foreign lands, but am residing now in the seaport town. I love the sea,' replied the stranger.

'It is evident then that you are not pure Sinhalese,' said the other. To this the stranger made no reply, but went on to further inquiries about the Reconcilers. 'Have they many of the poor amongst their followers?' he asked.

'They make no effort to secure them. But they are cunning enough to know that the householder is followed by his family and his slaves.'

'The priests are with them, are they not?'

'Of course they are. They, on their side, maintain that the Reconcilers are very good Buddhists, while the Jewess and her party can easily prove that all their wonderful doings are sanctioned expressly by the lotus-mouthed Lord of the doctrine. I said that they did nothing for the poor. That is not quite correct. There was a great almsgiving at the Sálakaggam[1] of the Maha temple the other day, distributed chiefly at the expense

[1] 'There is nothing new under the sun.' The Sálakaggam was the 'soup-kitchen' of Anuradhapura, where rice was distributed to the poor on presenting the tickets—little pieces of ola-leaf—with which they had been previously provided.

of the Greek gentleman, who is one of the founders of the new religion, and who stood with the priests, smiling most beautifully and compassionately on the poor slaves as they came presenting their tickets. There is great poverty in the city, and many a man has been obliged from want of food to send away his slaves. Oh yes, the Reconciler is popular with the lower as well as the higher classes, and with the very lowest.'

'Not a bad way to public favour,' remarked the stranger.

'Ah, well! "snipe can travel along the same road as elephants," as our friend in there would say;' and he nodded towards the room where Kiri Banda was still engaged in his business with the goldsmith. 'And there may be disciples among the poor as well as among the rich.'

'You spoke of the Greek gem-merchant just now. If I mistake not, I saw him on my way hither. He was in company with an elderly man of venerable aspect, apparently of the same race. Is he also one of the initiated? He looks as if he might well be their chief prophet, or the Reconciler himself.'

'No, indeed! Joseph the Syrian is not at all attached to the new faith. Some say that he and his Christian friends are exceedingly opposed to it. Though why they should be it is difficult to see, for that is the beauty of this new religion; it asks nobody to forsake the faith in which he has been brought up. It tells everybody that he is right; only he must add on a little bit of the Reconciler's teaching to make it perfect. They have a very persuasive way with them, those people.'

'Are all the Christians opposed to them?'

'Why, you seem to be all questions; I fancy that the first note you squalled out as a child must have been a note of interrogation.'

'Don't you mind him,' said another of the little party. 'There is nothing he likes so much as unrolling his gossip to those who will listen.'

'Well, the Christians are not numerous; they are all, or nearly all, of the foreign community, and the majority of them are not very particular one way or the other. They often come here to Jotthiyo on gem business, and when we talk about religion they put on a bland, superior sort of a smile, as if they were above all need of it, and it was a sort of thing which did very well for inferior persons like ourselves.'

'Have you heard that the Mihintala Thero has thrown off his robes and become a Christian?' asked one of the party.

'No, I have not heard that, and I happen to know that it is not true—not yet,' replied the chief gossip. 'For I saw him enter the Maha temple to-day with his robes on. You should be more accurate, my friend, when you come here with your news.'

This rebuke produced a faint smile (hearty laughs are rare in Sinhalese gossip), which meant that such a reproof from such a quarter was singularly out of place. Heedless of this, the speaker went on: 'Not but that it is probable enough that he may throw off his robes some fine day, or have them taken from him—which is more likely. I have a brother who is an attendant at the Maha temple, and he tells me that the Thero is to be tried for heresy as soon as the Wass season is over. It will serve him right if he is dismissed. And a little bird has whispered to me that there will possibly be graver charges than that of irreligion or unorthodoxy against him. Why should he be dissatisfied with a religion that was good enough for his ancestors for hundreds of years past? It is good enough for me—why not for him? All this comes of thinking about things. What is the use of thinking? It is about the worst occupation a man can take to. It is sure to bring him into trouble.'

'Your life will be one of great peace, my friend,' said a gruff voice from behind, as Kiri Banda and Jotthiyo returned to the shop.

'We praise independence, but my experience is that independent thinking is great foolishness. Many a man has lost his head by it.'

'Yours is safe enough, friend!' retorted Kiri Banda.

'Let the priests settle our religion for us, I say. Let them do our thinking; they are paid for it.'

'And precious little some of them do for their pay,' growled the one dissentient; for it must be admitted that independent sentiments were not much in favour in Anuradhapura.

'Anyhow, we cannot be wrong in following our betters. Our heads are safe while we do that.'

'You are a wise man, my good Jantu. Avoid thinking, and keep your head on your shoulders. Bow low at the cracking of the whips, and if one is laid across the back, ask for another. "You can bear the bite of the crocodile, though not the prick of the kohila thorn."'

'There you are, at your proverbs again! If report speaks truly, you must be getting familiar with the crocodile bites in your present situation. I hate the conceit of people who are always answering you in proverbs. They make it pass for argument, and think a proverb should decide every discussion.'

'Proverbs contain the wisdom of the ancients, my friend; and I would advise you to take to them. They will save you from thinking for yourself.'

'We were talking before you interrupted us,' said Jantu, 'of the Mihintala Thero and the Christians. And here is a stranger to Anuradhapura, who is deeply interested in your employers and their doings. Perhaps you will enlighten him a little.'

The only reply was a sleepy look, which indicated that Kiri Banda had finished his contribution to the conversation.

Not ill-pleased at the opportunity afforded him by Kiri Banda's reticence, Jantu proceeded to relate to the stranger a narrative of some of the wonderful doings at the shrine of the Reconciler. There were stories of jewellery which had long been lost found in the most unlikely places; and as the stories were being related, Jotthiyo, unobserved, with a curious twinkle in his one eye, bent low over his polishing wheel, which he worked in the simplest way with the string of a bow, moving it rapidly to and fro.

Then came the most precious bit of gossip of the day, which Jantu whispered into a circle of heads drawn together by a significant intimation that something unusual was coming. 'Scarcely anybody knows it, and you must not mention it for anything, but the king and chief queen and all the court are greatly agitated. They have suffered a terrible loss. The royal sapphire, the glory of the regalia, has been stolen. It was to be the right eye of the new statue of the Vanquisher, which the Prince Detu has just completed, and which will be the finest piece of sculpture in all the city. The king had sent it to be tried before finally fixing it in the socket at the Nethra Pinkama.¹ And while it was in the prince's studio for that purpose it disappeared under very suspicious circumstances, and it is said that the Mihintala Thero has something to do with it. But that cannot be possible. What do you say, friends?'

The only reply was a groan, which went round the circle.

'I have nothing to say against the Thero, except that I cannot see why he should go setting himself above the religion of the country. Depend upon it, he has been contaminated by those Christians. I shouldn't wonder if they have something to do with the loss of our resplendent gem; for you see it is our loss. The king had dedicated it to the Deliverer on our behalf. And now it is gone. Could there be anything more unlucky?'

The only reply was another circulating groan.

'But you must be sure to say nothing about it! I understand that steps are being taken which, with the aid of the Reconcilers, are sure to result in its recovery. There is nothing that that Jewess cannot do. The Reconciler knows everything, and he will tell the king through Leah the Jewess where the glorious gem is concealed.'

'I thought,' said the stranger, 'that such supernatural power as the Jewess claims could only be obtained by a pure life and much fasting, in repeated births. The holy Doctrine teaches us that only the

¹ The ceremony of painting the eyes.

Arhats possessed such power. And here is a wonderful thing: all this great Buddhist city seems to be united in giving praise to a woman, and that woman one of whose antecedents you know nothing except what she herself chooses to tell you. I cannot think that this is good Buddhism. What does the prince of sages say? "That which is called woman is sin."'

'Ah, that is where you are wrong, in thinking for yourself. I suppose that comes of your travel in foreign lands—I think you said you had spent much time in such countries. If the Mihintala Thero had stayed at home all his life, he would not, perhaps, be in trouble to-day.'

'What will be done if they do not find the jewel before the day of the Nethra Pinkama?' asked one of the party.

'Why, we shall be put off with something inferior, perhaps something made up by our friend Jotthiyo here.' This was said in an attempt to draw the goldsmith out, who sat on a mat, still bending the upper unclothed part of his body over the wheel, which buzzed and hissed as he applied to it a magnificent 'cat's-eye' which he was in the act of polishing, and which, as he held it up every now and then to the light, displayed the dazzling ray which the goldsmith seemed to have caught and bound to the stone across its polished surface. He was too deeply absorbed in the beauty of that white line which vibrated on the stone to pay any attention to the remark. But a deep groan once more went round the circle.

'I have heard too—and my brother, the attendant, has good means of knowing—that the ceremony at the dedication of the new image is to be the grandest that has ever been known. The king and all the priests in Anuradhapura are to be present, with elephants innumerable. But that will not compensate for the loss of the gem. You must be quiet, and say nothing, for if the people get to know of it they will, perhaps, have their revenge on the Thero and the Christians. We should be careful to say nothing which will inflame their anger.'

'But the Christians,' said the stranger—'I cannot see what they have to do with it.'

'That is because you are a stranger, you see. The old Syrian merchant whom you saw with Alypius the Greek is very friendly with the Thero, and he has a beautiful daughter, who, they say, has tried hard to draw him away from the faith of the glorious prince of the sages. Ah! there is always a woman in it!' And Jantu sighed, and the company groaned again, but this time with a satirical intonation: for Menika, Jantu's wife, meek and submissive as she looked when walking behind her lord to the temple, or setting the food before him in company, while he on such occasions assumed an air of great contempt for his women-kind, nevertheless in private was a most impatient listener, and her sharp tongue, it was well known, had much to do with his frequent visits to Jotthiyo's shop.

'Yes,' said the stranger, 'there is always a woman in it, and a woman may yet be the ruin of Anurad-hapura. I mistrust that Jewess!' This he said as if talking to himself, and about some one of whom he knew something. Then turning to Jantu:—'But what about this Christian lady, the daughter of the Syrian, where is she?'

'She has been staying in a village at some distance from the city. And I have heard that the lady who accompanied the Princess of Kalinga when she brought the Sacred Tooth, a learned Pali scholar, is there too. I have no doubt that they will try to wean her from the faith.'

'You seem to have some special grudge against the Christians,' said the stranger.

To this Jantu made no reply, but went on to say, 'It is rumoured that Alypius is anxious to have the Syrian's daughter to wife.'

'But surely he is not going the right way about it. If he forsakes the Christian faith, it must only be more difficult to obtain her hand. Besides, marriage would disqualify him from possessing the high supernatural powers claimed by the Reconcilers.'

'There you are mistaken again; but it is excusable in a stranger. He says that he forsakes no faith, but is anxious to reconcile all, and he does not himself lay claim to the supernatural power you speak of. That all lies with the Jewess and the astrologer, Kapuranda; but he has not been very successful, and we have heard very little of him of late.'

'I see—it is the woman again!'

'What woman? Menika has not—I mean—were you talking of the Jewess?'

'Never mind. When did you say the Thero is to be tried for heresy?'

'After the Mahinda festival is over, which concludes our Wass season.'

'That will be soon, will it not? I have heard that it is a splendid ceremony. I think I will wait for it.'

'Now I can tell you all about it, if you will wait

for a few minutes '—seeing that the stranger had risen to go.

Kiri Banda, who had also risen, remarked: 'The more you scratch, the more you must scratch. The more you talk, the more you must talk.'

In a short time the shop was cleared of all save the goldsmith and his workmen, who sat on their log-stools or their mats at their work, while Jantu's tongue wagged as if it would never have done.

CHAPTER XV.

LEAH'S CONFESSION OF FAITH.

The clergy have in their treasury an infinity of precious things and Mo-Ni beyond price. The king having entered into this treasury, beheld a jewel Mo-Ni, and immediately felt a desire to carry it away.—PILGRIMAGE OF FA HIAN.

'LET us have a look at the situation, my friend. Where do we stand?'

The speaker was Leah the Jewess; and the friend was Alypius, who, on his return to Anuradhapura, had made a point of proceeding as soon as possible to Sarana, as the head-quarters of the Reconcilers was called, to consult with the presiding genius of that establishment.

'That is a question I should like you to answer. I am not blind, and I am not, so I am vain enough to think, quite a lunatic; but I must confess to some difficulty in seeing where our plans are carrying us. I hope you see it clearer than I do.'

For answer Leah smiled on her friend half pityingly.

'Whatever may be the issue,' Alypius went on, 'my present position is not altogether a pleasant one. I would it were possible for somebody else to do some of the work assigned to me in the scheme.'

'That is the result of your visit to Jambugama. I might have known that your courage would be weakened by such intercourse. But let us look at our position and prospects. I think we have every reason to congratulate ourselves. The Reconciler is winning his way rapidly into popular favour. We began at the right end. The conversion of an Adigar is worth a hundred of the rabble—nay, more—for the hundred are sure to follow, as we have already experienced.'

'We should remember, however, that the tail is as likely to follow when the head runs the other way.'

'You are depressed, Alypius, when you should be rejoicing. You look at everything now in the gloomiest light possible; and all because you have had a nay from a mere chit of a girl. Much do you know of the female character! But she will soon be at your feet.'

'She will never be there alive, or voluntarily,' sighed Alypius.

'Why, the man must be really in love! Listen to the deep sighs rising from that manly breast!' And Leah laughed a great laugh of derision. But seeing that she was going too far for the patience of her colleague, she continued—'After all, you are not singular, my friend! The history of mankind is full of such instances as yours. Let the thought that you are one of a glorious company of fools console you in your depression of spirits. Don't frown; I understand you. You are mad with yourself for a weakness to which you have been driven by an irresistible fate. But weakness is the last thing a woman will forgive. I know the creature better than you do. Your experience has been limited, you know. And, besides, it takes a woman to understand a woman. I know her. What she likes above all things is a great audacity, which will stop short of nothing in order to win the desired object—it being always understood that the desired object is herself. And that is why I so strongly advise this step, at which you display so much hesitation.'

'I have been wondering,' said Alypius, 'whether you possess such a thing as a heart. Affection, and such affection as mine, you certainly can never have had.'

An unusually serious expression came into the face of the Jewess. There was a brief silence, and then a sigh. 'Yes,' said Leah, 'I can sigh as well as you; even now, at my age, as I think of some experiences in my past life. Of that past life, little, if anything, is known in Anuradhapura. But there was a heart within me once, and I lost it in the usual way. He became a Christian; he had been a heathen before, and his Christianity made him meek. These Christians glory in their humility, and I got to hate him for it. They say that that was the great characteristic of the Nazarene, and His disciples are like Him, or profess to be like Him, in patience and meekness. I suppose it is that which makes them boast so freely of that ignominious death to which their Leader was put, the cross of shame. Imagine it! How could meekness ever be a virtue in a man desiring to obtain favour in the eyes of a woman? And he, the man of whom I speak, became a Christian, and passed through a great change, as he said, and as he evidently did. Wilful and impatient of all control, he became meek and humble, and I grew to despise him for it, and to detest the faith which had made him so weak. There—that will do. Let us have done with these stupid reflections. I may say, however, that the more he gave way to weakness and humility, the more daring and proud did I become. I hesitated at nothing to gain my end, and—well, at the last, this meekest of men suddenly displayed a courage and power of endurance which I had not thought possible to such as he. And at that time I could almost have repented and given him all my best affection; but it was too late. I had sold myself to another.'

'I am beginning to understand you now,' said Alypius. 'And that is, no doubt, partly why the Christians are so obnoxious to you.'

'Let us have done with that! What is the use of thinking of the past? I have buried my past. I am now like a soul after migration into a new birth. Why, I have passed through a score of births in my time! And I am still far on the right side of the period at which, according to one of the doleful hymns of our nation, the average life is supposed to say farewell to the world.'

'It is not so easy to bury one's past. All the gods in our pantheon—and we have added a good many lately—cannot prevent a resurrection. I wish sometimes I could begin life again.'

'That is because,' said Leah, 'your views of the future are so gloomy just now, and because you are losing heart. Fits of depression in the present are always accompanied by resurrections of the past. I avoid them, and therefore my life up to the time of my coming to Anuradhapura disturbs me as little as if I had come straight from the Tusita heaven, whence they say our next Buddha is to come.'

'Your past has not been very heavenly, I imagine,' groaned Alypius.

'I say I have buried it, I tell you! And I should think there will be but little danger of resurrections in such a place as this. This is not a time for depression, when our mission for the regeneration of men by the aid of the Reconciler is so successful. My ambition is being realised more rapidly than I had hoped for. The invisible Reconciler who reigns in Sarana is the true ruler of this great city to-day. The king bows at his shrine, and consults him more than he does his ministers and his priests. The princely artist is now one of his most frequent worshippers, and is constantly imploring permission to see the great Master, that he may produce his similitude in wood or stone for the adoration of the multitude. Little he knows of the nature of the multitude. The chief queen is our most devoted adherent; and, let me tell you, when we secured her we secured the State. The entire priesthood—and the city seems to me sometimes as if it were laid over with yellow by the robes of the multitudinous order—is altogether on our side, with one or two exceptions which we shall now easily dispose of.'

'I am afraid it will not be so easy as you think. It is true that Abhayo Thero is losing favour, but one can never be sure of what may happen in such cases, especially as the prince is only half-hearted in taking up the prosecution. He finds it hard to break altogether with his old friend. Then there is Thuparama, who is continually asking for proofs and requiring explanations of discrepancies. Our position, of which you have given so glowing a description, is not by any means assured yet.'

'Well, it is of no use talking with you about our prospects in your present state of mind. But Kapuranda the astrologer, who ought to know his people if anybody does, is as sanguine as I am. What a miracle of ingenuity we have in that corpulent little person! How admirably the shrine he constructed answers our purposes, and with what satisfaction do the votaries receive the little bits of ola with the replies of the Master to their numerous questions! Little do they think that the Reconciler in preparing those replies has access to the horoscopes of all the chief personages in the city, and is familiar with the secrets of the State and of all the leading families. You may rest assured, Alypius, that, with the very slight exceptions you have referred to, this city believes as profoundly in the Reconciler as it does in the Buddha. The rate at which we have gone up in the faith and esteem of the public of Anuradhapura is amazing, even to one of my experience.'

'Yes; and to quote one of those simple Sinhalese proverbs which that sleepy idiot Kiri Banda is so full of, "If you jump up, you will fall down!" And we should be prepared for such a contingency with plenty of padding, to make the fall as easy as possible. I doubt very much whether there is so profound and so popular a belief in the Reconciler as you imagine. The people will go with the nobles, and the nobles will follow the priests. At present they seem gullible enough on the whole, but there are a few who doubt, and their doubts may be our ruin. We may see Lucian's farce in "The Council of the Gods" become a grim reality when the right of the Reconciler to sit on Olympus may be put to the most searching tests.'

'Never mind, friend! We will be ready for them. Our powers of invention are not yet exhausted. But should the calamity come about, which, I am persuaded, only exists in your diseased imagination, I doubt not I shall be prepared. It is not by any means my intention to stay here for ever. I have never yet been to Rome, and if our business in Sarana continues to flourish at the present rate, it will be easy for me in the course of a year or two to visit the imperial city in a condition not unsuited to my ambition. Our gains are not small, as you know. I have always told you that the most productive gold mine in the world is human gullibility; and I am following the example of the people of the country, who invest their wealth in jewels, as the best form for security and conveyance. By the throne of Solomon! or the Sacred Tooth of Gautama! or the sceptre of Jupiter!—or whatever you will—I believe Sarana to be the finest gem-pit in the kingdom! And I know a good stone when I see it, as you can testify. I doubt if Jotthiyo himself is a better judge. Wait a moment, and I will show you something which may lift you out of your cheerless mood and put a little life into you!'

Leah retired into another room, from which she soon returned bringing with her a strongly-bound box, which, after securing the room from intrusion, she opened, displaying a collection of jewels resting on cushions such as even Alypius had rarely if ever seen brought together in one place before. He looked at it for a few moments in entranced amazement, and then Leah saw a look in those dazzled eyes which made her wish that she had not been quite so confidential. It was not that the number of the jewels was so great, but the quality seemed perfect. There was scarce a stone that contained a single flaw. The colours were gorgeous. There was one set which Leah had fancifully arranged in the form of an arch, resting against a cushion covered with pale blue silk, composed of magnificent sapphires, rubies and opals. This especially claimed the admiration of the Greek. It was a necklace, which Leah's fancy had arranged like a miniature rainbow with its glory solidified.

'But,' said Alypius, 'I miss from this glorious collection the royal gem which was to have been the right eye of the new statue of the Buddha.' And he looked closely into the face of the Jewess to see what effect the hint might produce.

'Ah, if we could only secure that,' returned Leah, with apparent sincerity, 'my collection would be complete! We shall see. I may have something to tell thee about that before long.'

'As I look at all these treasures,' said the Greek, 'it seems to me that my share in the profits of the gem-pit, as you describe Sarana, has been a very disproportionate one. The Reconciler has given me nothing like that, and I know that Kapuranda has received much less than I. Such a partial distribution of favours is not seemly in one holding such a position.'

'You jump too readily to conclusions, my friend. This was not all made in Sarana, though many of the stones were presented by my admirers here. This is the result of many years of toil and—well, ingenuity. This is the only time they have ever been exhibited. I have been known to the world as—let us say—an excellent woman living in deep poverty, either involuntarily or voluntarily, for my soul's good. And at times in my wanderings over the earth I have suffered persecution, I have endured starvation, I have been brought down within sight of Sheol. And that rainbow band of beauty which you see there has been, together with another treasure, still more precious, my consolation and my hope. Oh, the beauties! To feel that one has such wealth and power concealed in one's dress, wrapped up in a bit of cloth! With that secure, what is the disfavour of kings, of bishops and priests? And what is the evanescent applause of the multitude compared with those glorious colours, which will endure as long as the world lasts. The coins which the foreigners are bringing to Anuradhapura now from the mint of Heracleia will, in time, be battered beyond all recognition, or will be worthless curiosities to future generations. These treasures, struck off from the great mint of Nature, will retain their value everywhere and for ever. This is the true universal coinage stamped with the image of the great god of light.

'I remember your saying once that you wondered whether I really had a religious faith. I will give you now a confession of faith! This is my religion!' pointing to the dazzling contents of the small strong box. 'I believe in jewels! They are hard, solid, beautiful facts. They are the eternal truth which men talk of as only symbols. Am I alone in this worship, this faith? Nay! what does your trade teach you if not this, that jewel worship is the most popular religion in the world? Look at the engraving on this stone! It is, as you know, the "gem of theosophy," Serapis, the lord of the subterranean world and its treasures; and with him you have here in the one headpiece Ammon and Phœbus, all personifications of the Solar Genius, and all united in that indissoluble bond of bright hyacinth. Depend upon it, Alypius, the jewel is the true Reconciler. There you will find all mankind agreed. The figure which forms the intaglio may be matter of dispute, but all will agree in the value of the gem. You sell the stones, and you enlarge on their religious efficacy and on their healing virtues, and you find that you can adapt them to any religious system that was ever framed, and call them by the name of any god that was ever worshipped, and all will buy and adore—of all creeds and all nations—except perhaps a few morose Christians and philosophers. Philosophers indeed, as if this were not the highest philosophy!

'And mark!' continued the Jewess. She had now taken a standing position in her excitement, and was talking with passionate earnestness to Alypius, who was struck with a certain fiery beauty in her features, which the passion expressed in her eyes seemed to throw over her face. 'Mark this! When human language fails men in their attempts to describe the holiest, the brightest, and best, their only resource for metaphor is in precious stones. The mountain-heights of human perfection are always crowned with gems. Plato's "New World" is like the Jerusalem of Solomon's days. "Silver is nothing accounted of" in it. The ordinary stones of it are the gems so much prized here. And the ideal city of the Christians has for its foundations precious stones. Is it not the same with our Buddhist friends? The translations that have been given me of the Pali verse in which the priests sing of the past glories of this city are full of descriptions, in which their greatest kings are likened to precious stones; and above all, are not their three Saranas, "the Buddha, the

Doctrine, and the Order," the three divine gems? There is jewellery in all religion, my friend. Men may say that it is a woman's religion. Fools! How they talk, as if a woman's religion ever went below a man's! Her instinct will carry her much nearer the truth than man's vanity. For the so-called vanity which lies in woman's attachment to precious stones is not half so vain as man's affectation of indifference.

'Look at them, Alypius! Look at these pure crystals now, as the light shines on them. Have I not reason to be proud of my religion? Let me give you my creed. "I believe in the Sardius, the Topaz, the Carbuncle, the Emerald, the Sapphire, the Diamond, the Ligure, the Agate, the Amethyst, the Beryl, the Onyx, and the Jasper!" Those were the twelve mystic stones in the breastplate of the High Priest, on which my ancestors saw the splendours of the Urim and Thummim rest. You see our ancient faith has not all departed from me. You have been dazzled with the beauty of that arched band of gems. Look! I will show you greater things still!'

And saying this she, having seen again that there was no possibility of intrusion, drew from a secret drawer at the bottom of the box a small breastplate exquisitely worked and embellished, in which were set the twelve gems which she had mentioned in her confession of faith, and in the order given. By the loops, which were also made after the fashion of Aaron's breastplate, as described in Holy Writ, she laid the wonderful plate on her bosom, and—to the Greek—she appeared to become at once transformed. Her figure seemed to rise into a queenly stateliness which was far removed from her ordinary appearance. Her long hair, which was still as black as in her youth, fell from under her little circular cap down about her shoulders. Her eyes appeared to him to shine with a greater brilliance than the jewels which flashed on her breast. It was to him like a figure which embodied in itself a combination of priestess and prophetess.

'Do I believe in jewels?' she continued, in what appeared the language of a sublime passion: 'This is my religion. Here is my creed. This breastplate has often been my salvation. I believe in the stones, though I have so little faith in man and in the inventions of man. I believe in the power of these gems. Behold in me a descendant of a priestly line. No! I have not buried all the past. There are some of the gems out of which their natural lustre dies,[1] when I wear this plate, because of my unworthiness. But while it recalls an evil past it gives me protection in the present, for while I wear it I bear a charmed life. It was a passion of mine continued for years to obtain possession by any means. Why should any human interest stand between me and the attainment of such an object—of jewels—either the same as or corresponding to those which once flashed on the breastplate of Aaron? stones the most celebrated for their beauty, brilliance, and magic powers. I believe I have succeeded in obtaining some that are the very same. What histories some of these stones could unfold, were they once endowed with the power of speech! Some of them have embellished heathen shrines, and some have been amongst the choicest treasures of kings. They come from various lands throughout which the tribes of our people have been scattered. You are thinking of their market value, and of

[1] An ancient superstition.

the wealth in money that they represent. What! sell
this, for which I have endangered my life over and over
again; these beauties with their wonderful history!
No, I will die first! What life of man could be compared in value with such a treasure as this? But there
is still one thing wanting to make it complete. One
thing which I would give this right arm to gain. It
is my dream day and night. To secure it I would
endure any hardship. I would still cross oceans, and
journey on foot over burning deserts. For it I would
brave the hatred of men or the scorn of women. There
is no danger or risk that I would run from, were it
necessary to the accomplishment of this great object.

'Hast thou ever thought,' and Leah leant forward,
speaking in a hoarse whisper, while her eyes blazed
with a fierce, hungry passion, 'of the Urim and Thummim, the stone which was the chief glory of the sacred
breastplate? Where is it? It must be somewhere
in the wide world; and it is the profoundest ambition
of my life to secure it. It is not yet amongst my
treasures; but I have a faith that I shall not die without
seeing that desire realised. It may be near now. All
my life in all its variety of experience shall all be bent
to the attainment of that one object. For that I have
come to this island of gems, and with that end in view I
submit to the most searching examination every stone
of importance that I know of, at all answering to the
reference in the Hebrew scriptures to that jewel of
divine radiance. When that is found, I shall have
grasped the true Sarana, the gem of gems.

'Am I mad to have told thee this? I, who am
usually so cautious and reticent. Nay, for I think
thou canst help me in thy calling, and that discovery

shall bring thee wealth untold. But dare not to think
of obtaining these treasures by fraud or violence. I
tell thee, the fate of Sisera, who fought against Israel,
would certainly be thine.' And as Alypius looked
into the face of the Jewess he felt that the hands
of this Jael would know no trembling in applying the
hammer and the nail.

After a brief pause the breastplate was put back
and the box securely fastened, and then Leah became
her old self. 'I should have been a fool,' she said, 'to
show the treasures to other than yourself. But our
interests are now so inseparable that I can apprehend
no danger. And if our scheme succeed, as it is
certain to, when the incomparable Irene becomes the
bride of Alypius, she shall be dowered with jewels
which might well be the envy of a queen. What
about her father, the old Syrian?'

'So far as he is concerned, our plan is carried out
to the letter. But I cannot help reflecting on myself
for the impositions I have practised on his simple, con-
fiding nature. He has no head for business, and it has
not been at all difficult to persuade him that our firm
was approaching its ruin. His chief thought was of
the numerous friends who would be involved in the
catastrophe, and of the disgrace which would be attached to Christianity in Anuradhapura through his
apparent dishonesty—as if I should have nothing to
fear on the score of character, in such a case. However,
I believe the old man would sacrifice his life if necessary
to avoid such a calamity. So sensitive is he in all such
matters. It was also not difficult to persuade him that
our salvation as a firm lay in the pearl fishery, which
has just commenced, and that it was necessary for him

to go and look after our interests there. And—well, he is now in a small vessel, whose crew are in my pay, which is bound for the fishery, but which I imagine will not reach it very quickly. At any rate, it is out of his power to interfere with our plans for the next two or three weeks. But I shrink from the use of force.'

'Be a man, Alypius! I tell you they like it! She must be brought to Sarana.' And Leah carried away her precious box, and the Greek took his departure.

CHAPTER XVI.

CONVERSATION AND CORRESPONDENCE.

By the power of this Pirit, may you possess freedom from all dangers arising from the malign influence of the planets, or the demons presiding over them.—GOGERLY'S TRANSLATION.

ANURADHAPURA was getting hotter than ever as the days went on, and the monsoon lingered. The rains from the north-east had hitherto come with almost unfailing punctuality at the close of the third month of the Wass season (about the middle of October). And now it was the 'robe-month,'[1] and still the rains came not.

The poor and rich alike had poured blessings on the memories of the kings who had made the great tanks of the city. It was in such a time as this that they realised the blessedness of these immense works of the bygone centuries. But now, even in the great tanks, the water was getting low with the evaporation produced by the terrific heat, and the water that was left had to be carefully guarded and distributed.

The drought had brought with it much poverty and sickness. The hospitals[2] and the 'rice-kitchens' were

---

[1] So called because it is in this month, at the conclusion of the Wass, that robes are presented to the preachers.

[2] Hospitals were established in various parts of the city, according to the Mahawanso, by Dutugemunu B.C. 137.

crowded with applicants, and the chandálas, whose duty it was to go through the various streets of the city every day for the removal of the dead, found the work even greater than the large numbers of people of their low caste set apart for that office could properly perform.

Multitudes of people besieged the temples. What could the gods be about, to delay the rains so long? Were they angry with the land? Where was the sin which had offended the gods? These questions and more like them were circulating amongst the people. They were asked by the gossips one day in the shop of Jotthiyo the goldsmith, and Jantu thought he had no difficulty in answering them. There were heresy and crime in high places, he said. And he looked at Jotthiyo, as if he thought he had at last said something which should arrest his attention. But the buzzing and hissing of the goldsmith's wheel never stayed.

There was to be a great torchlight procession of priests that night through the principal streets of the city. And Jantu, who loved a procession almost as much as he did a gossip, had made up his mind to be present. With his movements, however, we have but little to do in this chapter.

Two men were standing on the flat roof of the house of Joseph the Syrian, watching the line of the procession, as in the course of its progress it went round the king's palace, and passed on through the northern part of the city. They could see by the aid of the torch-light the foremost priests sprinkling water over the people and the houses as they marched along the street. They could hear the cries which came from the vast concourse of people following, who had faith that such a ceremony, in which such numbers of holy men were engaged, must bring the desired rains. They could also hear occasional stanzas which the priests chanted slowly as they marched.

'It is the Ratana,—the Sutra of Jewels,' said Abhayo to Thomas, for they were the two who were watching the procession so intently. And the Thero began to translate some of the verses as they fell upon the ear beginning with, 'Oh! all ye demons who are assembled, terrestrial or celestial, may you all possess happiness! Listen attentively to the things spoken!

'Therefore, ye demons, attend! Be friendly to the race of man, and unremittingly protect those who by day or by night propitiate you by offerings!

'Whatever wealth there may be in this or in other worlds, or whatever superior gem in the heavens, these cannot be compared with the Buddha. This gem-like Buddha is superlatively excellent. By this truth let there be prosperity!'

And concluding with the adoration of the three Saranas:—

'Ye demons, who are here assembled, celestial or terrestrial, we adore Buddha, the Tathāgata, worshipped by gods and men. May there be prosperity!

'Ye demons, who are here assembled, celestial or terrestrial, we adore his Doctrines, the Tathāgata, worshipped by gods and men. May there be prosperity!

'Ye demons, who are here assembled, celestial or terrestrial, we adore the associated Priesthood, the

Tathāgata, worshipped by gods and men. May there be prosperity!'[1]

'It is one of the Buddha's protection discourses,' said Abhayo.

'Do you think that Gautama really taught his disciples to use those words?' asked the Christian presbyter.

'I think there cannot be much doubt of it. It was one of the earliest duties that I can remember to commit to memory these and other discourses of a similar character, to be used for the exorcism of evil spirits and to invoke the protection of the inferior gods, as our friends yonder are doing now.'

And the Thero pointed with his long naked right arm to the priestly procession moving slowly between the long lines of torches. He continued:—'My venerated old tutor—who is now fast approaching the end, and will soon drop out from the procession of human life—he repeated the words to me. He learnt them from the lips of his tutor, and so the succession might be traced back to Mahindo and his colleagues, and through them back to the Buddha himself. For eight hundred years and more has the protection been daily repeated among the multitudes of the followers of Gautama by the members of the order which he established.'

'Does it then take the place of prayer?'

'It answers for both prayer and worship in one sense. In another it does not. For there is not one of those yellow-robed brethren who will not claim superiority to the gods whose aid they are now invoking.

---

[1] Gogerly's translation. The Mahawanso gives a full account of such a ceremony in a drought which occurred at a later period.

The discourses were given by the Buddha to be used as charms to avert calamity. One or more of them are chanted on almost every occasion of public or private importance. And the "saying of Pirit" in a house, whether the palace of a king or the leaf-hut of a beggar, is universally regarded as a sign of attachment to the Buddhist faith. But to be effectual it must be repeated by a brother of the order.'

'What a contrast,' said Thomas, as if speaking half to himself and half to his friend, watching the lines of light as they were passing back by another street to the king's palace, and listening to the dying wail of the invocation to the demon-gods, 'what a contrast to the prayer which the Christ taught His disciples to say!'

'I remember it,' said Abhayo; 'and I have often thought of the difference between that short beautiful prayer which our friends repeated to me once in this house, and which I shall never forget, and such words as those we have now been listening to—vain incantations to appease the wrath of angry demons. Already have I felt its sweetness and power. I have never heard anything like it. When I first heard it, I went away repeating the words to myself: "Our Father! Our Father!" They were the words I had been wanting to say for years. The thought that is in them had been struggling in my mind with a variety of doubts. There were vague ideas and aspirations which before could not be expressed. And that word seemed to put me on my feet before the Great Architect of the Universe. It was the first time that I ever felt that I could pray. It was a revelation to me, which quieted the excitement of my mind and the struggles within me. "Our Father!" It was like the crystallising drop which, falling on a solution seething with a conflict of the elements, suddenly calms the agitation, and produces a mass of solid beautiful crystalline forms.'

'I have known others,' said Thomas, 'on whom it has acted in the same way with a like result.'

'I had come to the conclusion that there must be a God—the Supreme Creator and Ruler of the Universe. I had confessed my doubts to the Senior Thero.[1] I talked with some of the brethren in the pansala about it first. Some were sympathetic. There was one who scoffed, and in his folly said, "If there be such a God, let Him strike me dead!" And I remember that my doubt increased because no dreadful result followed the blasphemy. But afterwards I reflected that that would be a poor way of vindicating the majesty of such a God as I sought. That was not the kind of sign that the world needed, that I needed to put my mind at rest in faith. I should rather doubt the more if that had happened.'

'Why, my friend,' interrupted Thomas, 'that thought could only have been brought thee by the very Spirit of the Christ.'

'It may have been so. I do not know. But this I know, that as I walked back to Mihintala repeating the words to myself, after having heard Joseph recite solemnly and touchingly the great simple prayer of his Lord, I said, "This is the sign that I wanted. There is such a God; and now I have found His name. *Our Father! Our Father!*" You asked me soon after I came to-night of my progress towards the truth. That

---

[1] Auricular confession is provided for in the regulations for the priesthood.

is where I stand. That is my religion. I can say "Our Father which art in heaven!"'

'Thank God!' said Thomas, reverently. 'Be assured that thou art not far from the kingdom. If thou canst so use the great prayer, thou wilt soon, I doubt not, be led to recognise in its Author thy Redeemer and Friend.'

After this they fell into conversation about their mutual friends, about Joseph's return to Anuradhapura, and his hurried departure for Mahatotai.

Thomas produced a letter which had come only the day before from Irene, and they withdrew to a room below, where by the aid of a great copper lamp, in which several burning wicks floated in oil, he made the Thero acquainted with much of what the letter contained.

'It is now a week since my dear father left us, and the time has seemed long, but we have had much to interest us. I daresay you will understand that by WE I mean Anula, the Indian lady of whom you have heard before, and the important young person who is now writing to you. The week has been full of events, and I greatly regret that I cannot send full descriptions of them to my father, but you may possibly find an opportunity of communicating with him. If so, I pray you to forward this letter to him, to let him know what we have been doing, and that, although he has only been gone one week, and will probably be back by the end of another, he is constantly in my mind and in my prayers.

'The first thing of interest which occurred after my father's departure was a religious ceremony which was held in Sikki Banda's house, at his desire, with the purpose of averting the influence of evil omens. These superstitious people imagine that such omens have been unusually bad and unusually numerous of late. They do not say so to me, but I feel sure that some of them are thinking that the presence of the foreigners has brought them ill-luck. Sikki Banda's harvest has not been so large or so profitable as he expected. He says that when he has given to the Mihintala treasurer the quantity due to the priests, whose monastery was endowed centuries ago with all the village and fields of Jambugama, he will have very little left for himself and his people.'

'It is very true!' interpolated Abhayo. 'Vast numbers of priests are maintained in this city and at Mihintala in idleness at the expense of the poor villagers. Buddhist kings, in gratitude for victory, or deliverance in battle, or as marks of special favour to friends in the order, would grant deeds of gift for the maintenance of an image-house, or a monastic establishment. Whole districts have been given to the brotherhood of Mihintala in that way. There are at present over a thousand wearers of the yellow robe on the Holy Mountain, and all, or nearly all, are supported by these endowments, which afford an unlimited license of oppression. The knowledge of this has long been to me one of the most harassing features of my position.'

'I can understand,' said Thomas, 'the value of endowments for education, and the propriety of maintaining them. And I can understand that where Buddhism is the national religion gifts of that kind in perpetuity would be thought necessary by your rulers, to preserve the sacred edifices, and to maintain continuous services in the holy places; but even looked at from a Buddhist point of view, it must be both wrong and unnecessary to make the land and the cultivators support such vast numbers of lazy monks.'

'True, it is inconsistent with the teaching of the Buddha that the "order" should receive such endowments. The strictest poverty is enjoined on us. We are supposed to collect the food for each meal from the householders, and to have no property, with the exception of three cloths of various kinds, in which we wrap ourselves, a girdle, the alms-bowl, a razor, a needle, and a water-strainer. But an evasive distinction is made between the individual and the community. As individuals we are still under our vows of poverty, but as communities we are the proprietors of wealth greater than that of royalty itself. And that we may seem to maintain the rules of the "order" forbidding us to acquire wealth in any way, all the secular work connected with our vast properties is carried on by lay-treasurers and other secular officers. There is quite a large establishment of that kind on Mihintala. And there are inscriptions on stone there, made by one of our royal benefactors, giving rules for the guidance of the lay-officers in administering the estates, as well as for the monks themselves. In the history of our land, the piety of kings, with their merit, has been measured by their gifts to the priesthood, and mainly by such gifts their station in the next birth has been determined. It was this inducement which made the kings give away the land from the people to the priests. If feeding one priest is an act of great merit, what must be the merit obtained by gifts which will suffice for feeding thousands in everlasting succession?'

'But surely a king cannot expect his successors to be bound by such wicked contracts made for the purpose of securing merit to himself! This state of things may go on until every inch of land in the kingdom is possessed by the priests. It will soon become the clear duty of the rulers to wrest such possessions from the wiharas and pansalas, to save the country from ruin. I do not see how such contracts can be more binding than the foolish dedication, of which I have heard, which was made on the arrival of the branch of the Bhoditree, when a deed of gift was made to it of the entire island.'

'It may be,' said the Thero, 'that righteous and unselfish kings may arise and put an end to this misappropriation of property, and the tyranny that it gives rise to, but I am afraid it can never be under the influence of the Buddhist faith. The temptation to accumulate merit of that kind is too strong. Accumulating merit for the kings means accumulating misery for the people. But this is a long interruption which I did not intend. Pardon me!'

Thomas went on with the letter.

'A large room was converted into a kind of preaching-hall for the ceremony, or series of services, for it has already lasted four days, and may continue two or three days longer. It began with the bringing of a relic—a hair from the head—of the Buddha (for such the poor idolatrous people claim it to be, and Anula says it is almost as sacred as the Tooth itself, of which Anuradhapura is so proud) from the village temple. The villagers say that this sacred relic is as powerful in protecting from evil as the personal presence of the Buddha himself would be. The casket containing the relic was placed in great state on a table of carved ebony, near which two priests sat on high seats reading from their scriptures. When the reading was finished the sacred cord called the Pirit Noola (the protection string) was tied around by the wall inside the room, the ends being fastened to the reading chairs, and then laid on the table which supported the relic. Then a large number of priests began chanting the Pirit verses, holding the sacred cord while they sang, in order that they might have a direct bond of connection with the relic.

'The services are all conducted in Pali—the sacred language—and I believe that, with the exception of the priests, Anula is the only person in the village who understands it. The people reverence her greatly, and seem to imagine that she must be supernaturally gifted. A learned woman is a marvel to them. But her attachment to me is regarded, I am certain, with great suspicion. And, indeed, sometimes I cannot understand how we came to love each other so dearly. I can understand my affection for her, because she has qualities of mind and heart which are most attractive and beautiful, in spite of her heathen superstitions; but it is marvellous that she should have become so attached to me, and I think it is, although she does not confess it, a manifestation of the attractive power of Christian truth. I believe that the Spirit of our Divine Saviour is working upon her mind. And she is struggling hard to overcome it. She talks of a love for me, but I believe there is in her, in spite of all her protestations, her religious observances and penances, a growing love for Jesus of Nazareth.

'She acknowledges that her mind is full of doubts,

but she says that the struggle will cease, and the doubts will no longer trouble her, when she has taken the decisive step of joining the Buddhist sisterhood of female recluses in Anuradhapura, which she has determined to do as soon as she can get away. And that will be soon now, for the messenger who takes this to you brought her a message from the queen and the Indian princess, urging her to take this step, and saying that a suitable escort would soon be sent for her to take her back to the city. It is possible that I may avail myself of the same opportunity of returning, if my father does not come back before. But I cannot bear the thought of Anula becoming like the shaven-headed women whom we see sometimes parading the streets near our house (which may God have in His loving protection—the best "Pirit!") with flower-offerings and with begging-boxes! You have never seen her, my dear pastor, but if you could see her, even you would say that it was revolting to think of shaving that beautiful head, with its rich masses of flowing black hair. I think Kumari has transferred all her adoration from me to the lady with "the resplendent head," as she phrases it.

'Now I am falling into that light style of communication which, I am afraid you will say, is characteristic of the sex to which I belong.

'I am writing a long letter, but I must find space for a description of what occurred here yesterday. You will know that this month is called by the Sinhalese the "robe month." And yesterday the great ceremony from which the month takes its name took place in Jambugama. Nearly all the village engaged in it. Anula was exceedingly busy during the early part of the day, and Kumari went about looking very important, because she was permitted to join in the preparations for the making of the robe. She seemed to regard me with great pity because I had no part in the matter.

'The robe had to be made from the beginning to the end in one day! Kumari and several other girls of the same age went out to the cotton bushes, as soon as it was dawn, to bring in the pods that were required. And very pretty they looked as they came in, bounding with the excitement of the occasion, bringing their little burdens to the reading-hall. In the hall Anula sat on a mat on the floor, surrounded by the women of the village, some of them opening the pods, others cleaning the cotton, and others spinning, while girls handed it, when ready, to the weavers outside, who sat at the looms making the cloth.

'When the cloth was finished, it was handed to the priests, who immediately set to work with their needles. When the work of the needles was concluded, the robe was handed to the dyers, who had prepared for that purpose a dye obtained by the boiling of the roots of certain trees. And in a very short time the important garment was ready for presentation to the fraternity. A council of priests was then held, for the purpose of deciding who the recipient should be. It seems that the rule is that it should be given to the most destitute, but the practice is to give it to the chief preacher at the Wass.

'I have written of these things at such length, because I think you will like to know something of the religious life of the people.'

Here Thomas put aside the letter. The metallic basin which formed a part of the water clock kept in the room had fallen to the bottom of the vessel in which it was placed. The Thero arose, gathering his robe about him, saying, 'I may not wear this much longer! I must hasten away now. My dear old tutor, of whom I spoke to you, needs my presence.' And saying this he took his departure.

CHAPTER XVII.

IN WHICH ABHAYO THERO GOES TO MIHINTALA FOR THE LAST TIME.

There was there a Samanean of exalted virtue, one who observed the precepts with exactitude, and lived in the greatest purity. . . . When he was dead, the king, having consulted the rituals and the sacred books, conducted his funeral as beseemed an Arhat.

FA HIAN'S PILGRIMAGE.

'WHY are you going towards the sacred tree when everybody else is on the way to Mihintala?'

'Because I am not "like the short-tailed cow who ran because the others ran,"' replied Kiri Banda. 'But you look as if you were out for a great festival, Jantu! Menika is with you, I see, and all your women-folk. Is it a pilgrimage?'

'It is like you to pretend not to know what is calling so many people out in this direction to-day, although, of course, there are not such crowds as there are at the great ceremonies, or as there will be in a few days at the Mahinda festival. The holy hermit of the Mihintala rock-cell is dead, and they say that the funeral rites will be attended by thousands of priests, and even by royal personages, and carried out in a manner suited to the spiritual rank of so virtuous a character. And as we have not been to the Sacred Mountain for so long a time, Menika thought—that is to say—I thought'—and Jantu glanced back to where his followers stood at a respectful distance in the rear—'that this would be a sight worth seeing, and that the journey on such an occasion might bring us much merit, though the women can only watch the procession from a distance.'

'It would require a great deal of merit,' returned Kiri Banda, 'to take me such a distance on such a day as this, through all the glare of the dagobas and temples that one has to pass between on the way to Mihintala. Why, the sun is almost hot enough to burn the old monk without the aid of a torch!'

'By the way,' said Jantu, 'who will apply the torch? It seems that the old hermit had no relatives. Abhayo Thero was his favourite pupil, but under present circumstances he will surely not be allowed to light the pile! Do you know, it is my opinion that the gods are punishing the city with this terrible drought because of the wickedness and heresy of that man who is still wearing the robe of the order. Else why was it that that solemn and magnificent procession of the priests who chanted Pirit through the principal streets the night before last failed to bring the rains?'

'I have an idea of the reason,' returned Kiri Banda, with half a wink of the eye which was turned from the gossip. 'The gods are angry with certain persons with long tongues who are setting the city on fire with scandals concerning some of the holiest men in the priesthood. There is one especially whom I might name, who will require to be sacrificed, I imagine, before the powers of the air will let the rains come. A word of advice, my friend! It will take more than a journey to Mihintala to acquire merit sufficient to cover the sins of the person I am speaking of. "Some people shut the doors of their own houses, and busy themselves in driving away dogs from the houses of others." There are sins that are quite as bad as heterodoxy with regard to the faith.'

'That is true,' said Jantu, lowering his voice; 'and I may not have been all that I should have been; but they say, and you must know something of it, with all your knowledge of people's private affairs, that the Thero of whom we have been speaking has stolen a gem; not an ordinary stone, but the divine jewel which the king had given to the new statue of the Buddha! What do you think of that?'

'I agree with the proverb, that "it is easier to argue with a thousand intelligent men than with one fool."'

Jantu was ready with an angry retort, but a curiously sharp and decided cough from Menika attracted his attention. And although she looked as meek as ever, it was evident that standing so long in the hot sun had exhausted her patience, and that the cough was equivalent to a command to move on.

Kiri Banda went on his way, and Jantu's little family procession moved towards Mihintala. As they passed each little shrine erected at a street-crossing, the head of the family would join the palms of his hands together and lift them reverentially above his head, acts of worship in which the family followed. 'Talk to me of my sins, indeed!' said Jantu, after he had passed in that way many street-corners with their pedestals of granite supporting small metallic or stone images of Gautama, before which, on a ledge of granite,

Q

the women had placed their offerings of flowers, now being rapidly withered by the fierce rays of the sun.

But let us go back a day or two, and follow Abhayo Thero to the deathbed of his old tutor.

It was the morning after his conversation with Mar Thomas. Abhayo saw, as he sat at the entrance of the cave in the early dawn watching the withered, shrunken form propped up on dried grass, that the end was drawing very near, and that his oldest friend would probably take leave of mortality in the course of the day, to enter on—what? To go whither? These questions would keep recurring as he sat there with the dying man's early morning meal—which he had prepared according to the regulations for sick diet—waiting until he should awake from a doze into which he had fallen.

Presently the hermit awoke. He could scarcely see, but he knew that the light was filling his cell. It gave him pleasure, and he said slowly, 'How good it is to feel the light!' And then, 'But this is the last time. There will not be another dawn for me! Abhayo! art thou there, my son? How beautiful the light is! But I must take leave of it this day. I ought not to love the light, I know. But how hard it is to extinguish all desire! My brethren say that I, like the Blessed One, have conquered the five deadly sins, that I am drawing near the end of the Fourth Path. That is what I have lived and struggled for. I have my doubts, my son! But my brethren are wiser than I. It may be as they say; what thinkest thou, Abhayo?'

'It is hard to say; but why talk of that now? I have brought thee food, my best of friends! Food prepared with my own hands, such as thou wilt love to eat even now!'

'Hush, boy! Talk not of loving food. I should love nothing. I care nothing for food, but I do love the light, and the light is going from me. I have lived in the light, my days have been spent watching the light grow and cover the world, and then die again; but I could always look forward to a beautiful morning coming on the morrow. Now I have reached a day when it will die, and never come again.'

'But there is rest near. Think of that, my dear old master!'

'True, lad! But it is rest in the darkness, and I love the light! What is Nirvana? The scriptures say that it is what succeeds when the lamp of existence is burnt out. That is darkness, and I love the light. And I—come near, Abhayo!—I—love thee, my son!'

'Eat a little food, my father!' said Abhayo, in a voice almost choked with emotion. 'It will make speaking easier. Much talking now is not good.' And without waiting for consent he held the leaf on which the food rested to the old man's mouth.

After a brief pause, the dying man went on again slowly: 'Dost thou remember, my son, our talk of prayer, the night before the Wass began? I said I would pray for thee. Since then I have prayed. Every day, I have thrown out a prayer from my lips, in the hope that it would be caught by some god who could give thee aid. But is it right for me to pray? Prayer means desire, and desire is evil. Besides, the gods are our inferiors. We are of the sacred order, and above all the gods. And I—my brethren tell me that the merit of my life and of my previous births is so great that I could command the services of all the gods in all the heavens. Such is the power, they say, of him who lives in the chief path. I have tried, my son—I would do anything for thy good, but the very effort has shown desire, and the demerit has weakened my power and confused my mind. Nay! do not trouble. I can talk better to-day than for many days past, but I feel that the light is going.

'It is good to pray, child; I have felt it good, even though one sees not whither the prayers go. How much better it would be if we could reach a great strong god who was able to help! Ah! if the Buddha were alive, perhaps he could help. The light is still going—and my mind gets confused.'

'There is such a God, my beloved master. I have found Him at last, and to Him I pray.'

'Found Him, my son! Who is He? Where is He?'

'Our Father!' replied Abhayo, solemnly and emphatically. 'It is the great God who gave us the light and gave us life.'

'"Father." Thy father died when thou wert a babe, Abhayo. He was tall, as thou art. He was more like his paternal ancestors, who came from the north of India, than he was like his mother's race. He was my friend. He was a favourite of Maha Sen, and he was heretical too. It is in the blood, perhaps! Have I told thee this before? Of course I have. How well I remember when they brought thee to the pansala! The sturdy little fellow, what legs and arms he had! And how quickly he learnt the names of the Blessed One! I have loved thee as my own child, Abhayo. Oh, the madness of it—that I should talk of love and child--

but it is true. I have tried to be to thee as a father. What was it? Say the name of that God again, my son?'

'Our Father,' repeated Abhayo.

'Yes, I was saying I have tried to be a father to thee, but oh, how little could I do! What power is there in these limbs? And sometimes my mind is confused. The light is still going, my son! How little can I do for myself! And yet they say that my power is above all the heavens, if I would only exert it. I might have worked miracles, as other Arhats have done. My brethren say that I have told them wonderful things in my dreams, that in such dreams I have shown myself possessed of a knowledge of all the past, and have travelled in many worlds; but my mind is not clear, and the light is going! Thou shouldest have a stronger than I to care for thee. Say it again, lad! Who is He?'

'Our Father,' repeated Abhayo again, 'my beloved teacher. No father could have been more tender or more fatherly than thou hast been with me. God is great, and He is like thee in thy love. He is thy Father too, the Giver of light.'

'My Father—Our Father, the Giver of light,' said the dying man. 'Send for the brethren, boy! the light is going.'

They came, the senior monks, and sat around the rough couch chanting the stanzas appointed to be said in the presence of one who is about to die; while Abhayo, in tears, supported with his strong right arm the hermit's head, with no thought of how soon the touch might be unclean.

The monks chanted the stanzas, but the dying man

heard not. He had gone back into the past. He was in the pansala with the boys about him, full of young life writing on the sand and repeating the sacred names. And then he was in the ordination hall witnessing Abhayo taking the vows.

The monks chanted on. Their weird song told all the dwellers on the sacred hill that the holy Arhat was about to accomplish the victory of Nirvana.

The old man struggled. 'Art thou here, Abhayo? Yes, I feel thy arm. No arm like thine!' Then he dozed again, and the chant of the monks continued. Then he woke again, and said faintly, only Abhayo could hear him: '"Our Father," the light is going, let it come again to-morrow!' There was a last flicker, and the lamp had burnt out.

Abhayo stayed all that day and the next, to render what assistance might be required from him for the cremation ceremony, which was fixed for the evening of the next day.

Jantu was not disappointed in his expectations. In spite of the doubts expressed by Abhayo, the monks of Mihintala reported to the king that the hermit had died an Arhat, and the king had commanded that the funeral should be conducted with all the magnificence that the ritual for the dead would admit of, for no monarch could be so great as the man who had trodden the chief path, and vanquished desire. Prince Detu, Dharma Sen, and others of high rank attended the funeral in great state.

Two thousand priests walked in slow procession to the burning-place with the body, which, wrapped in the robe of the order and covered with a white cloth, was supported on a bier carried on the shoulders of the slaves belonging to the monastery, preceded by the death-drums. Arrived there, they arranged themselves in a vast circle around the pile of costly and fragrant wood, over which a canopy of beautiful decorations in flowers and leaves rested on tall arches formed of the stems of graceful palms. The body was placed on the pile, and the cloth which covered it presented to the priest appointed to recite the offices for the occasion. He chanted selections from the Sutras in praise of the holy ones who had attained to Nirvana, the great crowd of priests joining in the refrain at the end of each stanza. He sang of 'the wise ones of the earth, who having no desire, and having destroyed the cause of their existence and completed their Karma, are extinguished like the lamp,' the men who had broken the 'five fetters' in which mortality is enslaved: (1) self-delusion, (2) doubt, (3) dependence on religious ceremonies, (4) the passions of the body, and (5) all hatred; the Arhats who had conquered all love of life, all desire for life hereafter, all pride and self-righteousness, and who had triumphed over ignorance.

A brief pause ensued, in which a breathless silence was observed in the immense crowd. After which the officiating priest intoned a few stanzas from Buddha's discourse to the bereaved:—

'In this world the life of man is one without a cause.

'Unknown, miserable, a little thing—and even that mixed up with sorrow.

'There is indeed no means by which those born could be prevented from dying. Even after arriving to old age, there is to us death. One dies; such is the nature of a living being.

'The young and the old, the ignorant and the wise,

whosoever they be, all come under the influence of death, all stand as it were on death, or end in death.

'Even thus the world is afflicted with death and decay; therefore wise men, knowing the course of things in the world, do not give way to grief.

'Even if a man lives a hundred years or more, he is separated from his relatives and yields up his life in this world.

'Therefore, hearing the words of the holy ones, overcome the lamentation arising from seeing one's dead body and knowing, "He will not be found by me again."

'He who seeks his own happiness should draw out from him the darts of his bewailing and many expressions of grief and sorrow.

'He who, not clinging to any object, has drawn his darts out, will arrive at a tranquil state of mind, overcome every kind of grief, and become sorrowless, undisturbed in mind.'[1]

The three Saranas and the five precepts of the Pan-sil were then repeated by both priests and people, after which more wood was piled on above the dead, and a flaming torch put into the hands of Abhayo Thero. He took it listlessly, scarcely thinking of what he was doing, but rather of the stanzas on bereavement which had just been chanted, and which seemed to him, though he had often heard and spoken them, so helpless and hopeless, so different from the words of the Christ. He could easily make himself alone in a multitude, and now as he walked three times around the pile—instead of reciting the 'Refuges' three times, as he was expected to, he said as if to himself—in contrast to the

[1] From Sir M. Coomara Swamy's translation.

words of the Buddha he had just listened to, the words of Jesus which had been translated to him from Thomas's manuscript of St. John's Gospel:—'*I am the Resurrection and the Life. Whosoever liveth and believeth on Me shall never die.*' This he said three times, and then put the torch to the pile, which was immediately wrapped in a great blaze.

It was his last Buddhist ceremony, and as he stood looking at the leaping flames, it seemed to him as if he were watching the burning of himself, of his past life, and of his old creed.

The brethren of the monastery had been kind; the chief Thero especially, who had resisted all attempts to prevent Abhayo from performing the last sad act of respect to the dead—the last but one, for the last was to come, when in ten days they would return to the burning place to collect the ashes. And even this would be permitted to Abhayo, so the chief Thero said, in talking to him after the funeral; but an earlier date had been fixed for the investigation of some heavy charges against him. It was considered of sufficient importance to hold the chapter for the examination in the Brazen Palace, and it was to be held on the day after the Mahinda festival, which was only seven days off. The old priest spoke in words full of sympathy, for he had been proud of this eloquent member of his establishment. But Abhayo looked as though such events in the future were small matters.

That evening, in the dusk, Abhayo Thero passed Jantu and his little family procession on the return journey. Menika was critical. She thought it was a stupid custom which kept women away from funerals, and she poured a torrent of wrathful words on her husband for being so long at the burning-place; as if all the funeral arrrangements had been in his hands. Jantu tried, with no great success, to divert her attention to the notables who were returning to the city.

'There,' said he to Menika, as the tall monk went by at a swinging pace, 'you have seen him before. That is the Mihintala Thero. It was he who applied the torch after all. I shouldn't wonder if he is going now to see that one-armed Christian priest. They tell me that they have become close friends. Ah well! We shall soon see what we shall see.'

Abhayo was going, as Jantu had conjectured, to see Thomas, and would return no more to Mihintala.

CHAPTER XVIII.

FRIENDLY CONTROVERSIALISTS.

... It seems a restlessness of heart, a silent yearning,
A sense of something wanting, incomplete.
BROWNING'S *The Ring and the Book.*

'IF this will not bring the rains, nothing will but the punishment of the guilty persons on account of whose sins this terrible drought has come to us.' It was Jantu who was speaking to his usual audience in the shop of Jotthiyo, and he was speaking of the elaborate preparations which were being made for the Mahinda festival.

'Why should this bring it more than any other ceremony?' asked one of the little party, the one who has already been introduced to the reader in connection with the gossip at the goldsmith's as a stranger to Anuradhapura.

'Because the king, in establishing it, made all the route of the procession as like as possible to the decorations which King Bimbasara made for the road on which the glorious Buddha walked on his way to Wesali, where the people were dying by thousands of the pestilence which a long drought had brought on them. And as soon as the Prince of the Sages began the journey the rain fell, and the kingdom was saved. My brother says there is no doubt that such a procession will compel the demons who are holding back the monsoon to loosen their hands. We shall see! My opinion is that the rains will not come till the great jewel is recovered for the image of the Vanquisher, or till the evil-doer who has stolen it meets with his just punishment.'

'Are they making diligent search for it?'

'It is said that the strictest investigation is being made privately. It would soon be discovered if one of us were suspected; at any rate, there would be very little delay in dealing with such as we are. We should soon be brought to the ordeal under such circumstances. But when it is a priest it is a different matter.'

'But you are not certain that the priest has done it,' suggested one of the company.

'I am not far from it, then, I can tell you!' replied Jantu, snappishly. 'And there is somebody else who knows, or ought to know, as well as anybody, and he is as certain of it as I am, and that is Kapuranda the astrologer. He was talking to a lot of us about it last night, and, as he said, it is our property that is stolen, for the jewel was, in a sense, a gift to the city. I wonder the people do not rise in a mass to crush the priest and his friends the Christian foreigners, for there is no doubt that the gem is somewhere amongst them.'

It was true, as Jantu had suggested, that the astrologer had spent much time in impressing his suspicions with regard to the lost gem on the minds of the people. And, as a consequence of such insinua-

tions and the wide circulation obtained by Jantu's
gossip, the tide of popular indignation was rising high
against Abhayo Thero and the Christians. In the
opinion of the multitude, some colour was given to the
suspicion by the Thero's avoidance of all publicity in
these days.

He had given his word that he would appear in
answer to the charges which had been preferred against
him. Meanwhile, he spent most of his time with
Thomas in the study of the Christian Scriptures. It
was his duty, he said, to weigh the evidence for the
claims put forth on behalf of Christianity. He had
learnt much, and his faith had grown, but he could not
rest with his present attainments. There was still much
of uncertainty in his mind. And he wanted to be
very certain before he took the final step which would
sever him from the associations in the midst of which
his life had been spent. All this was to Abhayo a
matter of much greater importance than the formal
impeachment for heresy which was now drawing so
near.

As to the other suspicion, which had been hinted
at by the senior Thero, he had scarcely given it a
thought, except that the chief priest must have been
talking in parables, and probably meant something
about the damage he was doing to the 'gems' of
the Buddhist faith. His duty was clear, and he felt
compelled to proceed with the investigation of the
supernatural claims of the Christian religion. And
it was natural to a man of his intensely earnest
character that he should not be satisfied with anything short of the fullest light attainable, and that
he should pursue such a course, regardless, for the

time, of all claims which were not a matter of life and death.

During one of these days of study, another letter arrived from Irene, a portion of which Thomas translated to his friend.

The letter was very much occupied with Anula. 'She is determined, as I told you in my last,' wrote Irene of her friend, 'on entering the Buddhist sisterhood. And since I wrote you she has been telling me much of what her life will be when she has taken the vows. How I wish I could dissuade her from taking that step! It is true that the act is not irrevocable, but it will be hard for her to return to such a life as we have lived here. It will mean death to our friendship.

'I am afraid that my knowledge of Christianity is weak and small, and my advocacy of it is too feeble in dealing with such a faith and such a nature as hers. If she had an opportunity of listening to your presentation of the truth, the result would, I cannot help thinking, be very different. I told her so the other day. She smiled sadly, and said that nothing could break her determination. She feels that she is losing ground, and talks of life as a constant battle between that which produces merit and that which produces demerit. Often I cannot follow her in her metaphysical talk. She uses many words which I cannot understand, and when the words are explained, sometimes I find great difficulty in grasping the ideas. She says that the great mystery of Karma is not easily understood, any more than certain mysteries of the Christian faith which I have been talking to her about.

'As far as I can understand it, however, it means the result of life, which result, according to its goodness or badness, influences the further course of the stream of transmigration. She illustrated it to me one day by means of a pair of scales, one of which she called "Kusal" (merit) and the other "Akusal" (demerit). The entire balance she called "Karma." She poured grains of sand into both scales, making them nearly balance each other, and said, "My Karma was once like that, but for a long time it has been going like this." And she went on gradually transferring grains of sand from the good to the evil side of the balance until the "demerit" scale greatly outweighed the other. When I told her that I thought she must have been mistaken, that the turning of the scale had not been apparent to her friends, she began to talk of the old subject of evil desires interfering with holiness, and of how people often make religion an excuse for the gratification of evil desire. I am certain that she has long been struggling with a great passion which is very much stronger than any affection which she may feel for me, and which she thinks is bringing her Karma down on the wrong side, and this she is determined to conquer in the life of a recluse.'

At this point in the reading, Thomas turned to his friend, to ask if that was a correct representation of the Buddhist doctrine. There was no answer; and then he saw that Abhayo was leaning forward with his head on his hand, as if labouring to conceal some strong emotion. He went on reading:—

'When she talked of the balance and the scales, I asked her where the weigher was in her illustration. It could not be complete without that. She knew what

I meant, and said that it weighed of itself. It must, of necessity, rise or fall, according to the scale into which our actions or thoughts are thrown. But I think she is learning to see—I cannot say, I may be too sanguine—that there must be a Judge with the scales, and that there is much in the scheme of " Karma " which could only be accepted with a belief in a Supreme Intelligence governing the world. That it is so is partially evident from the fact that she seems compelled often to use the word " Karma " where we would use the name of God when we speak of His almighty power and guidance. It appears impossible even to atheists, such as these poor Buddhists are, to live without recognising in some way and under some name the great creating and controlling Mind of the Universe.

'Another debatable subject in our little controversies is the question of the existence of the soul and its immortality. She answers me still with talk about the mystery of Karma and of transmigration. She talks of repeated births into states of life, which follow as a natural result of the Karma in the previous life. "It is a mystery," she says. I have replied that it is not that which puzzles me so much as the contradictions in the teaching concerning the soul, and such contradictions appear to me fatal to intelligent faith. "How can personal identity be maintained if there is no soul? And in this personal identity every Buddhist appears to believe. Sikki Banda, for instance, attributes his bad harvest, poor fellow! and all his ill-luck, to sin in a previous birth. And in the birth-stories which you have been telling me from time to time, you know the Buddha claims to have a knowledge of all the lives through which he passed before he became Buddha.

What does he mean when he says, 'In that birth I was Ráma,' or 'I was the hare'? What is the *I* in that case, if it does not mean the soul?" I could not follow her in her reply, but I could not help feeling that there is in it all, in spite of the Buddhist's denial, a dim intimation of the life and immortality which Jesus has brought to light in the Gospel.

'I wonder if there were ever two such girls as we are, engaged so frequently in such conversations! But the conversations arise only out of our love for each other, and each of us desires to convince the other of what she thinks is the truth. We do not spend all or even most of our time in this way, however. We often have a romp with the children, and we take daily walks. But I am expecting every day now that the escort will arrive for Anula, and then we shall be separated. That I cannot bear to think of. It seems intolerable that one so gifted, so beautiful and high-minded, should occupy so degraded and degrading a position as the regulations of the sisterhood demand. She tells me that one of Gautama's ordinances for the nuns is this:—"The female recluse, though she be a hundred years old, when she sees a Sámanéra novice, though he be only eight years old and just received, shall be obliged to rise from her seat when she perceives him in the distance; go towards him, and offer him worship."[1] He—Gautama—seems to have had the lowest opinion of our sex. Anula tells me that he is reported to have said on one occasion: "That which is named woman is sin." I do not understand how a woman, and especially such a woman as Anula,

[1] Hardy's *Eastern Monachism*.

can follow a saviour with such views of womanhood. That funny Kiri Banda says, "the more a woman is beaten, the more she likes you!" It may be on that principle that women are so attached to the Buddhist faith. It is strange, at any rate. How unlike Jesus of Nazareth! And yet Alypius and his party are for ever insisting on the resemblances between Christianity and Buddhism!

'What a long letter I have written you again! It occupies my mind in my dear father's absence, and though you may not approve of all the chatter it contains, I know you will be glad to hear from me, and you may be interested in our religious controversies. How I long for my father's return! Sometimes I cannot help feeling as if the bad omens which the people talked of when he left would be realised. But such thoughts are wrong, I know.

'The drought is terrible. The village tank is quite dried up, and the stream by which we used to sit in the evenings has long ceased to run. The poor cattle are dying for want of grass. What will the country do if the monsoon delays its coming much longer?

'In a few days the time mentioned by my father as his probable time of absence will have expired. May our Father in heaven have him in His holy keeping!'

Thomas found, on finishing the reading, that Abhayo was not inclined to return to his studies. He sat for some time in gloomy silence. Then he arose, saying to himself: 'And so we wander farther and farther away from each other!' And expressing a wish to go where he might be alone, he retired.

Thomas, who sat wondering for a time at the Thero's strange words and manner, fell into a sleep on his couch, overcome by the heat of the day.

If he had known Irene's position at the time that he was reading her letter, sleep would have been impossible. She was at Sarana with the Reconcilers, a most unwilling guest.

The escort for Anula had arrived at Jambugama on the day after that on which the letter was dispatched. That letter had been delayed for a day or two on the road by the neglect of the messenger. The escort had brought a message from Alypius to the effect that he had heard from his partner Joseph, who was on his way back from Mahatotai, suffering from fever which he had caught there, and he would like Irene to come as far as she could to meet him. He was not dangerously ill; but he would like the first face he saw in Anuradhapura to be hers.

Irene's excitement was intense. She could scarcely wait for the moonlight, in which the party had decided to travel, on account of the great heat of the day. She took no heed of the country through which they passed, and the beauty of the roads winding along under the palms and other trees in the light with which the moon flooded the land. Nor did she listen to the conversation, if such it might be called, of Kumari and the myna, which philosophic bird the little maid had, after much entreaty, been allowed to take with her in accompanying Irene back to the city.

Anula comforted her as best she could, and when they at last got to a part of the city where the man in charge of the little party said they would have to separate in order to reach their respective destinations, she offered to continue the journey with Irene, partly because she wished to prolong companionship with her friend as much as possible, and also because of an indefinable dread on her friend's account, which had been strengthened by the omens she had consulted before starting on the journey. For Anula was not altogether above the superstitions of her time and people. But for the urgency of the occasion she would not have started at so inauspicious a time. She was beginning to believe that ill-luck was inevitable to these foreigners, and to those who associated with them. But, for all that, her association with Irene had been a pleasant, restful interlude in her life, only too pleasant and too restful, she said to herself. And now the time for parting had come, for the leader of the escort declared that Anula's proposal was impossible, as far as she was concerned; but the escort could be divided in such a way as to make the rest of the journey, which would not be far or difficult, perfectly safe for each of them. So it was arranged, and with great emotion on both sides the two friends took leave of each other, each thinking that it was not likely they would meet again.

It was not without some suspicion of Alypius that Irene had entered on this journey. But she put the suspicion away from her directly, thinking it unworthy of her to imagine for a moment that the Greek would act with anything but straightforwardness at such a time. If she had known the city better, and understood the route by which she was being taken, her suspicions might have been confirmed. But of the way she was quite ignorant, and imagined herself on the road to Mahatotai, until the party halted at the headquarters of the Reconcilers, where she was received by Leah with a 'Welcome to "Sarana"!' Then her suspicions rushed back upon her like a flood, and a great fear arose within her.

CHAPTER XIX.

TROUBLE AT SARANA.

Like going to make bears dance in the midst of a religious festival.—SINHALESE PROVERB.

It was the great day of the Mahinda festival, and multitudes of people were pouring out of the various streets in the direction of Mihintala, to see the king bring the golden statue of Mahindo down the great stairway of the Sacred Mountain.

Religious festivals and processions have been frequently referred to in the course of this story. They were, and are still, the great features in the life of the people, the chief objects of public interest. Other events are dated from them, and it is to such occasions that the masses of the people look for almost the only variety which breaks the dull monotony of their existence.

The people of Anuradhapura loved a procession, and it must be admitted that this passion of theirs was fully provided for by the priests and those in authority. In the larger streets, especially in the southern and eastern parts of the city, where the ecclesiastical buildings were most numerous, scarcely a day passed without a procession of some kind, large or small; and when they were not visible in the streets, they might often be seen moving in slow and solemn march in the galleries around the great dagobas.

There was no denying that Anuradhapura was well supplied with such attractions; but, with the exception of the festival held in honour of the arrival of the Sacred Tooth, there was nothing even in that city of religious shows which could vie in pomp and magnificence with the festival which King Meghawarna had instituted to commemorate the advent of the great Buddhist Apostle to Ceylon. And in spite of heat and drought and pestilence, the multitudes moved out of the city towards Mihintala, for, added to the great attraction of seeing the procession start, was there not the hope that they would bring the rain with them on their return? that it would fall on the scorched land as it did when the Buddha walked to Wesali?

With the multitude of course went Jantu, and with him Menika, the children, and some slaves, who brought up the rear of the little family procession.

The crowds passed the shop of Jotthiyo, wondering much to hear the goldsmith's wheel buzzing and hissing on such a day as this. Even Jantu, knowing his habits, was surprised, and would have stopped to expatiate on the spectacle he was missing, but for the sharp, warning cough which came from Menika. A merry twinkle flashed in the eye of Jotthiyo as the party passed on at the order of the cough. The Sinhalese can make a cough mean a great deal, and Menika's was unusually expressive.

They had not gone very far when they were joined by the Sámanéra, Jantu's brother, who made himself of service in describing the pictures with which the road leading to Mihintala had been decorated on either side for the great procession. Nothing could be more picturesque or striking than the aspect presented by the long walls of bright colour formed by the side-pictures, interspersed by the freshly-gilded dagobas and shrines, and the numerous arches of wood and leaves which, in a variety of shapes, spanned the sacred road. But Mihintala itself was the crowning spectacle. Gay banners streamed from all the temples and other edifices on the hill. And the multitudes of people in holiday attire, and thousands of monks in their yellow robes, covered one side of the hill—the side of the ascent—with great masses of bright colour that were perfectly dazzling.

Nor was it less striking to look down from the hill on the vast crowd below, which, as the *Mahawanso* says of the attendance at the first of these festivals, 'was like unto a great ocean.' All about the east gate of the city and around the foot of the hill it was like an immense fair. There the people were supplied with refreshments of various kinds, and the cries of numerous boys might be heard announcing the sale of sweetmeats of the highest order of confectionery at the cheapest rates; while others proclaimed the virtues of the betel-leaf, which they sold together with the areca-nut and lime, all ready for mastication.

But all the cries were suddenly hushed, and the talk of the crowd, which had sounded like the noise of the sea, was suspended for a few moments, when the bands of music on the hill announced the commencement of the ceremony. And the brief silence of the multitude of spectators was followed by a tremendous shout, in which a hundred thousand voices seemed to unite, as the king, gorgeously robed, and bearing in his hands the golden image of the Buddhist Missionary,

THE SACRED BO TREE.
(*From a photograph by Scowen & Co., Colombo.*)

came down the granite stairway, heading the magnificent procession of priests and princes and officers of state.

Nor was the spectacle less imposing that night when the procession moved slowly through the worshipping crowds up the sacred road towards the city. It was a perfect dream of Oriental splendour. Thousands of lamps sparkled on the arches and illuminated the road, as the long line of the royal cortège, guarded by the flashing spears of the soldiery, following the elephants bearing the images of Mahindo and his colleagues, marched solemnly, to the chanting of the priests, through the great avenue of pictures, which represented, first, the five hundred and fifty birth-stories of the Buddha as Bodhisatwa, then the legends concerning Gautama himself, and, finally, mythical and historic scenes in which the conversion of King Piya Tissa and the planting of the Bodhi tree had great prominence.

On arriving at the Maha Wihara, the statue, after being carried three times in procession around the sacred tree, was deposited by the hands of the king in the shrine prepared for its reception, where it was to remain until the time appointed for conducting it to the wihara built for it near the royal palace. And so ended the great ceremony.

The dawn was rapidly breaking in the sky when Jantu and his little party, tired and sleepy, were leaving the enclosure of the Sacred Bo. 'And still there is no rain!' murmured Jantu.

'He! he! he! Nor any sign of it that I can see. Everybody is going home groaning in the same way, and looking up at the sky, which is as cloudless as ever.' It was Kapuranda the astrologer, who at once entered

into an earnest whispered conversation with Jantu—
and then, as the party left, remained behind saying
to himself: 'That will be the end of him. There is
nothing like working through the mob after all. They
know now—thanks to that old gossip—why the rains
are delayed. He! he!' Thus chuckling, he stood for
a moment in hesitation on the beautifully carved moon-
stone at the bottom of the flight of steps leading up to
the platform of the Bo, and then saying, 'There will be
no visitors at Sarana to-day,' he waddled away as fast
as his corpulence and the abundant clothing swathed
about his loins would permit. He was going to the
goldsmith's shop.

As he had calculated, Jotthiyo was alone. The
gossips were probably fast asleep in their own homes,
tired and exhausted with the part they had taken in
the great festival, as were also the workmen in an
adjoining room. But the goldsmith was as fresh and
his eye as bright as if he had spent the night in the
most invigorating rest and sleep, as, indeed, he had.

'You were at Sarana yesterday, he! he!'

'Yes, I was,' returned the goldsmith, strange to
say not disinclined for a talk. 'And I am going again
to-day. That is a bit of information which will give
you no surprise. And you did not come here on purpose
to get it.'

'No, indeed; but I am anxious, my friend, that our
plans—now that they are so near completion—should
have no flaw in them. Remember, nothing must come
between us and the prize! I never knew a goldsmith
outwitted yet, and I am certain that old Jotthiyo is not
the one to let the precious opportunity slip when it is
so nearly within his grasp.'

A glance from the eye of the goldsmith indicated that he might be trusted to that extent. 'Let me have a look at the substitute!' said the astrologer.

The goldsmith led the way to the strong box, and exhibited what appeared to be a magnificent sapphire of very large proportions.

The astrologer held it up to the light and examined it carefully, and then grinned with a chuckle of immense satisfaction.

'We must not be too confident, however,' said Jotthiyo, 'for we have to deal with one of the best judges of gems in the city. It is only a question of time, and, probably, not a very long time. She is bound to discover it sooner or later, and is much more likely to do it sooner than later. But some time will elapse before she does find it out, and perhaps sufficient for our security. The risk is great, but the prize is worth it.'

'I should think so indeed! Why, if you could bring all the precious stones which have passed through your hands into one dazzling pile of gems, it would not compare with it in value.'

To this the goldsmith responded with an enigmatical grunt, his only comment on unprofessional opinions; and then went on to say, 'I was there all day yesterday, as you know. Jantu and the rest of the gossips passed this on their way to Mihintala, regarding me as a born idiot or a perfect marvel of industry, because I kept my wheel going on such a day. As you can imagine, the wheel stopped when the city was emptied, and I was very soon on my way to the shrine of the Reconciler!'

'I guessed as much,' said the astrologer; 'and this

morning you will be as little likely to be disturbed, for nearly all the city is asleep; and in the after part of the day, if I mistake not, all the excitement will centre at the Brazen Palace. A better time could not have been selected. But we must, as you say, have a care, and look well at all the possibilities. The Greek, Alypius, has cast covetous eyes on our object, and but for the fact that he is so intensely absorbed just now in his love affairs, he might prove a formidable rival. It would be a shame to let such a prize as that pass out of our nation, he! he!'

'I am not afraid of the Greek. I believe he is a coward at heart,' returned Jotthiyo; 'but the Jewess is cast in an altogether different mould. Sometimes I can more than half imagine that she is the prophetess and miracle-worker she claims to be. And as to the jewel, she seems to want it more for the purposes of her magic, for a mighty charm, than anything else. She told me that when it is fixed in a certain wonderful breastplate which she will put on, it will give her a power more miraculous than anything she has yet laid claim to.'

'And that piece of work you are going to do for her to-day. You are to be well paid for it, are you not, eh?' And the astrologer chuckled with intense satisfaction.

'The Jewess could not obtain my help without letting me know something of her secret, and I have no reason to complain of her terms. I imagine that your friend, the prince's pupil, must have been still more liberally paid, for no friend of yours would undertake such a risk as he did for Leah without abundant compensation.'

'You may depend on that,' replied Kapuranda, 'but the poor young man is living in constant dread of discovery. We must get him sent out on a long journey, or there may be difficulties.'

'It is a good thing for us that Kiri Banda, with his everlasting proverbs, is out of the way,' Jotthiyo went on to say. 'He knows too much, and I am not at all certain that he is to be trusted.'

'I have been doubtful of him myself lately,' said the astrologer; 'but you may be sure that Alypius has sent him on such an errand as will keep him away from Sarana while the fair prisoner is detained there.'

'Yes; and it is not unfavourable to our plans, I can tell you, that she should be there, to divert the attention of the Jewess, and prevent too close a concentration in watching my work. We may be thankful that she is occupied with some other considerations as well as that in which I shall be engaged. I heard the young lady sobbing yesterday as if her heart would break, and calling out at intervals for her father and Anula, her Indian friend.'

'And they are far enough beyond the reach of her voice—at least her father is—and the Indian lady is with the sisterhood, they say, and about to take the vows. You may trust our two friends for making that all secure. They do not stick at much, and we may guess that we shall not be very tenderly dealt with if we fail. But it is worth the risk, and we must not let the prize go out of the hands of faithful Buddhists, to be carried away by foreigners.' And the astrologer shook his fat sides with laughter over his little joke.

After wakening the workmen and making certain arrangements, this singular pair went out, and walked through the city together for some distance, until they reached a street-crossing where they parted company; the goldsmith travelling with short, quick steps to Sarana, and the astrologer to the Hall of Mystery, where it was agreed he should await Jotthiyo's arrival soon after midday; and the little fat man waddled along with many a chuckle and with a look of infinite self-satisfaction on his countenance.

There was no doubt in Irene's mind, when she saw where she had been brought, as to the nature of the plot into which she had been entrapped. Even then it was more of her father that she thought than of herself. She could now see the treachery of Alypius in her father's departure; and the possible peril of his position made her, after the first outburst of indignation, careful not to give way too much to the rage with the wicked schemers which burned in her heart.

Alypius found that his audacity and courageous affection, as he called it, so far from creating a favourable impression, as Leah had predicted, had made him more hateful than ever. But he was not slow to discover the impression produced on her mind by the knowledge that her father's safety was in his hands. As Jotthiyo had overheard, she wept and sometimes cried aloud during the first day, while little Kumari, her fellow-prisoner, tried to comfort her. And even in the midst of her sorrow, the sight of the myna, with his head perked on one side, eyeing the new aspect of things with a comic solemnity, made her burst into an hysterical fit of laughing, followed by much sobbing, angry with herself that she could laugh under such circumstances.

For a prisoner, she was treated with considerable

kindness by Leah, who used all her powers of persuasion on behalf of her colleague, without avail. And Irene was not without hope. 'Visitors will be coming to the shrine,' she said to herself, 'and I will make myself heard then.'

But the day passed without the arrival of any of the disciples of the Reconciler, an absence which Leah had calculated upon. And now it was the second day at Sarana, and no visitor had come save the goldsmith, the movements of whose tools she had heard in another room. She tried to attract his attention, but without any result, save to bring Leah in for a moment, in a state of great wrath; and the goldsmith's wheel went on hissing as if nothing had happened.

Then she found that Kumari was gone, and thought it probable that she had been dragged away by Leah to punish her for her cries. But the myna was left, and again she laughed hysterically, as she watched the absurd antics of the bird and listened to its chatter. And still it was her hope that she could not be kept concealed long in a place of religious resort so popular as she understood the shrine of the Reconciler to be.

In the afternoon the Jewess came to her in good spirits. She praised her beauty, and promised her that she should not be long detained. She gave her comforting words concerning Joseph, whom she declared to be in no danger. And then she opened her jewel-case and laid before her a wealth of precious stones which, she said, should be Irene's if she would consent to be the bride of Alypius. She then arrayed herself, to Irene's amazement, in the necklace of beautiful gems which it had been her fancy to arrange in the form and with the colours of the rainbow. After which, with an

s

excitement which almost amounted to frenzy, she put on the breastplate, from which the mystic gems flashed a splendour which had at first a dazzling effect on Irene's eyes.

'There!' said the Jewess, 'I knew it. I have got it at last. Thou art dazzled by the glory of the Urim and Thummim. Art thou not also a child of our people, though a Christian? My words would seem madness to other ears, and it may be that they do to thine!' She was right there, for Irene had begun at first to doubt her own sanity, and to think that it must be all a strange, weird dream. Then the question suggested by Leah had occurred to her.

The Jewess went on: 'Ah, if thou couldest know how I have lived and striven for this, how I have risked all things, life and honour! Look on it, girl! On the great sapphire there! How does it appear to thee? I have travelled in nearly all lands in search of these gems. Thou hast read, or heard thy people speak, of the breastplate which the high priests of the house of Aaron wore in the Holy Sanctuary of Israel. It has been told thee of the chief gem on which the glory of the Divine revelation rested! To find that stone has been the great object of my ambition. I have enough left in me of the old faith of our fathers to put that before everything else in life, to secure the lost gem which formed the Urim and Thummim of the sacred breastplate. Look again, child! How does it appear? Thou art not impressed by it as at first. And now, as I look at it, it is not of that azure which one should look for—like the blue of the heavens concentrated. Look again, child! Nay, there is something in the old superstition; it pales on account of my unworthiness!

And so do my sins rise up against me now, when the great object of my life is within my grasp. I was afraid it might be so. And now, thou beautiful child of the Syrian, thou shalt wear it on thy breast. Resting on thy innocence, it may reveal the mystic signs!'

Irene, half afraid of her, for she looked like a Pythoness, fired with unnatural energies, and willing to humour her, suffered herself to be arrayed in the wonderful breastplate.

Anybody but Leah would have been profoundly impressed with the beauty of the Syrian girl, as she stood there in queenly stateliness with the great flashing jewels on her breast; but the attention of the Jewess was altogether riveted on the stone, on which she expected to see a display of unearthly glory. Her eyes burned with a long look of eager intensity. This was followed by a shade of disappointment, which gradually increased as she drew closer and closer to the stone. Then she unfastened the breastplate, and having fiercely wrenched away the stone, she held it up to the light. One long look in that light, and she dashed the false gem to the ground, with an exceeding bitter wail, 'Lost! Lost! Again betrayed!'

It happened at that moment that the myna hopped on to the table, and looking into the face of the Jewess in its most philosophic one-sided manner, gave utterance to the pertinent question, '*What can I do?*' which sent Irene into another fit of hysterical laughter, and Leah into a boiling rage. But her anger was soon diverted from Irene to the goldsmith, on whose devoted head she called down the curses of the God of Israel, and of a miscellaneous enumeration of heathen deities. She declared that she would follow him at once and

have his blood. But what should she do with Irene?
It occurred to her then that the safest place for her,
till her return, would be the strong secret room which
the astrologer had made behind the shrine of the Reconciler. There would be no visitors, she said to herself,
on such a day, and if any came while she was away
they would only be too frightened to come near, should
they hear Irene's cries.

Willing to atone for her apparent rudeness, Irene
followed the Jewess, not without suspicion, through a
narrow, secret passage to the room which she said
would be much more comfortable for her. It was not
comfortable. It looked small, and it was certainly
dark, and she was turning to protest, when the door
was closed upon her, and she heard the clanking of
heavy bars outside.

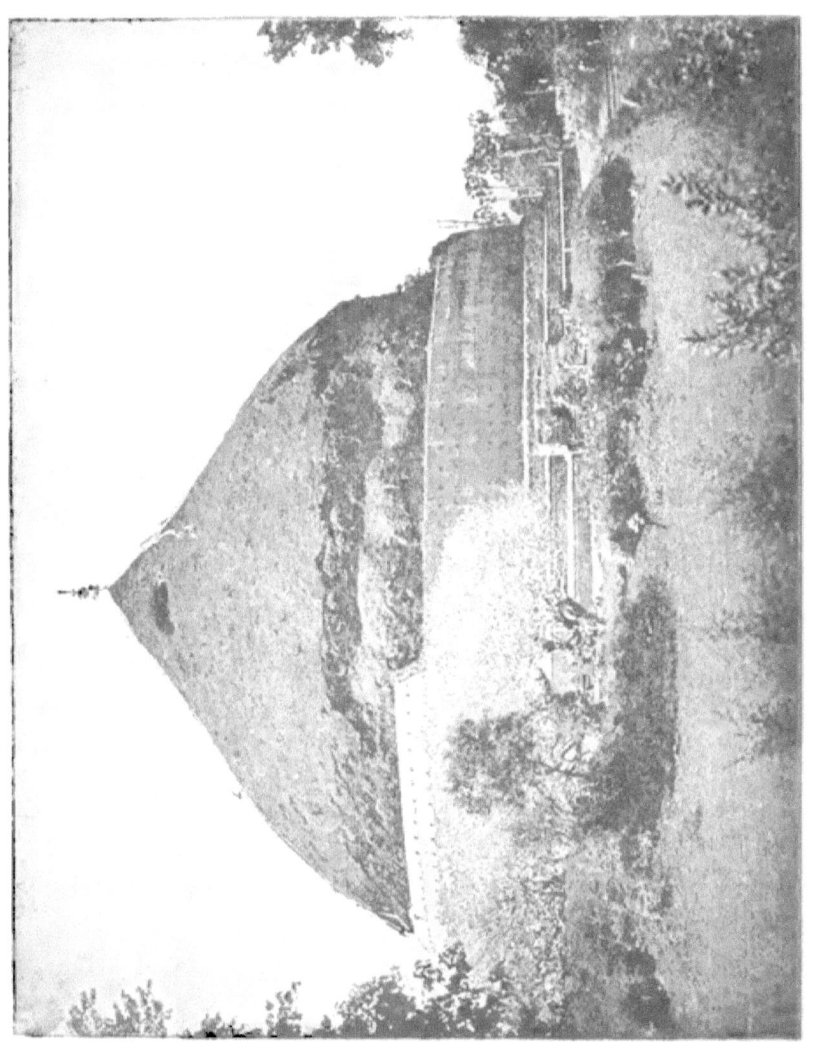

THE RUWANWELI DAGOBA.

CHAPTER XX.

AT THE BRAZEN PALACE.

> Then stand before that fact, that Life and Death
> Stay there at gaze, till it dispart, dispread,
> As though a star should open out, all sides,
> Grow the world on you, as it is my world.
> BROWNING'S *A Death in the Desert*.

THE Brazen Palace was the pride of Anuradhapuran architecture. Successive generations of royalty, after its erection by Dutugemunu, employed their resources on its repairs, on adding to its vast accommodation or adorning its walls. The old chroniclers never tire of describing the magnificence of this great structure, nor of detailing the labour and wealth lavished on it by the ancient kings.

And no one can walk through the avenues of stone in the great square of granite pillars which forms one of the most striking features in the ruins of the city, without being impressed with the thought of the religious life of the old capital whose chief monastery rested upon that wilderness of monoliths.

Built originally—according to the ancient historians—in fulfilment of a prediction by Mahindo, written on plates of gold, and from a design furnished by a heavenly architect, it became to the pious monarchs an object of almost as much care and devotion as the Maha Wihara itself, the great temple close by, whose edifices surrounded the sacred Bodhi-tree.

It was also the object on the destruction of which, in the unorthodox days of Maha Sen, the fury of the heretic was chiefly spent, and the commencement of its restoration was one of his first works of repentance. And Meghawarna's chief care on ascending the throne had been to complete the reconstruction of the magnificent monastery which his father had so ruthlessly destroyed. He had not been able to restore it to its pristine splendour or to its original size. It was once nine stories high. It was now only seven. Its rebuilding was, at the time of which we write, a matter of recent history. There were some old people in the city who could compare it with the colossal building which once stood on the same site; but even such declared that this was no unworthy successor, and nobody could look on the lofty pile without seeing in it a splendid tribute of devotion from the king to the priesthood.

It provided a thousand monks with residence, the upper apartments being occupied, according to the etiquette of the order, by members of the highest 'spiritual' rank, or of the greatest renown for sanctity; the elevation of residence being in proportion to reputation for piety.

In addition to the cells for the monks, there were rooms which had been built for meetings of the chapter, and for the larger assemblies of the priesthood. But the glory of the place was the great hall of the monastery, with its ivory throne, its pillars covered with gold, and its walls resplendent with inlaid jewellery.

It was here, on the day after the great festival of

Mahindo, that Abhayo's examination took place. The monks of Mihintala and the community of the Brazen Palace were in some way connected, and as Abhayo Thero belonged to the city almost as much as he did to the hill fraternity, by virtue of an office given to him in the days of royal favour, it was thought that this would be the best place for holding the investigation, and that it would tend to add to the importance and impressiveness of the occasion.

The knowledge that an assembly of such unusual interest was being held in the great hall of the monastery brought together large numbers of city idlers at an early hour in the afternoon of the day in the vicinity of the Brazen Palace. Among the first to come was Jantu, who was anxious not to miss any part of the proceedings visible to an outsider and a layman. It was not much that was open to him; but he could watch the arrivals of distinguished priests, and he could have a gossip with the crowd without; and Jantu also knew that before the day was out there would be a stir of some kind which would centre in that neighbourhood. He had been waiting since the shout of refection went echoing through the city from monastery to monastery, announcing the midday meal,— after which for the rest of the day all solid food was forbidden to the priests;—and he had entered into a calculation with reference to the hundreds of bushels of rice which the priesthood of Anuradhapura would consume in that one meal.

Under a tree near the Maha Wihara he sat down to eat his own food, which had been brought to him by a slave. This simple meal of rice and curry finished, he took out his betel-box, and having filled his mouth with all the necessary materials for a good chew, he passed it to some of his friends sitting near, and then stretched himself out to think. Talking was much more in Jantu's line than thinking, but he had been greatly perplexed to-day in coming to find the goldsmith's shop closed, and the goldsmith gone, nobody could tell him where, and he wondered what it could mean. Then he found it too hot to think, and soon fell asleep. And when he awoke again, people were gathering from all quarters, and numerous wearers of the yellow robe were ascending the stairs to the great hall of the Brazen Palace, and amongst them, to Jantu's great satisfaction, Abhayo Thero; for he—Jantu—had been more than half afraid that he might resign and escape the examination. Then, mingling with people with whom he seemed to have some secret understanding, who were sitting under the shade of a preaching-hall, Jantu entered into conversation.

The heat was terrible. And it seemed to be focussed in this part of the city, where the gilded domes and white pillars of dagobas and halls, and the metallic roof which gave its name to the Brazen Palace, flashed a dazzling, burning radiation on the whole neighbourhood like heat poured forth from mighty furnaces.

The numerous fields and gardens which added so much to the beauty of the city were now scorched-up and desolate. It was difficult to procure flowers for the sacred shrines, and those that were brought were shrivelled with the burning heat before they could be laid on the offering tables.

All animal life was oppressed with an intolerable heaviness. Scarcely a lizard chirped, and the dogs lay panting for breath on the sides of the streets, with their tongues out. Men who went abroad walked heavily and lazily, as if the air were loaded with a great fiery burden. And in the houses of the people women were leaning over gasping children and crying for the monsoon to come for their salvation.

Even Jantu found that until the evening came on the heat was too great for any display of enthusiasm on the part of the crowd slowly increasing around the great monastery.

And a heaviness characterised the proceedings within the hall in the earlier and more formal stages of the investigation.

It was held according to the form instituted by Gautama for the fortnightly examination of the priesthood. The chapter sat in a great circle on low cushions on the floor of the hall. After a preliminary service, in which two priests recited the regulations for the constitution and order of the proceedings of the assembly, one of them began the chief business of the day, the recitation of the laws of the Order as contained in the Book of Supreme Perfection. To Abhayo nothing could be more familiar than the entire service. How often had he listened to the voice of the officiating priest ringing out the words :—

'What is the first act of this meeting? To declare the purity of the venerable ones. I will recite the Book of Supreme Perfection; let every one of us hear attentively and consider it : if any one is guilty of a fault, let him confess it; if not guilty, he must remain silent. I shall conclude from the silence that the venerable ones are pure.' And he had joined his brethren in listening sleepily and carelessly to the enumeration of the prohibitions, as one of the many forms attached to his monastic life. There were the four great prohibitions, the violation of which would involve expulsion, followed by lists of numerous minor offences which would be punished with suspension, penances, and reprimand. He found himself wondering how he could have allowed his life to become so mechanical, and then fell to thinking of the dangers which beset all religious systems in a constant usage of unvarying forms. And now he was listening as he had never listened before. It was the last time he would hear the code recited, and he was going to break the silence with which he had hitherto taken part in this service. And now his brethren also were listening with unusual attention, for they knew that the solemn silence of the 'pure ones' was to be broken by the famous monk of Mihintala.

The offences demanding expulsion were recited:— (1) Giving way to carnal lusts. (2) Theft. (3) Murder or aiding to murder. (4) Boastfully and wrongfully professing to have attained the excellent perception of perfect wisdom—the wisdom of the Arhat.

Then the reciter addressed the assembled priests:— 'Venerable ones, the four Párájiká (exclusion offences) have been recited. If any priest has been guilty of any one of them, he can no longer remain associated with the order, but becomes as he was before. He has been overcome, and he is excluded.

'Therefore, venerable ones, I inquire, are ye pure respecting these things? A second time I inquire, are ye pure respecting these things? A third time I inquire, are ye pure respecting these things?'

This was followed by a long pause, during which all eyes were turned on Abhayo, who sat unmoved, in perfect silence. And as they looked on him sitting there in calm, unflinching fearlessness, the possibility that a great mistake in popular judgment had been committed dawned upon them. After the pause, the reciter went on:—'Ye are pure, venerable ones, therefore ye are silent: and thus I receive it.'

Then Abhayo spoke, and claimed to be free from all violation of the four great prohibitions. But he could no longer be a member of the order. He was there that day to resign his position in the brotherhood, and he would give them his reasons—reasons which they had a right to know—at the conclusion of the service.

He was perfectly calm, and could even listen critically to the recitation of the numerous sins which a priest might not commit. And he knew how impossible it was for the brethren to observe strictly some of the trivial prohibitions laid down in this catalogue for their guidance, and passed by all in virtuous silence.

Then, when the recitation was finished, he drew himself up and addressed the assembly:—'Venerable sirs, my lords of the Sangha! I have already by my silence declared my innocence of the transgressions which have just been enumerated. But I know something of what is in your hearts, and I know that the interpretation which you would give to some of the clauses of our ecclesiastical code is not that which I would give, and I freely acknowledge that according to the popular understanding of some of those clauses I should be condemned. And therefore have I spoken.

'It is no light thing for me to stand here and say that I am no longer of the Buddhist faith, and that this is my last day in the brotherhood; to lay aside this familiar robe will be almost like laying down my life. All my earliest associations are connected with it, and my dearest friends have worn this badge of the sacred order. And as I take it off, I know that it will be death to habits which have grown to be a part of my life, and to fellowships which have been with me from my childhood. It will take away from me old friendships. It will probably bring upon me the fury of popular indignation where once I received nothing but popular favour and applause. I lay it down, and it covers a past—in which there has been much that was pleasant to such a nature as mine—like the cloth which covers the face of the dead.

'As is known to this assembly, this step has not been taken in indecent haste. It is the result of a long and deep struggle, a terrible conflict in which the claims of Jesus the Christ and the claims of the Buddha have battled for the mastery; and now I am here to confess myself a disciple of Jesus of Nazareth.

'In all humility, conscious of the presence of so many wise and venerable men, my seniors, and in all honesty of conviction, I make this confession. It is not that I have broken the laws of the Sangha, so much as that I cannot now accept the first principles of the faith. I cannot repeat the Saranas, nor teach others to repeat them.

'I cannot take refuge in the Buddha, because I am now trusting in One who is holier and mightier than he. I said I would serve the best, the truest, and the greatest; and I say now before you all, if I can be shown a greater and a better Leader and Saviour than the Christ, I will follow him. I am thankful for the purity and beauty which characterised much of the Buddha's life, but it was not all pure and true; while the life of the Christ was like that flawless crystal.'

And Abhayo pointed to a fine jewel which sparkled in the canopy over the ivory throne. 'And that divine purity was maintained in the midst of all the evil of the world; and not by flying from the world.

'I take refuge in the Christ, because He is more than a Leader for mankind. He is also mighty to save! How few are there in this great city to-day, or in the world, who trust in the Buddha alone for salvation! What is this universal appeal to gods and demons by those who profess to follow the Sakya prince, and this willingness to compound with other religions, but a universal recognition of his insufficiency as a Saviour? I want a Saviour who is greater than the world, greater than man, and yet one who has lived the life of man, and can sympathize with me in my infirmities. I also want a Saviour who can never die. And therefore I follow the Christ.

'And what, venerable sirs, do we know with certainty of the Buddha? What historic evidence is there for the stories we relate of him? How obscure and uncertain is all our knowledge! Might I not with safety challenge the entire Sangha to produce the slightest contemporaneous evidence on behalf of the narrative generally accepted; evidence such as we have a right to ask when claims are put forth to the supremacy of the Universe and to reveal the only way of salvation?

'In the story of the Christ we have given us established historical facts supported by contemporaneous evidence. I have even seen a manuscript in which the account of the life of that Holy One was written by the hand of a disciple of one who knew Him and loved Him and was in constant association with Him. And we have the unquestioned testimony of men who lived at the time—and who were, some of them, enemies to the Christian faith—to corroborate the main facts of that narrative. And because of the certainty of the evidence I follow the Christ.

'In that life there are for me the holiest and noblest attractions. I contrast it with the life of him who, protesting against worldly caste, established the great spiritual caste of the "Sangha," and made it one of the three chief gems of the Universe. And I see in the Highest, who lived with the lowest and most sinful without contamination, showing how all family associations and the humblest relations of life might be elevated and made holy and heavenly, a truer Reformer than the Buddha. The Buddha was a poor sinner like myself, striving to work out his own salvation in his own way by his own unaided powers; and the redemption he gained was a joyless existence, with the prospect of a deliverance from life. I love to think of his great pity for all living things, and his burning desire for the salvation of men; but how sad it is for us, venerable sirs, to look on that picture which has been handed down to us in the traditions of the order, and observe that great character in all the loneliness of his attainments, utterly helpless and unable to save others. In the Christ I see a joyous hope for our race, an Almighty Saviour of men. Buddhism has brought me to recognise the need for a regeneration which shall come from above. And in Christ I now see that true Regenerator of mankind. And therefore I take refuge in the Christ, who is the "Lord from heaven."

'I can no longer take refuge in the Doctrine, the second Sarana of the Buddhist faith, because it is the product of the mind of man, and not a revelation from

the God of heaven, against whose purity and justice we
have sinned, and whose laws, written in our hearts, we
have transgressed. I recognise in it much that is high
and holy, which has been the teaching of the conscience
of the best men in all the ages. But I find all that
and much more in the teaching of the Christ.

'I cannot take refuge in the Doctrine, because it
does not recognise the existence of Almighty God, the
Ruler of the Universe, the Creator of the world, whose
existence, in the face of the indubitable proofs which
surround me in nature of the presence of a Supreme
Intelligence, it would be madness for me to deny or
ignore. And I follow the Christ because He teaches
me that that Almighty Intelligence is "Our Father."

'I cannot take refuge in the Doctrine, because it
furnishes no key to the mystery of life, because it does
not acknowledge the existence of the immortal soul in
man, without which recognition our best longings and
noblest aspirations have no foundation, and the greatest
problems of life go unexplained, and the demands of
eternal justice will go unsatisfied. I follow the Christ,
who " has brought life and immortality to light in the
Gospel."

'I cannot take refuge in the Doctrine, because of its
low views of human life. The Buddha teaches me to
regard all life as an evil. In that way have I looked
on it. All the world has been sad to me because of
that thought. I could see no good anywhere, and no
true joy or beauty in any form of existence. All nature
was in perpetual mourning, draped in the ineffable
sorrows of the curse of life. And as I looked at it and
thought of it, day after day, I said, "And is there no
end for all this, no hope?" And the reply of the

T

Doctrine was, and is, "There is no hope for life. There is no hope for thee except in leaving it. Live according to the precepts, and thou shalt have deliverance from the bondage of life." Then I asked, "What is the hope of deliverance which the Doctrine holds out to me?" And the reply was, "Thou shalt cease to be. Nirvana shall be thine at last!" And I felt that to be a deliverance which I could not desire, and against which my soul protested. There was no hope in the Doctrine.

'The Christ has taught me that life may be ennobled, that although there is in it much of evil and sorrow, the evil may be cleansed away and the sorrow turned into joy. And to me, now, life has a different meaning from what it had. I can see how it can be made a glad and glorious thing, and how I may comfort and gladden the lives of others. The prospect on which I look now is one of exceeding hopefulness for myself and for humanity, capabilities of a life of blessing and blessedness here, and hereafter a "heaven in which dwelleth righteousness."

'I cannot take refuge in the Doctrine, because it would teach me to destroy the holiest affections and noblest desires of the soul, to trample on the ties of family life and all earthly fellowships. I have had affections which I have tried to kill, in obedience to the Doctrine. I have been conscious that in those affections there was nothing unholy, and that consciousness has striven with the teaching which told me that they were dragging me down to perdition. The Christ has taught me to see that these affections may be leavened and kept pure with the love of the Holy God, and that they may thus be amongst the most blessed and elevating influences in life.

'I cannot take refuge in the Doctrine, because its tendency is contrary to that upward spirit of progress which should characterise the movements of men. Because in its low views of the life that now is, and in its gloomy prospects for the future, it is a discouragement to civilisation. And now I follow the Christ, who is at the head of the true regeneration and civilisation of mankind.

'I cannot take refuge in the Sangha. Venerable sirs, I have lived among you all my life. I have been one of you. And now it would ill become me to speak in other than words of gratitude for the kindness which I have received at your hands, and for the tolerance extended to me by you. Neither would it be becoming in me to point out the flaws in the "gem" of the priesthood. Are they not known to us all? Have we not often asked ourselves, "Are we worthy of a place in the three Saranas?" And I remember that I have been in my measure responsible for the sins of the Order, and therefore I will speak freely of that which is not personal. I cannot take refuge in the Order, because its daily life is inconsistent with the Doctrine. Because it absorbs the wealth of the land and oppresses the poor. Because it will strain the water, lest the smallest and meanest insect should lose its life, while its guilt and neglect are the ruin of thousands of human beings. Because it is a great priestly caste, to which it would have all men enslaved, and outside which, according to its teaching, there is no salvation.

'This day I renounce it, because the Light of Life is filling my eyes, and now I can see that Jesus only is the Way; that the "eight-fold path" leads through Him who is "the Way, the Truth, and the Life." And

I can see that the man who drives the plough, and the woman who sits at the loom, and—strange as it may sound in your ears—the little children at play, may live as holy a life and be as acceptable before God as any priest of any religion on the face of the earth.

'Christ is my Priest. He died for me, and He is now my ever-living Friend. It is not simply a doctrine which I have embraced in accepting this faith. It is a life. I thank you for the patience with which you have heard me. It has cost me much to say it, but I felt that it was my duty not to shrink from bearing this witness for the true Saviour of men here this day. You cannot know with what intensity I have resisted these convictions which have been slowly gaining upon me, nor how terrible has been the conflict between the old faith and the new. But Jesus of Nazareth has triumphed at last, and now I follow the Christ!'

It must not be imagined that Abhayo was able to say all this without interruption. Again and again there were cries of dissent, and many wondered at their own tolerance in allowing such things to be said; but there was that in the man and his speech which made him heedless of everything but the duty before him, and which compelled them to listen to the message he had to deliver.

They felt too that this was not the man to steal a gem. And it was with some shame that the matter was introduced. And the burst of honest indignation and surprise with which the charge was received by Abhayo made them wish they had never mentioned it. They said that, as he had not confessed to it in the regular way in the course of the service, they thought it right to tell him that all the city believed him to be the guilty man, and that the people charged the delay of the monsoon to his wickedness.

And as they spoke there were sounds from without which indicated the impatience of the crowd; for by this time large numbers had gathered to await the conclusion of the examination, and there were mutterings amongst them which predicted the rising of a tempest. 'It all comes of thinking for himself,' said Jantu. 'Why doesn't he think as other people do? And why did he take the gem?'

'That is what we want to know, and we want to know where it is. And know we will, if we can get him disrobed,' said several voices in the crowd.

'And there he is!' cried Jantu, as Abhayo appeared in loose white garments on the stairs at the entrance to the hall. 'Close around, and we will soon make him tell where it is!'

The priests begged him to return to the safety of the hall, when they saw the fierce looks of the angry mob.

Abhayo stood for a moment like a man in a dream. It was all so strange to be there in that unfamiliar costume and without the sacred robe. And what could the crowd mean by pressing towards him with threatening looks and gestures? And then, as men will often be impressed with little and unimportant things in moments of a great crisis, his attention was caught by the appearance of a man with one eye, standing on the outskirts of the crowd and watching the proceedings with a wicked, cynical delight; for Jotthiyo was there, thinking that this would be as safe a place as any, and that he would like to see how things were going in this direction.

The crowd came nearer and nearer. There was then a mighty rush. Abhayo stood with folded arms to receive the shock.

They closed around him crying,—'To the ordeal! To the ordeal under the Sacred Tree! The Good Serpent will tell us whether he is guilty or not!'

And Abhayo saw that to resist, even with his strength, was useless.

Some of the priests protested, but the majority of them thought it better to make no opposition to the popular appeal to the decision of the serpent.

CHAPTER XXI.

THE APPEAL TO THE SERPENT.

> On this occasion innumerable déwos and nagas assembled at this place, saying, 'Let us witness the contest between these two parties, the snakes and the Thero.'—TURNOUR's *Mahawanso*.

THE ordeal to which Abhayo was being brought at the close of our last chapter was probably a survival of the serpent-worship which Buddhism had professed to have replaced, but which it had rather assimilated by the encouragement given in both doctrine and legend. In this power of adaptation and assimilation may be found the secret of much of the success which, in the days of old, attended the propagation of the Buddhist faith.

The ordeal is not practised now, but a thousand superstitious and popular customs show that the religions of the ancient serpent and demon worshippers of Ceylon are nearer the heart of the people still than the teachings of Gautama.

In the midst of the howling multitude, Abhayo walked calmly, but conscious of the horror which awaited him under the Bodhi-Tree.

Through the nearest gateway the crowd struggled and pressed, and, thronging the galleries which surrounded it, they lifted their hands in adoration of the tree. And thrice they made the place ring with shouts in honour of 'the Nàga, the divine cobra, the guardian of the holy gems.'

The Nàga had been provided by Kapuranda the astrologer, who had secured for this purpose the most deadly of its kind, and he had had little difficulty in making the credulous Jantu and others believe that it was a descendant of that serpent from whose head the lost gem had originally come.

There on the Bhodimanda[1] (the highest platform surrounding the tree) an earthenware pot rested, on which all eyes were gazing, and before which some of the people were bowing in worship.

Abhayo looked at it, and as he looked and thought of its ghastly, deadly inhabitant, his blood ran cold. He could meet an open enemy. He felt that he could stand before the most venomous and most dangerous brutes of the forest, but this invisible horror made his flesh creep and took away his breath.

'Put in your hand!' shouted the crowd. 'If the good serpent bites, you will deserve the death; if not, you are innocent. In with the hand!'

Abhayo looked at the simple earthenware pot, which seemed to him to conceal a living hell, into which he was expected to plunge his hand through the thin leaf tied over the mouth of the vessel.

Then he looked at the faces around him, and saw that no appeal would be listened to, no justification would be heard. And looking at the determined faces around him made Abhayo calm again, as opposition always did, and took away the terror of the thing lying there concealed, waiting for the plunge of his hand.

[1] So called from its correspondence to the throne which Gautama occupied when he attained Buddha-ship under the Bo.

He called for attention, and cried: 'It is a dreadful death to die for an innocent man.'

'If thou art innocent, thou wilt not die. The good serpent will not bite,' they shouted.

Abhayo went on: 'I will not willingly submit to this ordeal. It would be sin against the good God in whom I believe, who made heaven and earth. He is my Judge, and not that loathsome, poisonous reptile.'

'Then we must force thee!' replied the crowd, headed by Jantu and Jotthiyo.

Their numbers overpowered him. They were dragging him to the ordeal, when they were suddenly arrested by the apparition of a beautiful woman, who, springing to the Bhodimanda, lifted the fatal vessel above her head, and in tones of passionate entreaty implored the infuriated mob to listen to what she had to say.

To the multitude, as they looked in their amazement on that magnificent figure, bearing in her uplifted hands the horrible tribunal, while the white drapery of her robes falling, left her rounded arms bare,—to the mass of the people it seemed nothing less than the intervention of a goddess from one of the heavens.

Let us now go back a little, to see what led to the appearance of Anula, for it was she, at such a time in so singular a manner.

It will perhaps be remembered that Irene's little Sinhalese maid, Kumari, managed to pass out of the room unobserved on the entrance of Leah, who was afraid lest the cries of her fair captive would attract the attention of the goldsmith working in another part of the house.

Leah had not missed the child until she had shut

Irene in the secret chamber behind the shrine of the Reconciler. And although it vexed her to find that the girl had gone, it was a matter of little importance compared with the great trouble of which her mind was so full just then. She would go to the astrologer and secure his help, she said, before she went in search of the goldsmith; and if there was any likelihood of delay in finding him, she would return at once to Sarana from the astrologer's and release Irene, for it was certain that she could not be kept long in such durance. It was possible, too, that she would find Alypius with Kapuranda, and both of them would probably assist her in recovering the sapphire from Jotthiyo. Such were her thoughts as she made her way to the astrologer's residence.

But Kumari's escape was not so unimportant a thing as it seemed. It was one of those little things on which events of great magnitude will sometimes turn. The little maiden was sharp and intelligent, as such Sinhalese maidens are now, and once in the open street she managed, by dint of numerous inquiries, though in a part of the city of which she had no knowledge, to find her way to her destination. For her destination was to reach Anula, whom she knew to be with the sisters of the faith in the nunnery.

Anula was congratulating herself that the final step which would decide the course of her life, and separate her from distracting associations and affections, was so near at hand. The conquest had been difficult, and was not complete. There were still lingering doubts in her mind, and the knowledge which she already had of the lives of many of the sisters did not tend to allay those doubts; but she had determined not to be influenced by such. She would rather look for example to such characters as Yasôdhara, the wife of the Buddha, and Sanghamitta, the sister of Mahindo, and others of the holiest women in the history of their faith.

But the victory was a sad one, and questioning in her mind, as might a general who has conquered in the fight when looking on his slain friends and comrades, 'Is it worth such sacrifice?' and then thinking it sin to entertain such a thought for a moment, she sat in the shade of the great rock in the garden attached to the nunnery, meditating.

It was while she was there, thinking of her self-conquest, that word was brought of a Sinhalese maid who had come in great excitement wanting to see the lady Anula immediately.

On listening to Kumari's story, given breathlessly and incoherently, she was not long in deciding that she would go to the rescue of her friend. She decided first by instinct, woman-like, and then backed it up with reasons afterwards as she walked rapidly along the hot streets escorted only by the Sinhalese girl. She tried to persuade herself that it needed this act on behalf of her Syrian friend to complete the annihilation of the great affection which had hitherto been the chief hindrance to the realisation of her ideal of holiness; for she had little doubt that the love of Irene had conquered the man and the priest in Abhayo, and influenced him in favour of Christianity.

She was so absorbed in these thoughts that she scarcely noticed the people gradually filling the streets as the day advanced, and she would perhaps have passed without recognition even so striking a figure as that of Joseph the Syrian, whom they met on the way, had it not been for the ejaculations of surprise and delight which came from Kumari, whose delight was increased by seeing with Joseph her uncle, Kiri Banda.

Rapid explanations followed, in which both parties had much to say about the wicked treachery of the Reconcilers, and both parties were speedily walking together with quick steps towards Sarana. And as they walked Joseph told Anula his story, of how the men in charge of the vessel delayed his landing, and finally set him on a desolate shore at a great distance from the pearl fishery, where he would probably have died but for the help given by friendly natives, who, induced by promises of much reward, brought him to the fishery, whence he managed to secure a boat for Mahatotai. It was on his way from the latter place to Anuradhapura that he met Kiri Banda, who brought a letter which Alypius had declared to be of urgent importance. He also told her of revelations which had been made to him by Kiri Banda concerning the lost gem which had been intended for the eye of the new idol, and of the suspicions which had been designedly cast on Abhayo.

All this helped to make the walk through the city an exciting and eventful one for Anula. But it was to be much more eventful yet. On their way they had to pass near the Maha Wihara and the enclosure of the Sacred Bo, which they reached just as Abhayo was being brought to the ordeal. They were told of what was taking place. They saw the infuriated mob moving in the galleries around the tree above them; they heard their wild cries about the theft of the jewel, the anger of the gods and the cobra, who was to arbitrate. There were men closing around him armed with long swordlike knives, who were going to force him to the awful test. Anula took in Abhayo's danger at a glance. There was not a moment's hesitation on her part. If she had paused to think about it, she would probably not have done so extraordinary a thing. Before Joseph could do anything to prevent her, she had gone in by another entrance, broken through the crowd where it was thinnest, and was soon standing, as we have seen, on the highest platform with the vessel of the ordeal in her uplifted hands.

The crowd drew back in the utmost astonishment. Nothing could have been more unexpected in such a place at such a time. The priests were greatly scandalised. Abhayo was at first more inclined than ever to imagine himself in a dream. Anula, without saying a word to him, called on the people to desist, crying out that she had something of the very greatest importance to say to them. Then briefly and passionately, while they were hesitating, not knowing what to make of such an appearance, she unfolded the story she had just heard from Joseph of the guilt of the Reconcilers, not doubting its truth, and speaking in tones which carried conviction, or, at least, doubt with regard to the charges against Abhayo, to those within the reach of her voice.

Jantu was thunderstruck. If it had been Menika herself, he could not have felt more powerless to urge on the attack on Abhayo than he felt now under the influence of the appeal from this wonderful woman. Her beauty was increased by the excitement ten-fold. She was dressed in the white garments usually worn when one has taken the vows of 'Sil,' and her whole appearance presented a grace and majesty which awed the multitude. Her eyes blazed with indignation as she spoke of the injustice they were doing to an innocent man, and denounced the iniquity of the wrongdoers.

Her hands trembled for a moment with the passion which inspired her. The great jar fell on the stone parapet, and out of a thousand fragments there sprang the hissing, hooded death!

The mob drew back in consternation and alarm. They trampled on each other. And those who could get away fled, for none would dare to lift his hand against the sacred serpent. They shrieked in their terror, and amidst the frightened cries there was one cry of real pain, which came from the goldsmith Jotthiyo, who was near the wall striving to cleave his way through the crowd and make his escape.

It was some time before quiet and confidence were restored, and not until assurance was given that the cobra had retired into one of the numerous crevices formed by the roots of the Bo.

At last Jantu spoke: ' It is the lady who came with the princess and the holy tooth-relic. She has a right to be heard. The women are greater than we think.' (Here Kiri Banda gave a loud cough.) 'Who was it that brought the conquering tree of wisdom to Ceylon? It was a woman. And was it not a woman who brought us the last great treasure which was once in the lotus-like mouth of the Blessed One, who gave us the precious gem of the Doctrine? And it may be that a woman has been sent to us again now, to help us to recover the glorious jewel designed for the new statue. If the priest is innocent, we will let him go. He will meet with his reward fast enough. Men who go about thinking for themselves, like he does, are sure to come to trouble sooner or later. But let us go now to Sarana to see if these things be true, and take the Thero with us. We will have the ordeal yet, if this information should prove false.' And Jantu looked around on the crowd with an air of great sagacity and importance, at this sudden development of a public character within himself.

A priest came forward to remonstrate, and suggested that a small deputation should be sent, headed by one of the order, intimating that if they went in a mob they would be repulsed by the soldiery. But a great shout went up from the people: 'To Sarana! to the Reconcilers!' and immediately they began to move away. And, without speaking a word to Abhayo, Anula, now overwhelmed with conflicting feelings, rushed to the side of Joseph.

CHAPTER XXII.

THE MONSOON COMES.

> . . . But alas!
> Men breathe forth passions which fall back in blights
> And stormy desolations, that defile
> The sky-born streams, and flood life's fields with woe.
> BAILEY'S *Festus*.

So absorbed had they all been in what was taking place under the famous tree, that no attention had been paid to the sudden change in the air about them and in the sky above. In the galleries about the Bo all was agitation; but all over the rest of the city a heavy stillness had settled, and the hot air was suddenly cooled. A sensation of awe seemed for the moment to silence all animal life, as it is said is sometimes the case in the hour before a dread battle. The lizards crept into the innermost recesses of deserted ant-hills; the frightened birds sought the thickest shelter they could find in the trees. The dogs wriggled their way noiselessly into such houses as would receive them. Men in the streets became solemnly glad as the skies rapidly darkened, and said to one another: 'It is come at last!' And the women left their gasping children to look out of doors, and returned whispering the tidings of approaching blessing: 'The monsoon is coming!'

On the great thunderclouds came, until the heavens were filled with their blackness. Then, just as the multitude was moving away from the sacred tree, out of the black cloud-masses a stream of flame seemed to leap into the very heart of the city and fill the great square with fire. The roof of the Brazen Palace blazed like a sheet of flame, and the crystal on the Ruwanweli tope looked like a ball of fiery illumination. It was but for a moment. Then the air was filled with the crash of thunder, as if all the dagobas in the city had fallen.

The crowd paused, holding their breath. Anula, who had but just braved so courageously the enraged mob, clung to Joseph for support. Then Jantu cried: 'Friends, the monsoon is come! the gods are with us! Let us away to Sarana!'

With a wild shout they ran, and as they ran the floods came.

While they are on their way let us look in at Khanda Rāja, the residence of the astrologer. That worthy has just bowed Leah out of the Hall of Mystery, having succeeded in persuading, or half-persuading her of his own devotion to her cause, and of his ability to lay his hand at any moment on Jotthiyo. A young Sinhalese man, who has been in concealment on the premises during the interview, is now admitted into the hall. He was the prince's pupil, a relative of the astrologer, who had been in hiding for some time, and in constant fear lest his part in obtaining the gem for the Reconciler should be discovered.

Kapuranda threw himself on a mat, and gave way to the enjoyment of a long series of chuckles.

'He! he! he! success at last! The game is won,

and I hold the prize! It has gone off admirably! That Thero will have met with his doom by this time. The cleverest woman in the world, the Jewess, must now own me master in her own arts. And I have disposed of Jotthiyo! And a man who can cheat a goldsmith is no fool!'

'No, indeed! But what have you done with Jotthiyo?' inquired the young man.

'Ha! ha! he will be far enough from Anuradhapura to-night, and for many nights to come; though I have asked him to come here to-morrow. I told him they would be sure to search for him at once. He acknowledged that they would. And at last I got him to see that the safest place for the precious stone just now is the Hall of Mystery. He thinks he will come to-morrow; but I think he will not. No, not for many morrows! It is his purpose, if the way is clear, to carry the great jewel to Mahatotai, where he is going to make a bargain with some foreigners, which he says will enrich us both beyond all our dreams of wealth. "Us both," indeed! How much should I see of that wealth? The cunning rascal! He knows how pious I am. And he made me swear by all the gods, and by the sacred Bo, that I would not deceive him, nor let the resplendent gem go out of my sight till his return. He! he! Trust old Kapuranda for that! Let us look at it now! I must not let it go out of my sight, you know.'

He brought out a parcel, which he seemed to handle tenderly and affectionately, chuckling all the while; and, undoing numerous folds of wrapping, he held the big crystal up, to catch the light coming in at the little window of carved wood.

'It is getting dark,' he said: 'the air is cool; the sky is covered with cloud; the monsoon must be at hand. That wicked Thero has met with his just punishment, he! he! The gods are satisfied, and are letting the rains come! But the jewel does not look quite what it did, and what it should. It must be the want of light. And yet——'

Just then the lightning flash of which we have already spoken poured its vivid illumination into every house in the city. Kapuranda fell back as if struck by it. But it was not the lightning which had so suddenly paralysed him. For a time he was speechless, and groaned heavily, to the consternation of his young relative. Then he said: '*I have lost it after all! He made a second substitute!*' And he flung the mock gem across the room. There we will leave him groaning in his disappointment and defeat.

On returning to Sarana, Leah's first thought was to look to the safety of her jewels. 'I have been deceived so terribly that I cannot be too careful,' she said to herself. It was her intention to let Irene go, after she had seen to the jewels. But, on approaching the strong box in which she kept her precious case, her quick eye discerned at once that it had been tampered with, though it looked much as when she left it. Breathlessly, she tried the secret springs. The lid flew open, the case was gone! Another had known her secret, and availed himself of it! Leah sank down before the rifled box, stunned with the treachery which had bereft her of the things she valued most in the world.

There she sat, holding her head in both her hands, as if she were afraid it would burst with the agonies of her great loss. Nor did she heed the lightning flash, the roar of the thunder, or the torrents of rain streaming down into the gardens outside. Nor did she heed the thud and splash of human feet which now and then might be heard at intervals in the storm, for they seemed no concern of hers.

Nothing interested her but the terrible, bitter sorrow which now filled her life. Nearer and louder came the thud and the splash. The lightnings flashed ever and anon, and the thunders of the monsoon rolled over the city; and she could hear in the midst of it all, coming nearer and nearer, shouts as of anger, which seemed to rise from a multitude of human voices, and she heeded them not, for all that was dear to her was gone. The jewels had been to her like living things, to which she had given all her love.

Nearer and nearer came the sound of the voices and the feet, until at last they entered Sarana. She heard cries about a sapphire! Then her interest was aroused, and she listened eagerly. But her hopes were dashed when she discovered that they had come to seek the lost jewel. And as she listened it became clear that the secret of her iniquity was in the hands of the mob now crowding in to the shrine of the Reconciler.

The room in which she was sitting was not very accessible. But she could not escape without attracting attention. She heard the people shouting for the Reconciler. They wanted to see the Reconciler. She heard the voice of Kiri Banda and the calls of Irene, followed by the moving and creaking of the woodwork separating the shrine from the secret chamber. Then there were cries of great joy in a language familiar to her, the tongue of her childhood, as father and daughter were locked in each other's arms. She heard the people comment on the beauty of this Reconciler, as they called Irene.

There was a loud laugh, too, at the appearance of the myna, who had flown to Kiri Banda's head, from which perch this bird of wisdom poured forth repetitions of the profound interrogation: 'No refuge. What can I do?'

Then she heard them go into the secret chamber, searching for the gem, and examining the contrivances which Kapuranda had made for the perfecting of their impostures. Baffled there, she heard them cry: 'Where is the Jewess? We must have the Jewess!'

Then the instinct of self-preservation rose within her. She would try to preserve her life, if it was only for revenge. Throwing off such robes as might interfere with her escape, she made a rush out of the room to a side-door, and was soon in the garden without. Her flight was speedily discovered, and Jantu with many others were running after her. She managed to elude their pursuit at first, and gained upon them considerably by taking to unfrequented streets.

The thunders of the monsoon were becoming less and less loud. But the rain still fell in torrents, and the water swirled and eddied in the narrow streets through which she ran. She was still in advance of her pursuers; occasionally she had lost sight of them, through the delays caused by doubts at the cross-streets. Once they turned in an opposite direction to that which she had come, and this gave her time, and enabled her to recover her breath while she crouched for a few moments in an open preaching hall at a street corner. How she blessed the monsoon which had driven the people into their houses, and caused the streets to be deserted by nearly all but herself and her pursuers!

And now they were gaining upon her. She heard the splashing of many feet and heard them calling on any who might hear to stop her. On they came with their long black hair streaming down over their backs, with their garments gathered up about their loins, that they might run more swiftly. They were getting nearer every moment, and she was so wet and so tired!

Then the darkness of the evening befriended her. She made another turn into another street, and felt that this must be her last. She could hear her pursuers in the distance. She was not sure, but now they appeared to have gone in another direction. She found herself at last before a familiar-looking building which she could not have seen, so dark was the evening, had she not come close to it. Even then the building called up associations in her mind of the old days of long ago. And she said: 'This is the church of the Christians, where they will always give sanctuary to those who want refuge.' All this flashed through her mind in a moment as she stood there in the pouring rain.

The door was open, there was a glimmering light within. She rushed in, and would have fallen faint and giddy on the floor, but for the quick support of a man's hand. The hand was scorched and livid. She could see that even then, in the light of the brass lamp which stood on the reading-desk; and she noticed the great Hebrew letters on the wall behind the lamp, and she read out the syllables as if she were in a dream. And a voice, which seemed to come out of a distant past—it was to her like the voice of the dead—said: 'Yes, it is the house of God. None are turned away from this Refuge!' There was a flash of recognition in the eyes of both. Her brain reeled, and she sank unconscious into the arms of Thomas, who had come into the little church, as was his wont, for evening prayer.

CHAPTER XXIII.

AFTER THE MONSOON.

<small>The eternal God is thy refuge, and underneath are the everlasting arms.—DEUTERONOMY xxxiii. 27.</small>

THE burst of the monsoon was succeeded by a few dry days of pleasant and beautiful calm. The drought had come to an end, and the pestilence was stayed. A new life had taken possession of the city gardens and fields, and the weather was delightfully cool.

Irene was moving about in the little garden of the quadrangle, rejoicing in the fact of being at home again. And home was all the dearer because of their late experiences. The garden had revived with wonderful rapidity under the influence of the monsoon rains, but it had been wofully neglected during the absence of the young mistress of the house. Every now and then Irene would hold up a big weed or a decayed plant, and shake it playfully at Thomas, who sat in the inner verandah looking on the garden with an expression of penitence for his neglect which was half comical and half serious.

The little garden seemed full of life. In the midst of the wild profusion in which the flowers had been allowed to grow, Anula and Kumari were as busy as Irene, occasionally assisted by Joseph, in reducing the wilderness to something like order. And there in the overhanging branches flitted the myna, chattering its phrases in its old inconsequent, solemnly humorous fashion.

'Sing, child! sing as you work!' said Joseph to his daughter. 'Leah wishes to hear you sing! The cool morning hour will soon be gone.'

And singing a sweet Greek melody or one of the Psalms, she brought back the wayward vine of a passion-flower, fastening it to the trellis, as when we saw her first. Nor was the picture less beautiful than when we first saw the Syrian girl in the midst of her flowers.

Anula looked deeply thoughtful as she worked under the direction of her friend. The flowers and the singing were not engrossing all her thoughts.

She had said to Irene when they arrived at home on the night of the monsoon—for they always talked of that eventful time as 'the day' or 'the night of the monsoon': 'It is of no use resisting any longer, dear friend! Now, like Ruth in the sweet story your father told us, I say, "Thy people shall be my people, and thy God my God!"' And all the pent-up emotion in Anula's heart seemed to be liberated as she threw herself in this covenant of love on the neck of her friend.

Irene's joy at this declaration was unbounded; but after a while she had replied: 'It shall be so, dear! Our home shall be thy home until Boaz claims thee!' And Anula knew that she spoke of Abhayo, and knew that her friend was not her rival.

We have been looking on the garden and its workers. Now let us turn to the verandah. There, lying on a couch, was Leah the Jewess. She was sick, sick unto death. The agitating experiences of that eventful day and night seemed to bring a hidden disease to the surface, and with it there came a fever which no remedy but the touch of death could allay.

Her proud, wicked heart had melted at last. And in place of the 'heart of stone' there was now the 'heart of flesh!' Thomas was nearly always by her side, nor could he do enough to satisfy himself in attending to her comfort. And after some loving and gentle attention, she would lay hold of his burnt hand and cover it with kisses and tears. Nor would she let him keep it out of sight, as had been his custom aforetime.

She would say that Thomas's love and forgiveness were helping her to understand the mighty pity of the great God, and the compassion of Jesus Christ. Her position was at the feet of the Redeemer with the poor woman who had sinned greatly and been forgiven much. She had no desire for the recovery of the lost jewels, except when she thought of how little was the service which she could now lay at the feet of Christ the Messiah.

The great sapphire had been found on the dead body of Jotthiyo, the goldsmith; and the 'serpent ordeal' had become more popular than ever, when it was discovered that the goldsmith had died from the bite of the cobra. And the people were looking forward with delight to the dedication of the new image of the Buddha.

The recovery of the gem had made it unnecessary to make further search for Leah. As to Sarana, the royal and priestly disciples of the Reconciler were not sorry to let the impostors escape. They were not proud of their connection with that popular shrine. But there were large numbers of people who, in spite of the exposure of the frauds passed on them, and the flight of the arch-deceiver, still believed in both the Reconciler and Leah. And it was not long before a shrine similar to Sarana was established elsewhere for their benefit.

Of Alypius nothing had been heard except that he had been seen hurrying, in the pouring rain of the monsoon-burst, through a street leading towards one of the wooden bridges which crossed the river. And as the bridge had been carried away by the tremendous torrent which had come with the floods, it was thought possible that the Greek had been borne away with it. When he was seen he had looked—so it was said—as if he were carrying something heavy under his cloak.

Leah seldom spoke of her late colleagues during her sickness. Her husband, to whom she had been so strangely reunited, knew all her sad, wicked story, and all had been forgiven. And now, notwithstanding great weakness, pain, and fever, she felt, as she listened to Irene's singing, that she had at last reached the truest and best refuge after all her wanderings.

Next to her husband she became most deeply attached to Irene. She said that she had sinned against her grievously. But of that the Syrian girl would not hear, and she surrounded the poor suffering penitent with sweet observances.

Sometimes Leah talked of a desire to live, that she might atone for some of the wickedness of her past life.

And then again she would say: 'How sweet is such a life as this, and oh, how short!' And on the morning of which we write she told Thomas that she had prayed to be spared to the next Sabbath. For on that day, the Lord's Day, Abhayo and Anula had determined to make public confession of their faith in Christ.

The Sabbath came. Leah was still living, but she was sure, she told her friends, that this would be her last day on earth. And she implored them to grant her one last request. It was that she might be carried on the couch into the little church, to be present at the holy service. With much reluctance the request was acceded to.

Abhayo and Anula stood before the congregation, and declared that they had taken refuge in 'God the Father Almighty and in Jesus Christ His only Son.' And in the name of the Holy Trinity they were baptised.

The congregation then sang the forty-sixth Psalm, beginning with, 'God is our refuge and strength, a very present help in trouble,' and ending with the words of blessed promise and assurance: 'Be still, and know that I am God. I will be exalted among the heathen, I will be exalted in the earth. The Lord of hosts is with us, the God of Jacob is our refuge.'

And the dying woman heard the voice that she had learnt to love so well, the voice of Irene, rising clear and sweet above all the voices in the congregation; and she felt the mighty comfort of refuge in the Eternal God.

At the close of the service it was decided that Leah was too weak to be carried back into the house. And there, in the church, she remained, in the midst of gentle, loving ministrations, to die.

When the day drew near to its close, and the hour for evening prayer was at hand, Leah's friends were all gathered about her couch. She wanted to see them all, she said.

She talked with difficulty, but she said something about Sarana and jewels. Thomas quoted from the words of the 'blessing of Moses, the man of God': 'Let thy Urim and Thummim be with the Holy One!'

Faintly she replied: '*Yes, the Urim and Thummim at last—none can take it away now—with the Holy One —with the Holy One!*' And, taking the burnt hand of her husband, she placed it on her head, where it rested as in loving benediction, while her soul passed away from a life of storms into the quiet and assurance of the Eternal Refuge.

Within the church, it was a Sabbath peace, emphasised by Death. Without, immense processions were marching through the streets of the city. The bands were playing, and multitudes were shouting the three Saranas of Refuge, in the Buddha, the Doctrine, and the Order. It was the night of the dedication of the new Buddha.

* * * * * *

As soon as arrangements could be made to supply his place, Thomas went to India as a missionary amongst the Damilos, and he was accompanied by Abhayo and his wife Anula.

Joseph and Irene remained in Anuradhapura. And they were frequently cheered with news from, or of, their dear friends on the continent. They were told that the people amongst whom Thomas lived and laboured loved him so greatly, and esteemed the true piety of his character so highly, that they were accustomed to say it was as if one of the holy apostles of Christ lived in their midst.

PRINTED BY
SPOTTISWOODE AND CO., NEW-STREET SQUARE
LONDON

www.ingramcontent.com/pod-product-compliance
Lightning Source LLC
Chambersburg PA
CBHW022044230426
43672CB00008B/1069